Yale Historical Publications

Miscellany 89

THE ABBÉ DE CONDILLAC

After a painting by Beldrighi. Paris, Bibliothèque National.
Photo courtesy of Hachette, Paris.

THE GEOMETRIC SPIRIT

The Abbé de Condillac and the French Enlightenment

by Isabel F. Knight

17573

New Haven and London, Yale University Press, 1968

To Luise J. Zucker,

in gratitude

Preface

The prevailing state of mind among the men of the French Enlightenment was dissatisfaction. Sometimes it took the form of good-humored exasperation with human folly and gullibility; often it blazed out in bitter anger at the cruel irrationality of man's—or God's—inhumanity to man. In any case, the men of the Enlightenment felt—most of them—that the intellectual and social fabric of their time, together with the Christian cosmology which justified it, was coming apart at the seams, and deservedly so. Their job was to hasten the day.

Thus the prevailing mode of action among the philosophes was: ATTACK. They attacked the Church, they attacked the State, they attacked warfare, they attacked intolerance; they attacked the philosophical traditions, the social hierarchies, the educational system, and the economic organization; they attacked provincialism, prejudice, pretension, and pride. No person, no institution, no belief that was part of the Old Regime—the Establishment—was safe from their persistent, pugnacious, and revolutionary criticism. But the revolution they intended was not the bloody overthrow of kings and cardinals; they intended a revolution at once less violent and more profound. As Diderot put it, they meant to "change the general way of thinking." This accomplished, the Old Regime would perish of itself, and a new and better society, a society of free and enlightened men—free *because* enlightened—would rise on its ruins.

The new way of thinking preached by the philosophes was captured in a phrase: "the geometric spirit." If it triumphed, the geometric spirit would liberate men from the tyranny of superstition, prejudice, ignorance, theology, and metaphysics (near-synonyms in the philosophes' vocabulary) by teaching them to think clearly, rationally, and scientifically. The official theoretician of the geometric spirit was a professed Catholic, an inactive priest, and a political conservative: Etienne Bonnot de Condillac. More than anyone else, it was Condillac who systematized the geometric spirit, setting down its epistemological foundation and deriving from it a methodology whose universal application would, he felt, open the doors to all the knowledge available to man. He himself took the geometric spirit into psychology, linguistics, aesthetics, education, economics, and history.

This present study of the geometric spirit, as Condillac understood and practiced it, is meant to illuminate the texture, the inner structure, and the half-acknowledged tensions of Enlightenment thought—the intellectual life of the age as it was experienced by those who lived it. With this larger purpose in mind, I have not limited myself to Condillac's thought alone; I have compared his ideas, attitudes, and assumptions with those of his contemporaries and often of his predecessors wherever it seemed fruitful to do so. Thus I have tried to portray Condillac's mind both as a unique phenomenon and as a paradigm of the mind of his age.

One major aspect of Condillac's thought has not been treated here, except incidentally: his historical writings. More than half of Condillac's writings are devoted to history, and to deal with the subject adequately would have required several more chapters: on progress and decadence, on the relationship of the Enlightenment to the past in general as well as to certain crucial periods of the past, on historical causation, on the moral uses of history, on Providence, and on politics—to name only the most obvious. To attempt the task would have lengthened this work intolerably. But it is to be hoped that this significant gap in Enlightenment studies will soon be filled.

I have a special obligation to my dissertation director, Franklin LeVan Baumer: for his patient insistence that I get down to business and for his painstaking comments, which always had a way of pointing out problems I had not noticed and of clearing up difficulties that had seemed insurmountable. My understanding of some of the

philosophical issues discussed in Chapters 2–5 has benefited much
from long and exciting talks with my very good friend Adele
Spitzer. If my handling of them still bears the mark of the amateur,
it is not her fault. I should like also to acknowledge a longstanding
debt to Mark H. Curtis and Trygve R. Tholfsen for having first introduced me to the excitements and rewards of intellectual history.
My greatest debt is to my husband, Alan Knight, for reading and
criticizing the entire manuscript, for going over my translations
from the French, for sharing the burden (and the fun), and for
cheerfully tolerating a degree of domestic neglect that would have
provoked most men to justified complaint. Busy as he was with his
own work, his presence and encouragement made my work possible. Finally, a warm and special word of thanks is due to my
small sons, Jonathan and Michael, for smiling so much.

I. F. K.

University Park, Pa.
October 1967

Contents

1. Condillac and the Enlightenment

In the spring of 1756 the Abbé de Condillac received—and declined —an invitation to visit Voltaire's Swiss retreat, Les Délices. Voltaire had hoped that he could give Condillac the leisure and facilities to write a work containing "all that man is permitted to know about metaphysics."[1] The invitation reflects the esteem in which Condillac was held by the philosophes; his refusal suggests the caution, amounting almost to fearfulness, with which he regarded them. Rousseau called him one of "the best thinkers and profoundest metaphysicians" of the century.[2] Diderot and d'Alembert praised his attack on *l'esprit de système* and borrowed from his writings for the *Encyclopédie*.[3] Indeed, as chief disciple of John Locke, idolator and popularizer of Newton, and one of the few systematic thinkers of the French Enlightenment, Condillac came close to being philosopher to the philosophes. Yet his books were commended by the Jesuits of Trévoux,[4] and his talents brought him

1. Voltaire, *Œuvres complètes*, ed. Louis Moland (52 vols. Paris, 1877– 85), *39*, 18. Unfortunately, Condillac's reply is not extant, so we can only guess at his reasons for not accepting. See Gustave Baguenault de Puchesse, *Condillac, sa vie, sa philosophie, son influence* (Paris, 1910), pp. 103–04.

2. Jean-Jacques Rousseau, *Emile*, Bk. II, in his *Œuvres complètes*, ed. V. D. Musset-Pathay (25 vols. Paris, 1823–26), *3*, 157.

3. Denis Diderot, *Lettre sur les aveugles*, in his *Œuvres complètes*, ed. J. Assézat (20 vols. Paris, 1875–77), *1*, 315; *Encyclopédie, ou Dictionnaire raisonné des sciences, des arts et des métiers*, ed. D. Diderot and J. d'Alembert (3d ed. 36 vols. Geneva, 1778–79), *1*, lvi. The articles "Divination" and "Systèmes" are taken word for word from the *Traité des systèmes*, but they are not signed. Rousseau suspected that Condillac might also have been the author of the article "Evidence": see Rousseau, "Notes en réfutation de l'ouvrage d'Helvétius," *Œuvres complètes, 10*, 198.

4. Not that the Jesuits of Trévoux always agreed with him, but they gave him generally favorable reviews containing only a few reservations; e.g. the *Essai sur l'origine des connaissances humaines* was described as a work "of the most sublime metaphysics," in which the author was some-

favors from the Court of France itself: on the recommendation of the Queen he was made tutor to the Prince of Parma and was later offered the post of tutor to the three sons of the Dauphin. For Condillac was discreet: despite his philosophical innovations, he maintained his religious orthodoxy to the end and kept his distance from those bolder spirits who would not bow to the Establishment.

Condillac's philosophy had a special relationship to the thought of his age precisely because of its ambiguity (one might say, its equivocation). There was something in his thought for everyone: for the radical, a thoroughgoing sensationalist psychology with hints of mechanistic determinism; for the conservative, a rational, ordered, and comprehensible universe presided over by the familiar and beneficent God of the deists; for the pious, an insistence on the spirituality and immortality of the soul and a conspicuous avoidance of direct offense to the authority of Church or Scripture. The very breadth of Condillac's appeal perhaps accounts for the fact that, despite his high standing, he had no real disciples among his contemporaries. His position was one of popularity rather than influence, suggesting that his books had more of the familiarity that confirms than the impact that converts.[5] His readers must have encountered his ideas with a sense of recognition, a feeling

---

times led astray by his confusion of sensations with ideas (*Mémoires pour l'histoire des sciences et des beaux-arts* [i.e. *Mémoires de Trévoux*], May 1747, pp. 800–08; see also ibid., Sept. 1749, pp. 1836–53; March 1755, pp. 641–69; Dec. 1755, pp. 2911–37).

5. Cf. Introduction, *Œuvres philosophiques de Condillac*, ed. Georges LeRoy (3 vols. Paris, 1947–51), *1*, xxxi; and Mario dal Pra, *Condillac* (Milan, 1942), pp. 357ff. This judgment was anticipated, albeit in another spirit, by Condillac's one enemy among the philosophes, Baron Grimm. Grimm quite obviously did not like Condillac, and his dislike was intensified when Condillac was dragged into a quarrel with Grimm's good friend Diderot about the invention of the statue-man. The tone of Grimm's reviews of Condillac's books ranged from the sarcastic to the vicious, with particular scorn for their lack of originality: "He has the air of repeating half-heartedly what others have revealed to humanity with genius," and,

that their own thoughts were here stated with new clarity and persuasiveness. It would seem that there was something typical, something broadly representative about Condillac: he conveyed a mood or expressed a set of attitudes which most of the philosophes found congenial and relevant, and which few of the antiphilosophes found offensive.

Toward the end of the eighteenth century, after Condillac's death, this diffuse popularity began to crystallize into a specific influence. The medium of the transformation was the salon of Mme. Helvétius, where a group of young men, notably Destutt de Tracy, Cabanis, and Volney, inspired by Condillac's methodological and psychological writings, created a program for the study of the human mind which they called *Idéologie*.[6] In this form the philosophy of Condillac achieved academic status as the official philosophy of the French schools during the Revolutionary and Napoleonic periods. After 1815 Condillac shared the fate of his disciples when a "spiritualist" reaction, led by the renegade *Idéologue* Maine de Biran, discredited the notion, basic to *Idéologie,* that the human mind is mechanical and passive. Throughout the remainder of the nineteenth century Condillac was regarded almost exclusively in the light of this dead controversy. Students of his thought either took for granted the image of his philosophy reflected in the work of the discredited *Idéologues* or else sought to rehabilitate him by connecting his philosophy with some momentarily popular doctrine—associationism, scientific empiricism, and even idealism.[7]

Nineteenth-century polemics about Condillac have been replaced by twentieth-century indifference to him. To be sure, his

about *Le Commerce et le gouvernement:* "it has the great merit of explaining, with a marvelous clarity and precision, what everyone already knows." Melchior von Grimm et al., *Correspondance littéraire,* ed. Maurice Tourneux (16 vols. Paris, 1877–82), *3,* 112; *11,* 54.

6. For a full account of this movement, see F. Picavet, *Les Idéologues* (Paris, 1891).

7. See below, "Bibliographical Essay," pp. 301–13, for details.

name appears in every handbook on the Enlightenment, with a paragraph or two on the statue-man, but there have been few serious attempts to analyze the details of his thought, only one attempt systematically to discuss the whole of it,[8] and none at all to seek in it, except in the most general terms, clues to the characteristic structure and peculiar tensions of the thought of the French Enlighenment. Interest in the period itself has not flagged: new interpretations continue to appear along with reassertions and revisions of old interpretations; and studies of the giants of the age—Voltaire, Montesquieu, Diderot, Rousseau—still compel attention. Of course, men like these were engaged in a battle with the established order, a battle for toleration, for free thought, for a more natural morality and a more rational society, a battle which has not lost its relevance or its intrinsic excitement. Condillac, however, stayed clear of the warmer controversies. He preferred to deal with problems of abstract philosophy, which could be contemplated in the quiet and security of his own study. There was in his life no drama, no heroism, no tragic conflict to compel our interest; nor were his writings graced by wit or brilliance, or rewarded with lasting influence. Yet to the student of the French Enlightenment the philosophy of Condillac is a rich source. He may have avoided the more conspicuous and more dangerous battles of his age, but he was deeply involved in subtler intellectual controversies, which were perhaps neither less intense nor less significant.

The philosophes, as everyone knows, believed in reason and in nature. They admired science, especially Newtonian science. They were dedicated to the hope that man's life could be improved (although not necessarily perfected) if the principles of reason, the authority of nature, and the methods of science were allowed to sweep away superstition, ignorance, intolerance, senseless customs, fallacious ideas, and outworn institutions. So much can be said with confidence. But when one examines their philosophy and

8. Dal Pra, *Condillac.*

their program in detail, the very elements which had seemed most clear and definite begin to shift, blur, and disintegrate. What did the philosophes mean by "reason," and how did their conception of it differ from that of the Cartesian rationalists or the Aristotelian rationalists? What exactly was their conception of nature? Did Fontenelle, Voltaire, Diderot, Rousseau, d'Holbach, and Condillac all see it in the same way? And if there were several conceptions current at the same time, did they have anything in common with one another—historically, logically, or psychologically? How did the philosophes think man was related to the world of nature: Was he a part of it or independent from it or both? And what about their admiration for science? Fontenelle was a Cartesian, while Condillac and Voltaire were Newtonians; Diderot disapproved of mathematics but his colleague d'Alembert was a brilliant mathematician; Buffon explored "natural history" instead of the more common "natural philosophy"; and Rousseau was an amateur botanist. From these several schools and branches of science the philosophes derived several versions of scientific method and more than several notions of how it should be applied outside the realm of natural phenomena. (There were many, of course, who insisted that nothing existed outside the realm of natural phenomena.) Nor did they agree about the things to be attacked. What, for example, qualified as superstition? Voltaire was a deist who would have crushed not all religious expression but only the Catholic Church; d'Holbach was an atheist who would gladly have abolished the whole business; Diderot was by turns deist and atheist "according to the state of his nerves"; [9] and Condillac lived and died professing the Catholic faith. Consider their philosophy of art: still steeped in the absolute principles of classical aesthetics, with its single norm of perfection imitating "nature," the philosophes yet were relativists. Having discovered other cultures, other arts, and other faiths, they no longer believed that the culture of France, or even of Western Europe, was the only "natural" culture. On the other

9. Preserved Smith, *A History of Modern Culture* (2 vols. New York, 1934), 2, 326.

hand, was not nature, including human nature, fundamentally the same under all the accidental accretions of time and place, and would not this basic uniformity produce a single art if creativity were free to follow nature? And what is one to think of the appearance of "sentiment" as an aesthetic category of the Age of Reason? The list of problems and contradictions is infinite. Moreover, the complexity of the thought of the Enlightenment is not revealed merely in contradictory attitudes taken by different individuals but often appears as well in contradictory notions held by the same individual. And when a man holds incompatible ideas with equal fervor, he may be supposed to owe his devotion to them to something other than their compelling logic; or rather, the logic that he finds compelling is not of a universal order but bears the mark of time and place and individual bias. It is for the purpose of untangling some of the threads of this complex thought that I have undertaken to analyze the philosophy of Condillac, in whom the divergent philosophical traditions and intellectual loyalties of his age came together in uneasy coexistence.

The life of Condillac may be briefly told, for it was to all appearances an austere life, a life that left behind few traces from which to reconstruct it. He kept no diary, wrote no memoirs, seldom corresponded. His biographer, relying upon family tradition, describes his personality as cold, dull, and unanimated—a description we can accept as true.[10] Otherwise, there seems no way to account for the fact that those indefatigable, uninhibited, and gossipy letter-writers, the philosophes, had so little to say about him. They all knew him; they ran into him in several of the more prominent salons; they read and esteemed his books; but although they talked about his philosophy, they rarely have anything to tell us about Condillac the man—evidence enough that he made little personal impression on his contemporaries. On the evidence at hand, one may conjecture that Condillac was retiring to the point of timidity, that he formed no attachments, provoked no quarrels,

10. Baguenault de Puchesse, *Condillac,* p. 20.

and kept to himself in spirit even when he was living the worldly life of a man of letters in Paris in the 1750s. As a result, we, like his contemporaries, can come to know him only in his intellectual life and perhaps in only part of that—the part he was willing to make public. The other dimensions of his being, what he loved, what he feared and hated, his pleasures, his passions, his indignations, and his private anguish—these remain forever inaccessible. Perhaps, out of some necessity for defense against the demands of living, he so successfully anesthetized his own emotions that they were inaccessible even to himself. There is something in the quality of his thought which suggests that his was an impoverished life, a life lived in only one dimension.

Etienne Bonnot was born into a family of the petty *noblesse de robe* on September 30, 1714, at Grenoble. He acquired the name by which he is known in 1720, when his father bought the nearby domain of Condillac. A sickly child, whose eyesight was so poor that at the age of twelve he had not yet learned to read, Condillac picked up the rudiments of an elementary education from a local curé.[11] In 1727, when his father died, he went to live with his oldest brother, Jean Bonnot de Mably, a royal official in Lyons. There he was for a time left much to himself, for he was so quiet a boy that his family regarded him as simple-minded. Such, at least, is the testimony of Rousseau, who was briefly employed in the Mably household as a tutor to Condillac's nephews.[12]

The details of Condillac's life in Lyons are obscure. Georges LeRoy believes that after a few years he was enrolled in the Collège des Jésuites there, although Baguenault de Puchesse does not mention it.[13] In any case, sometime in the 1730s another brother, the socialist Abbé de Mably, took him to Paris and entered him first at Saint-Sulpice and then at the Sorbonne to study theology. Condillac unenthusiastically completed the course

---

11. Ibid., p. 4; cf. Voltaire, *Œuvres complètes, 57,* 43.

12. Rousseau, *Emile,* Bk. II, *Œuvres complètes, 3,* 157.

13. LeRoy, *La Psychologie de Condillac* (Paris, 1937), p. 5; and his Introduction, *Œuvres phil. de Condillac, 1,* vii.

and in 1740 was ordained priest. Although he wore the cassock for
the rest of his life, he chose not to exercise the office. Instead,
sponsored by his brother, by Mme. de Tencin, and by the Duc de
Nivernais, Condillac entered into the social and literary life of
Paris.[14]

Dissatisfied with his formal education, Condillac set about
educating himself all over again.[15] He read the great philosophers
of the seventeenth century—Descartes, Malebranche, Spinoza, and
Leibniz—and formed a lifelong aversion to the kind of speculative
systems they had created. He preferred the English philosophers,
who were then at the height of their popularity in French intellectual circles. Condillac read no English, but Locke's *Essay
concerning Human Understanding* had been translated into French
by Pierre Coste in 1700, and he seized upon it eagerly, adopting
Locke's empiricism as the basis for his own philosophy. Although
it is not known whether he read Newton, who wrote in Latin,

---

14. Condillac's connections with Mme. de Tencin and the Duc de
Nivernais are not clear. The Tencin family was also from the Dauphiné
and distantly related to the Bonnot family, but Mme. de Tencin had left
the provinces long before 1740 and she died in 1749, just when Condillac
was becoming well known. Probably the Abbé de Mably, who already had
some reputation in 1740, was his brother's entry into Mme. de Tencin's
salon. (See LeRoy, Introduction, *Œuvres phil. de Condillac, 1,* viii.) From
three extant letters to the Duc de Nivernais (*Œuvres phil. de Condillac, 2,*
544–46) it appears that Condillac was on very friendly terms with him,
for he writes with a casualness, almost an intimacy, which is unusual for
him and most refreshing. Nivernais, who served the French government in
a number of ambassadorial posts, including that of Rome, was apparently
influential in getting Condillac the revenues of the Abbey of Mureau as
a reward for his services at Parma (see Condillac's letter to the Duc de
Praslin, *Œuvres phil., 2,* 547). Condillac's acquaintance with him probably
dated back to his early days in Paris (Baguenault de Puchesse, *Condillac,*
p. 15).

15. This is the customary interpretation of a remark made by Condillac
much later to the effect that such a new beginning is necessary upon leaving
school (*Histoire moderne,* in *Œuvres phil., 2,* 236). Cf. LeRoy, Introduction,
Œuvres phil. de Condillac, 1, viii; and Baguenault de Puchesse, *Condillac,*
p. 9.

he did read Voltaire's summary of Newton's works, *Eléments de la philosophie de Newton* (1738), and through this book he also became acquainted with the idealism of Berkeley. Condillac somewhat belatedly discovered Bacon—after the fundamentals of his own thought had formed—and found him to be impressively in advance of his time.[16] No doubt he read much more, but it was primarily reflection upon these philosophers that went into the creation of his first two books, the *Essai sur l'origine des connaissances humaines* (1746) and the *Traité des systèmes* (1749).

During these years of reflection and reevaluation Condillac renewed his acquaintance with Rousseau and the two became quite friendly. Rousseau recalled their friendship and its happy consequences for Condillac, in the *Confessions:*

> I was, perhaps, the first who discovered his abilities, and estimated him at his proper value. He also seemed to enjoy my company; and while, shut up in my room . . . near the Opéra, I was composing my act of *Hésiode,* he sometimes dined with me *tête à tête,* and we shared the expenses. He was at that time engaged upon his *Essai sur l'origine des connaissances humaines* . . . . When it was finished, the difficulty was to find a bookseller to take it. The booksellers of Paris are always arrogant and hard towards a new author, and metaphysics, which was not much in fashion at the time, did not offer a very attractive subject. I spoke of Condillac and his work to Diderot, and introduced them to each other. They were made to like each other, and did so. Diderot induced Durand the bookseller to accept the abbé's manuscript, and this great metaphysician received for his first book—and that almost as a favor—one hundred crowns, and even that he would perhaps not have received but for me. As we lived at a great distance from one another, we all three met once

16. *Essai sur l'origine des connaissances humaines,* in *Œuvres phil.,* I, 115.

a week at the Palais Royal, and dined together at the hotel Panier-Fleuri.[17]

It is not difficult to imagine what the three philosophes talked about at their dinners, since some of the ideas Condillac was working on at the time turned up a few years later in the writings of the other two. They must have discussed problems relating to sense experience, such as the contribution each of the senses makes to human knowledge, and the relativity of our knowledge to the kinds of senses man has. These were major themes in Condillac's *Essai* and in Diderot's *Lettre sur les aveugles* of 1749. They probably also talked about language, how it originated and how it came to develop as it did—another important subject in the *Essai,* which was taken up by Rousseau in the *Discours sur l'inégalité* (1754), where he credited Condillac with giving him his first ideas on the subject.[18] It would seem that Condillac repaid his friends for their help in the coin of ideas.

After the publication of the *Essai* and of the *Traité des systèmes* three years later, Condillac became fashionable.[19] Diderot introduced him around to all the philosophes of note and borrowed material from the *Traité des systèmes* to form the articles "Divination" and "Systèmes" for the *Encyclopédie.* Condillac's social world expanded with his reputation. Besides his customary attendance at the salon of Mme. de Tencin (until her death in 1749), he appeared at the gatherings of Mlle. de Lespinasse, Mme. Helvétius, Mme. de Vassé, Mme. Geoffrin, and Mme. d'Epinay—at least, so we are told in the traditional biographies.[20] Condillac's fame may have admitted him to the best intellectual society of Paris, but it was not enough to overcome the diffidence of his elusive personality.

17. *Œuvres complètes, 15,* 115–16; *The Confessions of Jean-Jacques Rousseau,* ed. Lester G. Crocker (New York, 1957), pp. 171–72.

18. *Œuvres complètes, 1,* 245.

19. See François Picavet, "Introduction" to Condillac, *Traité des sensations,* Pt. I, ed. F. Picavet (4th ed. Paris, 1919).

20. Ibid.; Baguenault de Puchesse, *Condillac,* pp. 13ff.

His presence at these salons has been noted only by those who were interested in him to begin with; nowhere in the many studies devoted to the salons does his name appear on the lists of guests. One can imagine him in that dazzling society: silent, withdrawn, overwhelmed. Whatever excitement attended the first appearance of the bright young metaphysician brought in by Diderot must have quickly died when it became obvious that he could not hold his own in the conversational competition of the salons.

Condillac's failure in the fast-paced atmosphere of the salons did not get in the way of his growing success with the printed word. In 1749, while he was resting at Grenoble after finishing the *Traité des systèmes,* d'Alembert brought him the news that he had been elected a member of the Académie Royale des Sciences et Belles Lettres of Berlin—perhaps on the recommendation of its president, the renowned naturalist Pierre Maupertuis.[21] Condillac was accorded this honor primarily in recognition of the *Traité des systèmes,* in which he had launched a devastating and original attack upon the despised metaphysical systems of the seventeenth century. The *Traité des systèmes* enjoyed a wider acclaim than the *Essai,* well-received though that had been. Even Grimm liked it, although his praise sounds grudging.[22]

Within a few months of the publication of the *Traité des systèmes,* Condillac was deeply engaged in a new project—or, rather, a new consideration of an old project: the reconstruction of the origin and development of human knowledge. By the summer of 1750 he had already formed his idea of a gradually animated statue as a device for demonstrating his theory that personality originates in sensation.[23] Unfortunately his work was held up by a prolonged illness and by his chronic eye trouble.[24] When the *Traité des sensa-*

---

21. Baguenault de Puchesse states wrongly that this was in 1752. See Condillac's letters to Maupertuis, dated 25 and 29 December 1749, *Œuvres phil., 2, 533.*

22. *Correspondance littéraire, 2, 204.*

23. Letter to Maupertuis, 12 August 1750, *Œuvres phil., 2, 535.*

24. Letter to Maupertuis, 25 June 1752, ibid., pp. 535–36.

tions finally appeared, in 1754, it was clear that his thought had deepened and in some respects changed. He was no longer writing in the shadow of Locke. He had in fact produced, in his analysis of the statue-man, the most rigorous demonstration of the sensationalist psychology of his century. However, his satisfaction with this work was soon disturbed by comparisons of his statue-man with a similar fiction of Buffon's, which had got the latter into trouble for advocating "materialism." To satisfy the authorities or his own conscience or both, Condillac hastened to restate his faith in God, free will, and the immortal soul—first in a brief *Dissertation sur la liberté* and then in the *Traité des animaux,* in which he refuted both Descartes's view of animals as machines and Buffon's notion that animals possess only a "corporeal" soul.

Condillac's reputation soon reached high places. Early in 1758, on the recommendation of Queen Marie-Leczinska, who was the Duchess of Parma's mother, he was invited to Parma to tutor the young Prince. Condillac evidently looked upon this invitation with more favor than he had Voltaire's of two years before. He took up his duties at Parma in March 1758 and remained there until January 1767. During those years he wrote for the Prince a *Course of Study,* which combined simplified versions of Condillac's earlier writings with a great deal of new material. The *Cours d'études* contained a *Grammaire,* drawn mostly from the standard French grammars of the day, but beginning with Condillac's own observations on the origin and structure of language; *De L'Art d'écrire,* a handbook of style; *De L'Art de raisonner,* a textbook of scientific method; *De L'Art de penser,* an analysis of the psychology of thought; and the *Histoire ancienne* and *Histoire moderne,* in which Condillac wrote a "philosophy of history" in Voltaire's sense of the phrase, supplemented by *De L'Etude de l'histoire* solicited from the Abbé de Mably for the occasion. In addition, Condillac compiled a *Dictionnaire des synonymes* for the Prince, which was found in manuscript after his death and left unpublished until 1951. In return for his services the Duke of

Parma obtained for Condillac the revenues of the Premonstraten-sian Abbey of Mureau and granted him a liberal pension.[25]

In January 1767, his task at Parma finished, Condillac returned to Paris. Although he had been away for nearly nine years and had published nothing since 1755, his reputation was still high. In 1768 he was elected to the Académie française. He was asked to undertake the education of the three sons of the Dauphin, the future Louis XVI, Louis XVIII, and Charles X, but he refused, for he had lost what little enthusiasm he had ever had for the busy social life of a Parisian man of letters.[26] He rarely attended sessions of the Académie and stayed away from the salons, devoting himself entirely to his work. His chief concern in these years was for the publication of the *Cours d'études*. Publication was begun at Parma in 1769 under the direction of the chief minister, Guillaume Dutillot, who was dismissed in 1771. His successor completed the printing in the following year, but he was unable to overcome the opposition of the Bishop of Parma to the distribution and sale of the books, an opposition evidently provoked by Condillac's criticisms of ecclesiastical politics and of Spain in his history. Condillac tried in vain to obtain the printed volumes, or at least the return of his manuscripts. Finally, permission was secured to publish them in France—perhaps through the intervention of Turgot, whom Condillac had known since the 1750s, when they had both frequented the salons of Mlle. de Lespinasse and Mme. Helvétius—and in 1775 the books and manuscripts were returned to him. The first edition appeared in Paris, although still with the imprint of Parma.[27]

In the meantime, however, Condillac had had enough of Paris. Seeking a quieter life away from the city, he purchased the

25. LeRoy, Introduction, *Œuvres phil. de Condillac, 1,* x; Henri Bédarida, "Condillac à Parme. Quelques Lettres inédites," *Annales de l'Université de Grenoble* (1924), *1,* 233–34.

26. Baguenault de Puchesse, *Condillac,* p. 143.

27. Henri Bédarida, *Parme et la France de 1748 à 1789* (Paris, 1927), pp. 115, 417–18.

château and land of Flux, near Beaugency, and in 1773 took up residence there with a favorite niece, remaining until his death seven years later. He was by no means idle during these last years in retirement. In 1776 he published a book on political economy, *Le Commerce et le gouvernement considérés relativement l'un à l'autre.* The same year he became a member of the Société royale d'Agriculture d'Orléans.[28] Shortly afterward the government of Poland asked him to write a textbook of elementary logic to be used in schools,[29] and the result was *La Logique,* which appeared in 1780.

Each year Condillac went to Paris for a brief visit. During one of these visits, in 1776, a strange and revealing encounter took place with his old friend Rousseau. Rousseau had just completed another of his many self-revelations—the dialogue *Rousseau juge de Jean-Jacques*—and, fearful that his enemies would destroy or distort it if the manuscript fell into their hands, he sought a way of bringing it intact to the world's attention. He tried to leave it on the high altar of Notre Dame to be found by a priest who, under the guidance of Providence, would be sure to deliver it to the King himself, but he was prevented from carrying out his fantasy by a locked door, which he took as heavenly disapproval of the plan. Then, in a state of despair, Rousseau heard that Condillac, whom he had "not ceased to esteem," was in town—another, and more favorable, sign from Providence:

> I took my manuscript to him, and I handed it over to him with transports of joy, with a beating of the heart which was perhaps the most worthy homage a mortal could render to virtue. Without yet knowing what it was about, he told me on receiving it that he would make a good and honest use of my deposit. The opinion I had of him made this assurance superfluous.

28. Baguenault de Puchesse, *Condillac,* p. 21.
29. See the correspondence between Condillac and Ignace Potocki, in *Œuvres phil. de Condillac,* 2, 551–53.

Two weeks later I went back to him, persuaded that the moment had come when the veil of darkness held over my eyes for twenty years would fall, and that somehow or other I would have from my depositary the enlightenment that seemed to me must necessarily follow from the reading of my manuscript. Nothing of what I had anticipated happened. He spoke to me of this writing as he would have spoken of a literary work I might have asked him to examine and give me his opinion of. He spoke to me of transpositions to be made which would put the contents in a better order, but he said nothing to me of the effect my work had made on him, nor what he thought of the author.[30]

The ageing Condillac, helpless in the face of Rousseau's anguished but nebulous demands, took refuge in blindness and offered to serve as Rousseau's editor. Bitterly disappointed, Rousseau refused the offer and regarded the friendship as ended.

Condillac made a last trip to Paris in the summer of 1780. Feeling ill, he returned to Flux as quickly as possible, sent for a priest, and affirmed his Catholic faith. On the night of August 2 he died "of a putrid-bilious fever." He told his niece that he had once taken a cup of bad chocolate at Condorcet's and had never been the same since; he had always detested Condorcet.[31]

Condillac left behind the unfinished manuscript of a last work, *La Langue des calculs,* in which he was still pursuing the goal he had pointed to more than thirty years before in the *Essai sur l'origine des connaissances humaines:* a way of casting philosophy into the precise terms of mathematics. Condillac's entire intellectual career may best be understood in the light of this quest. The image of certainty and clarity provided by numbers and their relationships dominated Condillac's mind. He was no great mathematician—he confessed as much to Maupertuis[32]—and his notion

30. Rousseau, "Histoire du dialogue *Rousseau juge de Jean-Jacques,"* in his *Œuvres complètes, 17,* 459–61.

31. Baguenault de Puchesse, *Condillac,* pp. 23–24.

32. *Œuvres phil., 2,* 534.

of mathematical method was limited to the simple equations of basic algebra. The analytic logic of algebra, the step by step progression through a sequence of identities, the manipulation of known and unknown quantities, the ultimate reduction of terms to a comparison with unity—these were the elements he wished to impose upon philosophy. More than that, these were the elements which made up the structure he saw in nature. Condillac the empiricist, whose first project was to replace the rationalist metaphysics of the seventeenth century with the empirical philosophy of Locke, was himself committed to a view of the universe as rationalistic as anything Descartes or Spinoza or Leibniz could have imagined. That is, he was committed to a view of the universe which assumed a fundamental order behind the empirically observable phenomena, an order more significant than the phenomena, which man can come to know because it is an order essentially congenial to his reason. It is the aim of this study not merely to demonstrate the fact of Condillac's basic rationalism but to show how it functioned in his thought: how it shaped and altered the empiricist principles he had acquired from Locke, how it determined the meaning he attached to those ambiguous and omnipresent words "nature" and "reason," how it acted as an unconsciously held metaphysics which comes through most clearly in his methodology, how it served as an anchor for his religious convictions, and how it gave him an image of man and his works not dreamt of in the empirical philosophy.

2. Metaphysics *en géomètre*

The science that does most to illuminate, sharpen, and en-
large the mind, and so should prepare it for all other studies,
is metaphysics. . . . There was a time when . . . of all philosophers, metaphysicians seemed to me to have the least wisdom.
Their works taught me nothing, for I found only phantoms in
them, and I blamed metaphysics for the befuddlement of those
who cultivated it. I then decided to dispel this illusion and
get to the source of so many errors. Those who had strayed
furthest from the truth came to be of most use to me. No
sooner did I learn the uncertain paths that they had followed,
than I thought I saw the direction I should take. It seemed to
me that one could reason in metaphysics and morals with
as much precision as in geometry; that one could form ideas as
exact as those of the geometers, and, like them, give precise
and constant meanings to expressions; in short, that one
could work out, perhaps even better than they have done, a
method that would be simple and practicable enough to
achieve certainty.[1]

All Condillac's works were colored by his early reaction against
seventeenth-century metaphysics. He had read the metaphysicians
in his first independent search for truth and knowledge and had
found their writings to be full of meaningless jargon and unverified
assumptions. His disappointment, and his conviction that the real
key to knowledge had been discovered by Locke, Newton, and
Bacon, started him on his long intellectual career, for it impelled
him to articulate his own vision of what metaphysics should be.

1. *Essai sur l'origine des connaissances humaines* (hereafter cited as
Essai), *Œuvres phil. de Condillac, 1, 3.*

He dreamed of a philosophy that would bear the marks of an exact science—precision, clarity, universality, certainty—and of a philosopher endowed with all the virtues of the great Newton.

Condillac's vision was the ultimate expression of the hopes, ambitions, and ideals of a generation imbued with what it called "the geometric spirit"—a term whose broadening application and changing content reflect not only the rising tide of science as the model of true knowledge but also a shift in emphasis within science itself. The phrase had been coined by Pascal to distinguish the method and temper of the mathematical sciences from the "subtle spirit" of philosophy.[2] In this way he hoped to protect philosophy from the influence of Descartes, who, more than anyone, had set up the precise and infallible deductions of mathematics as a universal method. It was Descartes who triumphed, as the "geometric spirit" spread its light in ever-widening circles of thought. Spinoza proposed to demonstrate his system of ethics geometrically, complete with definitions, postulates, axioms, propositions, and proofs, and capped with the final "Q.E.D."[3] Hobbes asserted that "they that study natural philosophy [which, for Hobbes, included man] study in vain, except they begin at geometry."[4] So it continued until, in 1731, Fontenelle, full of enthusiasm for the glories of science, suggested that all fields of thought and expression—not excepting even oratory—might profit from a touch of the geometric spirit.[5]

Condillac's ambition to reason in metaphysics *en géomètre* was far from original then; it was a reflection of widespread admiration for the achievements of science. But by his time the word "geometry" had become a kind of ritual invocation of a whole

2. Blaise Pascal, *De L'Esprit géométrique,* in his *Œuvres,* ed. Léon Brunschvicg et al. (14 vols. Paris, 1904–14), 9, 240–90; *Pensées,* sect. 1, No. 1, ibid., *12,* 9–14.

3. In *Ethica ordine geometrico demonstrata.*

4. Thomas Hobbes, *Concerning Body,* Bk. I, chap. 6, No. 6, in his *English Works,* ed. William Molesworth (11 vols. London, 1839–45), *1,* 73.

5. Bernard de Fontenelle, "Préface sur l'utilité des mathématiques et de la physique," *Œuvres* (5 vols. Paris, 1825), *1,* 54.

cluster of virtues associated with science of all kinds, including the antimathematical science of the empirical tradition. Condillac himself found geometry in its restricted sense the least satisfactory branch of mathematics, because its method is deduction from general definitions.[6] Thus, in becoming a talisman for the Age of Reason, the word "geometry" lost the very virtues it was used to extol—clarity and precision of meaning. "Geometry" as the universalized ideal of all enquiry was therefore entirely compatible with Condillac's empiricist and sensationalist philosophy.

Part of the explanation of the changing meaning of "geometry" lies in the history of science itself. The scientist has appeared in many faces, and so, therefore, have his imitators. There is a historical ambivalence in science between an empiricist, anti-intellectualist concern with brute fact, on the one hand, and an abstract, generalizing devotion to mathematics, on the other. The coming of age of a particular branch of science has commonly been marked by the resolution of this ambivalence in the work of a man great enough to comprehend both tendencies. Thus Brahe and Copernicus may be said to represent the methodological polarities in astronomy, as may Boyle and Descartes in physics; Galileo and Newton were the giants who united them.

Inevitably, the image of science in the minds of those laymen who have looked to it as a model for other disciplines has often reflected the same ambivalence in a simplified or vulgarized form. It has been suggested that as the Cartesian system gave way to the Newtonian, mathematics declined in prestige.[7] Diderot, for example, felt that the true spirit of science lay in the collection and classification of data and not in mathematics, which he regarded as a kind of game whose object has no existence in nature.[8] It also appears to be the case that among those who still stressed the

6. *Essai,* in *Œuvres phil.,* *1,* 25–26.
7. Paul Hazard, *La Pensée européenne au XVIIIème siècle, de Montesquieu à Lessing* (3 vols. Paris, 1946), *1,* 174–75.
8. Diderot, "De L'Interprétation de la nature," *Œuvres complètes, 2,* 9–11.

mathematical tradition, like Condillac and d'Alembert, a different
kind of mathematics from that of Descartes and Spinoza was meant.
Where the latter had been impressed by the logical imperatives of
deductive geometry, the mathematically minded philosophes were
interested in the philosophic possibilities of algebraic analysis.
Moreover, there was a growing tendency to try to assimilate mathematics to an empirical method in the manner of Newton, for, far
from rejecting mathematics, Newton had expanded it and put it in
the service of an experimental science whose fundamental data are
empirically derived and verified. Thus it may be said that while pure
mathematics, mathematics divorced from the observable world, had
markedly declined in prestige by the middle of the eighteenth
century, mathematics as a technique of empirical science remained
very much alive, and it was in the light of this conception of the
geometric spirit that Condillac set himself the task of working out
its implications for metaphysics.

Condillac early concluded that the chief cause of metaphysical
error was a false notion of the source of human knowledge. He
therefore determined that the first step of his own program must
be the establishment of a sound epistemology. With this decision,
he adopted a philosophical undertaking which, ironically, had
originated with the man he most condemned. It was none other
than Descartes who had raised the question of how a man can get
from inside his mind to the outside world and back again, and made
it the paramount problem of modern philosophy.

Why should the problem of knowledge have arisen at all? The
medieval philosophers had not been very concerned about it. Most
of them took it for granted that man is in direct contact with the
world around him, and they had Christianity, common sense, and
Aristotle to support their assumption. As Christians, they held
that man is the center and purpose of the created universe, which
had been placed under his dominion. It followed that the natural
world must be especially adapted to man's needs and capacities,
and therefore that man perceives objects as they are in themselves.
In other words, the medieval philosophers endorsed on theological

grounds the common-sense view that things are what they seem to be.[9]

Natural phenomena in a universe tailor-made to human specifications were gratifyingly easy to explain. Seeing man as a microcosm, the medieval philosophers understood the events of the natural world by analogy with human experience. They explained causality, for example, in terms of will and purpose, potentiality and actuality; thus a heavy object must fall because a lower place is proper to it by virtue of its form or potentiality. The projection of human patterns onto the external world was reinforced by Aristotelian science, which conceived reality to be made up of substances endowed with absolute qualities existing just as man experiences them, so that hot and cold—or heavy and light—were distinct and opposite properties. All this added up to a unified view of the cosmos in which the direct relationship between mind and reality was self-evident.

The epistemological security of scholasticism was finally shattered in the seventeenth century, primarily by the impact of the New Science of men like Galileo. The basic assumption of medieval science had to be discarded when man was displaced from his commanding position. Not only did man see his dwelling place removed from the center of the cosmos, but he had to face abundant demonstration that things are seldom what they seem, and that the nature of reality in the physical world is not defined by man's direct experience of it. The Aristotelian reality of substance and qualities gave way to a mathematically conceived reality of matter-in-motion. The most disconcerting thing about this strange new world of science was man's irrelevance to it. There was no longer any recognizable correlation between his perception of the world and the world itself. The real characteristics of the world, the primary qualities of extension and motion, were impersonal data

9. Although never *merely* what they seem to be, for the symbolic and analogical values of things were always of greater significance to the medieval mind than the merely literal; but insofar as natural phenomena were considered for their own sake, appearance was accepted as reality.

to be measured. The sounds, colors, and odors which make up the familiar world man lives in were reduced to the status of secondary qualities existing only in his mind.

The philosophical implications of the divorce between mind and external reality forced a reexamination of the nature and extent of human knowledge. Beginning with Descartes, epistemology became central and indispensable to all philosophical speculation, so that the characteristic problems of modern metaphysics have been at bottom epistemological. Philosophical investigation has tended to focus on such problems as the source of our ideas, the nature of mind, the nature of the relationship between mind and external reality (if, indeed, there is one), the nature of mental processes and perceptual operations, the possibility of knowledge, and the criteria of truth or verifiability. The subjectivist viewpoint of post-Cartesian philosophy derives from the epistemological problem, and the man-centeredness of its preoccupations derives from the related fact that science has been given jurisdiction over the world of nature—that is, over that part of reality which exists independently of man's activity. "Holding the findings of science to be the truth, it [philosophy] retracted its influence to problems of perception and thought. It became, largely owing to the influence of Descartes, increasingly subjective, concerned with modes of consciousness."[10] The eighteenth-century philosophers made a virtue of necessity, and declared that the proper study of mankind was man.[11]

There is a special difficulty in discussing the influence of different types of philosophy on intellectual history, because in the process of dissemination the differences between schools of thought

10. Meyrick Carré, *Phases of Thought in England* (Oxford, 1949), p. 226.

11. There were, of course, other and more positive factors involved in the new concern of philosophers with human problems, but I am inclined to believe that the relegation of the province of "reality," such as it was, to the quantitative methods of the scientist was of decisive significance.

tend to crystallize at the expense of often equally significant similarities. This difficulty can cause confusion in discussing the epistemological theories of Descartes and Locke as well as the enormous role the latter played in shaping the mind of the French Enlightenment against the native influence of the former. The well-known antithesis between Cartesian rationalism and Lockean empiricism was a legitimate inference from the tendencies of the two philosophies, and in the minds of their respective disciples and admirers this antithesis became the most important aspect of the relationship between them. And yet, if the epistemologies of Descartes and Locke are compared without reference to subsequent interpretation, it can be seen that in many important respects Locke was a Cartesian.[12]

In part, of course, this can be explained by the fact that they shared the general attitudes common to their century. That they should both look to science as the ideal of sound method and true knowledge was practically inescapable. But in addition, Locke owed much more to Descartes in the way of fundamental principles than even he realized, because Descartes, in making the first modern venture in epistemology, had established the groundwork for further speculation. First of all, Descartes made it clear that all thinking about epistemological problems must begin subjectively, inside the mind, because nothing outside it can be taken for granted. Descartes' realization that we are not in direct contact with the surfaces of things led him to recognize that our perceptions take place within our minds and are made up of ideas, and that ideas are not the same stuff as the physical realities which cause them. In this he was perpetuating the dualism suggested by the New Science, and he accounted for our experience of a physical world by a theory of representative perception. Our perception of

12. For discussion of the complexities of Locke's relationship to Descartes, see James Gibson, *Locke's Theory of Knowledge and Its Historical Relations* (Cambridge, 1917), and Leon Roth, *Descartes' Discourse on Method* (Oxford, 1937).

secondary qualities is caused by the physical attributes of things, but there is no necessary resemblance between them. In other words, the sensations we experience represent physical reality but are not identical with it.

The complex of ideas about perception which Descartes developed in connection with his epistemological dualism was basic to Locke's philosophy, but Locke took those ideas in the opposite direction and with them created a philosophy of quite another character. To begin with, Descartes belonged to a generation of system-builders, and for him the purpose of epistemological inquiry was to find a universal method with which to build a metaphysics expressed, in spite of its critical origins, in the Aristotelian language of essence and substance. As a result, the practical epistemological dualism with which Descartes began hardened into a dogmatic metaphysical dualism that set the tone of his entire thought and which incidentally ensured that Cartesianism would not long survive as a live option in philosophy, for the nature of Descartes' dualism widened the schism between mind and body until only God could close it.

Since pure thought is the essence and true activity of the mind, according to Descartes, truth can only reveal itself in the form of rational conceivability, and the ideal of knowledge must be that of abstract geometry, independent of the physical existence which we perceive so dimly. As for our sensory perceptions, even their value as representations of physical reality can be justified only on the grounds that God would not deceive us. Thus, although Descartes surprisingly turned out to be a dogmatic realist about the physical world, he was forced to base his realism on faith in the trustworthiness of God. Such a transcendental appeal was becoming more and more difficult to incorporate into a scientific world-view such as that held by Descartes himself. His own disciples, unable to juggle faith and reason with quite their master's aplomb, tended to take refuge in a frank supernaturalism. Surely Malebranche's assertion that every perception requires an act of God demonstrates more vividly than could any skeptic's argument that the bond between mind and matter had been irrevocably broken.[13]

Locke, on the other hand, did not wish to build a system or prescribe a universal method. His concern was to describe the particular ways in which we know, or think we know. His ideal of knowledge was not the self-enclosed and abstract perfection of geometry, which he found to be essentially uninstructive, but the fact by fact discoveries of observation and experiment. Locke was not embarrassed by his epistemological dualism because, staying uncommitted to any absolute statement about the nature of reality, he was not obligated to provide a metaphysical bridge between mind and the physical world in order to justify his reliance upon sensory experience. He was free to remain ultimately agnostic about the correspondence of our ideas to real existence, while asserting that we can be as certain of it as we need to be for the practical activities of life. Locke did not solve the problem which science had raised and Descartes had acknowledged, but he was in a position to make the best of it, and this has perhaps been the strength of the empiricist tradition in modern philosophy.

By the middle of the eighteenth century the philosophy of Locke had become authoritative not only in England but in France as well. Voltaire's tribute perhaps best explains why Locke took hold when Descartes did not: "So many philosophers having written the romance of the soul, a sage has arrived who has modestly written its history. Locke has set forth human reason just as an excellent anatomist explains the parts of the human body. He everywhere takes the light of physics for his guide."[14] In the modesty of his claims and the simplicity of his language and in his reliance upon the evidence of experience, Locke appeared to be the scientist of the soul, and nothing could have spoken more directly to the interests of the men of the Enlightenment, for whom the natural sciences were the pinnacle of human achieve-

13. Nicolas Malebranche, *De La Recherche de la vérité,* in his *Œuvres complètes,* ed. André Robinet (14 vols. Paris, 1958–64), 2, 312–20.

14. Voltaire, *Lettres philosophiques,* in *Œuvres,* 22, 122–23.

ment. Locke, along with Newton, was the intellectual idol even of
those who, like Condillac, were most conscious of his weaknesses.

Condillac's unbounded admiration for Newton, whose method
he hoped to approximate, suggests that, like many another thinker
of the second rank, he wanted to be the Newton of philosophy,
reconciling the opposing tendencies of empiricism and mathematics. And, indeed, his work contains both elements. On the
one hand, he adopted Locke's empiricist epistemology, and on the
other, he championed mathematics as the perfect language for
expressing and expanding knowledge. But the union of these
elements remained imperfect in Condillac, betrayed by his incor-
rigibly abstract turn of mind. Since this is not the place for a
detailed analysis of Condillac's use of mathematical logic, which
will be taken up in a subsequent chapter,[15] it must suffice here
to point out that instead of subordinating mathematics to the
requirements of the data by making it an instrument of measurement, comparison, and expression, he selected and shaped his data
to fit the logical structures of analytic algebra. His logic became the
master, rather than the servant, of his thought. In spite of his
empirical philosophy, Condillac was truly heir to the mathematical
tradition.

Condillac's taste for the simplicity and uniformity of mathematics, as opposed to the irreducible diversity of empirical data,
linked him in spite of himself to Descartes. Like Descartes, and
unlike Locke, Condillac was looking for a universal method suitable
for system-building, and both the *Essai sur l'origine des connaissances humaines* of 1746 and the *Traité des systèmes* of 1749 were
dominated by this preoccupation. His criticism of the metaphysicians was at bottom a thoroughgoing condemnation of their
methods, and the purpose of his investigation into how we acquire
knowledge was to find out how to acquire more knowledge.

Directing Condillac's quest was an orientation toward nature
which we shall encounter again and again in his thought and,

15. See below, pp. 61–63.

indeed, in the thought of his century.[16] He assumed that the ideal method is the one by which nature first taught man when he acquired the knowledge necessary for his survival, and that we must recapture this primitive experience if we want insight into the nature of knowledge and the best means of acquiring it. Now one of the problems about eighteenth-century naturalism, as A. O. Lovejoy and Basil Willey have made abundantly clear, is the multivocality of the word "nature."[17] For the sake of simplicity, however, its many meanings may be said to cluster around either of two poles: the view that the essence of nature is contained in the universality, simplicity, and order of its laws, or the view that it is contained in the diversity, complexity, and irregularity of its phenomena. This is the external side of the antithesis between mathematical rationalism and empiricism in the scientific study of nature. Condillac's naturalism, while containing elements of both views, leaned heavily toward the first.

The *Essai sur l'origine des connaissances humaines* must be understood in the light of the foregoing discussion of some of the pervasive elements in Condillac's thought, for it was these elements which determined his ultimate dissatisfaction with Locke's pioneer effort. Condillac considered Locke to have been the first to grasp the true source and organization of human knowledge, but he also felt that Locke had not gone far enough in his analysis of the understanding and that as a result he had left many unanswered questions and unresolved ambiguities. Instead, Condillac offered a genetic analysis of the understanding that would reduce it to a monistic system: "We must go back to the origin of

16. See Zora Schaupp, *The Naturalism of Condillac* (Lincoln, Nebr., 1926). Unfortunately, Miss Schaupp's otherwise useful reevaluation is rendered somewhat superficial by her failure to analyze the complex notion of naturalism.

17. Basil Willey, *The Eighteenth Century Background: Studies on the Idea of Nature in the Thought of the Period* (London, 1940); A. O. Lovejoy, " 'Nature' as Aesthetic Norm," "The Parallel of Deism and Classicism," and " 'Nature' as Norm in Tertullian," *Essays in the History of Ideas* (Baltimore, 1948).

our ideas, explain their generation, follow them to the limits
nature has given them, in order to fix the extent and boundaries
of our knowledge and to recreate the entire human understanding."[18] Condillac's program reflected a nearly universal conviction
of the French Enlightenment that the explanation of anything—
man, ideas, or institutions—lies in its origins.[19] This genetic
explanation is not the same as a historical explanation, which
became characteristic of nineteenth-century thought. The thinkers
of the Enlightenment were seeking not to explain how something
had developed in its uniqueness but, rather, to find the common
ground which constituted its universality. Condillac's genetic analysis was intended to find the fundamental basis of the human
understanding and the universal laws by which it develops its
operations and acquires its ideas. He expected to find that fundamental basis in a single principle which would explain all the
phenomena of the understanding in the same way that Newton's
formula of gravitation explains all the phenomena of motion:
"My plan is to reduce to a single principle everything concerning
the human understanding, and . . . this principle will not be a
vague proposition, nor an abstract maxim, nor a gratuitous supposition, but an invariable experience, all the consequences of
which will be confirmed by new experiences."[20] In other words,
Condillac intended, by the method of genetic analysis, to reduce
all the parts of the understanding to a least common denominator
that would be both logically and temporally prior to the rest.

By contrast, Locke's approach had been descriptive rather than
genetic, and piecemeal rather than systematic. He analyzed the
understanding logically into its separate operations and classified
ideas into their various types; he treated the understanding statical-
ly, as if it were a container or receptacle—or sheet of paper. Locke
described the understanding as "not much unlike a closet wholly

18. *Essai*, in *Œuvres phil.*, *1*, 4.
19. See Lester G. Crocker, *An Age of Crisis: Man and World in
Eighteenth-Century French Thought* (Baltimore, 1959), p. 181.
20. *Essai*, in *Œuvres phil.*, *1*, 4.

shut from light, with only some little openings left, to let in external visible resemblances, or ideas of things without; which, would they but stay there, and lie so orderly as to be found upon occasion, it would very much resemble the understanding of a man, in reference to all the objects of sight and the ideas of them."[21] Condillac, on the other hand, had a more dynamic conception of the understanding. For him the understanding "is only the collection or combination of the operations of the soul. To perceive or have consciousness, to give one's attention, to recognize, imagine, remember, reflect, to distinguish one's ideas, to abstract them, compose them, analyze them, to affirm, to deny, to judge, to reason, to conceive: there you have the understanding."[22]

Locke's static treatment prevented him from giving an adequate account of the activities of the mind. Although he had established to Condillac's satisfaction that the contents of the mind are acquired, he appeared to assume, in his dual attribution of knowledge to sensation and reflection, a kind of autonomous and innate power in the mind to work with its contents. Locke tended to call upon this faculty whenever he was at a loss for an explanation of psychological experience. For example, he presupposed the existence of an unconscious power of judgment to correct errors in visual perception, enabling us to perceive depth and perspective.[23] He also endowed the mind with an unexplained and apparently innate power to combine simple ideas into complex ones.[24] Condillac's persistent attempt to eliminate all autonomous activity from the mind may, I think, be explained in two ways. First, in common with the rest of the philosophes, he could not tolerate the inclusion of a mysterious or occult property in the mind which would lie outside the reach of analysis and explanation. Second, in keeping

---

21. *An Essay concerning Human Understanding* (II.11.17), ed. Alexander Campbell Frazer (2 vols. London, 1894; repr. New York, 1959), *I*, 212.

22. *Essai,* in *Œuvres phil., I*, 28.

23. *Essay concerning Human Understanding* (II.11.17), *I*, 185–89.

24. Ibid. (II.12.1–2), pp. 213–15.

with his desire to reduce all the elements of a thing to a least common denominator, he could not accept the proposition that there are *two* irreducible faculties of the mind: either they must both be reducible to an even more elemental faculty, or one must be reducible to the other. From Condillac's point of view, then, Locke had passed much too lightly over the origins of human knowledge and had contented himself with too many unexplored suppositions about the way the mind converts sensations into knowledge and thought. He regretted that Locke, who had worked on his *Essay* at intervals over a twenty-year period, had not taken the time and effort to reorganize and rewrite the book after his thought on the subject had matured. Since Locke had not done this, Condillac set out to do it himself.[25] Thus the *Essai sur l'origine des connaissances humaines* reflects the *Essay concerning Human Understanding* both as a pattern and as a point of departure.

Condillac's chief task was to account for the development of reflective intelligence without falling back on Locke's autonomous and somewhat mysterious faculty of reflection. This meant that he had to trace the progressive unfolding of the operations of the understanding from bare perception to reflection without appealing to any activity which could not itself be explained by prior operations or by the physical needs of the body. He began with "the impression caused in the mind by the action of the senses"[26] —i.e. perception or consciousness—as our most basic and immediate experience and the primary source of all our ideas. The first step in the development of mental activity out of consciousness is the creation of "attention" by our physical needs, which cause us to experience pleasure or pain in sensation. The accompaniment of pleasure or pain intensifies certain perceptions until they blot out consciousness of any other simultaneous perceptions. This intensification is attention, the sine qua non of the advance of the mind beyond the mere lethargic and discontinuous awareness

25. *Essai,* in *Œuvres phil.,* 1, 5.
26. Ibid., p. 10.

of its sensations.[27] Attention brings about this advance by forming the mechanism which converts simple sensations into the data of thought—the association of ideas. Since things attract our attention only by the connection they have to our needs, it follows that our attention takes in at the same time the need and the object or idea to which the need is directed. Henceforth, the link between the two which exists in nature also exists in our minds. Needs which are related to one another, the objects which satisfy them, the places where we have found those objects—all these begin to form chains of associated ideas which expand and multiply as our experience grows. Once a chain of ideas is formed, it is only necessary to attend to the first idea in the sequence to recall all the other ideas. This mechanism makes it possible for the mind to recall perceptions when the objects which cause them are no longer present to the senses.[28]

The most rudimentary form of memory is the ability to recognize a repeated perception as one we have already experienced. This is the foundation of all meaningful experience because it is the source of self-awareness. Unlike both Locke and Descartes, Condillac denied that self-awareness is an immediate and intuitive experience. Like any other idea, the idea of the self must be acquired from the raw material of sensation. It is our recognition of a repeated perception which makes us conscious of a continuous self to which the perception belonged before and to which it belongs again. Without this recognition each moment of life would seem to be the first moment of our existence and our knowledge would never extend beyond a single perception.[29]

Up to this point in its growth the understanding has been purely passive, subject to the accidental changes in the stimuli presented to it from outside. Even the memories or images of absent objects have been brought to mind by the chance presentation of objects associated with them. In other words, at this stage of

27. Ibid., pp. 11–13.
28. Ibid., p. 17.
29. Ibid., p. 14.

his development a man would not have the power of disposing of his own attention or of directing the course of his own thoughts. The invention of signs is the necessary step which provides him with the means of taking command of his mental processes. With the use of signs to stand for ideas, the way is opened to a full development of the powers of reflection, which is defined simply as the voluntary successive application of the attention to different objects or the different parts of a single object.[30] All the higher operations of the mind can then be derived from the faculty of reflection. To compare ideas, to judge whether two ideas are the same or different, to abstract a general characteristic common to several ideas—these are all simply different ways of running through a series of associated ideas, or, in other words, different manners of reflecting.[31]

Condillac discovered his Newtonian principle of the understanding in the ancient doctrine of the association of ideas.[32] The laws of association had been formulated by Aristotle to explain the workings of memory; he found that ideas are joined because of similarity, difference, or contiguity. The idea of association occurs in this form as a casual commonplace of little significance in a wide variety of philosophers from Epicurus to Descartes. Hobbes was the first modern writer to endow it with any importance, for he used it to explain a wider range of mental phenomena than those of memory. It appeared in Locke as an afterthought, a chapter added to Book II in the fourth edition of the *Essay* (1700) to explain human error and eccentricity by the adventitious association of intrinsically unrelated ideas. Hume used it in the *Treatise on Human Nature* (1738) in much the same way Hobbes had, and Hartley's *Observations on Man* (1749) finally established the well-known school of English associationist psychology, in which associationism was the basis for explaining the entire human understanding. Condillac, however, anticipated Hartley in this thoroughgoing associa-

30. Ibid., p. 22.
31. Ibid., p. 33.
32. Ibid., p. 4.

tionism by three years. Condillac's source for the idea probably cannot be established. Hume had not been translated into French by 1746 and Condillac read no English. He might have read Hobbes in French but there is no evidence that he did so. Neither Locke's use of association nor the traditional Aristotelian conception was broad enough to allow for Condillac's development of it into a universal principle. Perhaps the best that can be said is that the notion of the association of ideas was in the air. Condillac might have picked it up in conversation with someone who had read Hobbes or Hume. Or it might be simply another of those independent but by no means accidental simultaneous developments which mark the course of intellectual history. The association of ideas was a useful and satisfying notion for the eighteenth century, comprehensive enough to give a plausible explanation of our mental processes, concrete enough to be observed in action, and mechanistic enough to fit the scientific scheme of things. For precisely these reasons it was soon to serve Bentham as *his* Newtonian principle of moral science.

Clearly the association of ideas was the gateway to reflective thinking in Condillac's analysis. But besides explaining the ordinary activity of the mind, it also accounted for individual styles of thinking and deviations from the normal mental constitution. The association of ideas is a function of mental organization, and differences in that organization produce different degrees of facility. A man with very little power of association would be an imbecile; with an excessive facility in associating ideas he would be a madman, because his bizarre imagination would seize upon farfetched associations and combine ideas into fantastic sequences. Within the range of normalcy there is variation between the slow and careful associative process that produces profound thinking and the quick and fluent associations that characterize the graceful and witty mind. But the principle of *all* thinking, productive or frivolous, sane or fantastic, precise or careless, is the association of ideas.[33]

33. Ibid., pp. 18–19.

Condillac dealt with epistemology primarily from the point of view of the psychology of thought. He was interested in the way man used his mind and in finding a set of directions that would help him to use it better. Only occasionally and incidentally did he turn his attention to the more metaphysical aspects of epistemology—to problems of truth and reality—and when he did so, he tended, in disregard of his own commandments, to be careless, eclectic, and ambiguous. His usual method with such problems was to take a passage nearly verbatim from Locke and then, evidently dissatisfied with Locke's diffuseness or with statements uncongenial to his own assumptions, to cut the passage short and end with a hasty qualification put together on the spur of the moment. As a result, Condillac's metaphysics fairly bristles with inconsistencies and imprecisions baffling to the reader. Nevertheless, some observations may be made regarding Condillac's ideas about the self, the materials of knowledge, and their relation to external reality.

"Whether we ascend (to speak metaphorically) up to the heavens or go down into the abyss, we never leave ourselves, and what we perceive is never anything but our own thought."[34] This succinct statement of Condillac's most fundamental and consistently held epistemological principle leaves unanswered the question of the relationship between our thought and the external world. For the most part, Condillac did not depart radically from the theory of representative perception laid down by Descartes and assumed by Locke, but he did lean toward a withdrawal into a kind of solipsism in which the only "true reality" is in the modifications of one's own being.[35] It is through these modifications—that is, through sensory experiences—that we come to know both ourselves and the world beyond ourselves. Condillac did not accept the proposition of both Descartes and Locke that we have an immediate and intuitive experience of the self. He argued instead that we come to know ourselves as the unchanging substance to

34. Ibid., p. 6.
35. Ibid., p. 50.

which modifications happen. Condillac might have said, "I am modified, therefore I exist." The discovery of the self occurs prior to the projection of sensory experiences onto the outside world, which is a necessary and inevitable step in human awareness, but one which takes away from our experiences their "true reality." For our ideas of light, color, and sound are real, true, clear, and distinct only so long as we see them as belonging to ourselves. As soon as we abstract them from their subject, our own being, and consider them apart from ourselves and existing in combination outside us as "objects," error becomes possible.

Inconsistencies in Condillac's treatment of error in sensory experience reveal that he failed to face squarely the problem of reality created by the subjectivist epistemology. He accepted the Cartesian charge that sense perception is an unreliable source of knowledge and set about erecting a sensationalist epistemology which could claim to take that unreliability into account, but at the crucial moment in his argument Condillac turned away from the issue into a question-begging conclusion:

> There are three things to be distinguished in our sensations: 1. The perception that we experience. 2. The attribution we make of it to something outside us. 3. The judgment that what we attribute to things belongs to them in fact.
>
> There is no error, no obscurity, and no confusion in what happens within us, nor in our external attribution of it. If we reflect, for example, that we have the ideas of a certain size and a certain shape, and that we attribute them to a certain body, there is nothing here that is not true, clear and distinct. . . . If error enters in, it is only insofar as we judge that such a size and such a shape belong in fact to such a body.[36]

36. Ibid., p. 9. Similar statements may be found in both Descartes and Malebranche: René Descartes, *Les Principes de la philosophie* (Pt. I, chap. 68), in *Œuvres*, ed. Charles Adam and Paul Tannery (13 vols. Paris, 1897–1913), 9, 56; Malebranche, *De La Recherche de la vérité*, in *Œuvres complètes*, 1, 77–78.

So far Condillac has simply restated the Cartesian criticism of
sensory experience in a way which implies an answer to it. We
derive all our ideas from sensation; those ideas are clear, distinct,
and true, and it is equally clear, distinct, and true that we refer our
ideas to an external source. As long as we draw no conclusions
about the real, objective nature of the external source, we are on
firm ground. Condillac seems to be answering the Cartesians with
a radical idealism similar to Berkeley's. But he did not stand his
ground. He went on to give an illustration of his position which
utterly destroyed it. "If, for example, I see from afar a square
building, it will seem round to me. Is there then obscurity and
confusion in the idea of roundness, or in the reference that I make
of it? No; but I judge that building to be round; there is the
error."[37] Now this sort of error is worlds apart from the kind of
radical doubt that the Cartesians cast upon sense perception. They
had in mind a basic inadequacy of man's senses, an unbridgeable
gap between the nature of mind and the nature of external physical
reality. Condillac's reduction of this problem to mere faulty perspective changes its whole character, because it makes of it a
correctible defect in perception. We can find out that the "round"
building is really square by walking up closer to it. We can, in
other words, correct our erroneous observation by more observation. And, indeed, Condillac himself asserted finally that the judgments we make about sensory perceptions "can be useful to us
only after a well-considered experience has corrected their defects."[38] One is back, then, to a common-sense empiricism which
presupposes the external world and its accessibility.

Turning from the unsolved problem of the objective nature of
reality to the subjective assessment of it, Condillac stated that
ideas are the link between our discrete, unorganized sensations and
knowledge. It is by being formulated into ideas that "thought"
(a general term for Condillac, meaning everything the mind experi-

37. *Essai*, in *Œuvres phil.*, *1*, 9.
38. Ibid.; cf. *La Logique*, in *Œuvres phil.*, 2, 373: "Thus the senses themselves often destroy the errors into which they have made us fall."

ences) constitutes knowledge. A thought becomes an idea when we take cognizance of it as representing something other than itself, whether that something is an external object or an internal operation. Most fundamentally, a perception is a simple idea, provided it is clear and distinct. Condillac had taken over the Cartesian criteria of clarity and distinctness, but he used them in a different way. Not only did he find clarity and distinctness in perception rather than conception, but he had emasculated them as criteria of truth by limiting the nature of truth. "What is more clear than our perception of sound and color! What more distinct!"[39] But what is the truth which the clarity and distinctness guarantee? When we have a clear and distinct idea we know that it is true that we have such an idea, for an "idea" which is not clear and distinct is in reality no idea at all.[40] The "truth" so verified has been reduced to a tautology.

Finally, then, we must ask where our thoughts and ideas come from. Thought has two sources. In the first place, we acquire thoughts through specific sensations, such as light, color, pleasure, or pain. Or, rather, these unorganized sensations *are* thoughts—the very first thoughts we have. The second source is the mind's own activity. For our next thoughts consist of the ideas we form by reflecting on the internal operations which sensations give rise to, such as perceiving or imagining.[41] The mental activity of reflecting involved Condillac in the same epistemological ambiguity for which he had criticized Locke. In developing the psychological processes of the mind, Condillac had deprived reflection of its autonomy by making it depend upon the mechanical association of ideas. But in his epistemological theory of the origin of ideas he tried to achieve the same end simply by making reflection appear later than sensation. Mere temporal priority, however, does not of itself establish a genetic priority, and since Condillac probed no deeper into the relationship of reflection to sensation,

39. *Essai,* in *Œuvres phil., 1,* 8.
40. Ibid., p. 10.
41. Ibid., p. 6.

the essential ambiguity remained unsolved in his first book. The
mind still appeared to be endowed with an unexplained and innate power incompatible with his strict empiricism. His own
dissatisfaction with this state of affairs led him to turn his attention to the problem again in the *Traité des sensations,* where he
worked out his theory of the origin of ideas more rigorously, and
succeeded in eliminating innate reflection. The *Essai,* however, at
least established that, for Condillac, there are no ideas which are
not acquired: that is to say, there are no innate ideas.

In the middle of Condillac's *Essai sur l'origine des connaissances
humaines* there is a long section entitled "On the Origin and
Progress of Language." Detailed discussion of Condillac's theory of
language will be taken up later, but it might be well to consider
here the place and relevance of a study of language in a work of
metaphysics. The explanation lies in part in a novel interpretation
of "metaphysics." Metaphysics had traditionally meant the systematic investigation of the ultimate nature of things, of the
underlying substance of Reality, of the first principles (substantively
understood) of philosophy. In this sense metaphysics was in bad
odor among the philosophes, who regarded the quest for "essences"
as futile and nonsensical. Although they rejected the Aristotelian
and scholastic understanding of the term, however, not all philosophes gave up the term itself. Instead, it began to take on a new
sense as the investigation of the nature and conditions of human•
knowledge in order to establish the methodological principles and
techniques by which all investigations, including those of science,
must proceed.[42] Thus, said Condillac:

> Of all the sciences metaphysics is the one which best embraces
> all the objects of our knowledge. It is at once a science of
> sensible truths and a science of abstract truths: a science of
> sensible truths because it is the science of that which we per-
> ceive by sensation within us, as physics is the science of that
> which we perceive by sensation outside us; a science of

42. See Smith, *A History of Modern Culture,* 2, 160.

abstract truths because it is metaphysics that discovers principles, that forms systems, and that provides all the methods of
reasoning. Mathematics itself is only a branch of metaphysics.
It presides therefore over all our knowledge, and this prerogative is due to it, for since it is necessary to treat the
sciences relative to our manner of conceiving, it is for metaphysics, which alone knows the human mind, to guide us in
the study of each. Everything, in some respects, is in its
province.[43]

Condillac's understanding of the function of metaphysics foreshadows the twentieth-century notion that the philosopher's business is to clarify concepts and to analyze language—that is, to
keep the tools of thought sharp and serviceable. Inevitably, philosophy so understood becomes far more concerned with the names
of things and concepts than with the things and concepts themselves. This attitude parallels a like tendency in epistemology
when ideas are made to mediate between our minds and "reality."
In both cases there is a shift in focus, a retraction of the gaze
from "real" objects to the ideas or sensations or names which represent those objects to us, and which become more "real," by
virtue of their immediate accessibility, than the objects themselves. Ideas and names, then, become less instrumental, less restricted to their imputed function of pointing beyond themselves
to "reality," and come to take the place of the entities they had
merely stood for in the older philosophies. Thus Condillac's meta-

---

43. *De L'Art de raisonner,* in *Œuvres phil., 1,* 619. Bacon also classified
mathematics as a branch of metaphysics but for quite different reasons.
He defined metaphysics as the study of formal and final causes, and the
subject of mathematics as determined or proportionable quantity, which
appears to be "one of the essential forms of things." Moreover, observed
Bacon with a perceptible sneer, metaphysics is the study of abstractions, and
"it being the nature of the mind of man (to the extreme prejudice of
knowledge) to delight in the spacious liberty of generalities . . . the
mathematics of all other knowledge were the goodliest fields to satisfy that
appetite." Francis Bacon, *The Advancement of Learning* (III.2), in his
Works, ed. J. Spedding, et al. (14 vols. London, 1857–74), *4,* 369–70.

physics is about ideas, his epistemology is about sensations, and
his methodology is about names. The world of his concern and his
philosophy is a greatly diminished world. He does not presume to
range the cosmos or penetrate to the nature of things, because he,
like most of his contemporaries, believes that it is not given to
man to do so. It is enough for him to clarify the contents of
our minds, and since those contents are largely made up of words,
with or without ideas attached, the origin and progress of language
becomes an appropriate object of study.

Besides the interest in words which was intrinsic to his general
philosophical posture, Condillac had a more direct concern with
language. Language provides a crucial link in his psychology of
thought by converting the initially passive operations of the mind
into active ones. It is Condillac's thesis that it is language, and not
an autonomous power of the soul, which gives man control over
his faculties. But having asserted and demonstrated this thesis, Condillac was further responsible for demonstrating that language itself
is not a special and innate endowment of the human mind. To do
this he had to show how language originated and developed according to principles compatible with his system. In addition, the link
between Condillac's epistemology and his methodology was his
theory of signs. The process of naming is a step in acquiring knowledge, but its present thoughtless haphazardness causes a great deal
of error. Half the methodological battle will be won if we can recover the way in which man first named things under the pressure
of need. Then every word he possessed was attached to a clear and
distinct idea, and meant the same to everyone who uttered it. Only
in arithmetic has this clarity and accuracy been maintained.[44]

The recognition that words are necessary not merely to communicate but to think was a cornerstone of Condillac's psychology
of knowledge and thought. In the development of the reflective
intelligence the stage at which the distinctively human character
of man's mind emerges from the passive animal experience of
externally determined stimuli is the stage at which he invents

44. *Essai*, in *Œuvres phil.*, I, 105.

signs to stand for ideas. Only then can man take control of his thoughts, his memory, and his imagination. Only then does he become an active thinker capable of initiating a chain of associations at will. Thus "the use of signs is the true cause of the progress of the imagination, contemplation, and memory."[45]

But what about the invention of language itself? Does that not suggest a creative faculty in man, independent and self-generating? Condillac's answer to this question was to demonstrate that signs could have been invented with nothing but physical reactions to outside stimuli and the mental mechanism of the association of ideas. Natural cries and gestures, with which the body spontaneously expresses feelings and responds to external events, make up the raw material of signs. Habitual repetition of a cry or gesture in a recurring situation sets up an association between the two, so that the cry or gesture comes to signify the situation or the emotion the situation provokes. When man recognizes the principle that sounds or gestures may stand for things, he can begin to invent signs deliberately. With this act of choice, accidental or natural signs become "les signes d'institution," signs established by man's will and made general and permanent by convention. Hereafter the connection between signs and the things they stand for may be an arbitrary one, whereas the primitive, undeliberated cry or gesture always had a natural link to its object. Once the creation of signs becomes intentional, it also becomes careless, as man, no longer controlled in his choices by simple need, becomes inattentive and inconsistent. As a result, he makes up many words which do not represent clear and distinct ideas, words which he uses as though he understood them when in fact they have no meaning at all. This problem—which today would be called the problem of semantics[46]—was Condillac's entry into methodology, for he insisted that no productive thought can take place in any discipline until its vocabulary has been clarified. His model for the renewal

45. Ibid., p. 19.

46. See below, Chap. 6, for more extended discussion of Condillac's theory of language and the historical antecedents of his concern with semantics.

of language was mathematics. Numbers were his ideal signs because they are precise, they mean the same things to all who use them, and they may be analyzed into a common denominator —one—for accurate comparison.

The materials of knowledge, the operations of the mind, the origin and growth of language—these subjects were treated in the *Essai* not for their own sake but as preparation for the concluding section, "On Method." The purpose of the *Essai,* after all, was to try to fill the need for a satisfactory method of investigation. Condillac asserted that the critical philosophers, Descartes and the rest, could not provide adequate constructive programs because they do not get back to the source of error, eradicate it, and start anew. As a result, they merely fall from one error into another. Error, says Condillac, arises from our habit of reasoning on things without clear and distinct ideas of them. We acquire this habit as children when, haphazardly and unreflectingly accumulating sense impressions, we build up a stock of uncritically held ideas, like Bacon's Idols of the Cave. When we first begin to reflect, we find these ideas in our minds and call them "reason," "natural light," "principles engraved on the soul," and so on, and having attributed them to God, we mistake them for true first principles. The way we form our language reinforces this inexact thinking. We learn language before the age of reason, and except for words to make known our needs, chance largely determines what words we hear and what ideas we attach to them. Joining signs to things has become so natural to us by the time we have attained the age of reason that we tend to think that names refer to the very reality of objects and explain their essence. Descartes and Malebranche claim that our passions lead us into error, but Condillac argues that language is a still more fundamental cause. Passions may lead to the abuse of a vague principle or a metaphorical expression for self-serving purposes, but it is vagueness and metaphor which create the possibility of error in the first place.[47]

47. *Essai,* in *Œuvres phil., 1,* 104–05.

To eliminate vagueness and to purge our ideas from error, Condillac set forth a critical method which was a more radical version of Cartesian doubt—Cartesian doubt, perhaps, as Bacon would have conceived it. For Descartes' deficiency was that he only doubted the *truth* of his ideas; he doubted whether they corresponded to objective reality, but he did not doubt the ideas themselves. He doubted whether two and two make four and whether man is a reasonable animal, but this doubt assumed that he had ideas of "two," "four," "man," "reasonable," and "animal," so that he fell right back into the errors caused by taking ideas for granted.[48] Condillac argued that we need a fresh set of ideas and a new language to express them. To give plausibility to this suggestion, he hypothesized a newly created man, a man with the full faculties of reason but having no ideas (since ideas come only from experience). By placing this man in different situations and imagining the sense impressions he would experience, a new stock of ideas can be created. If the stock is gradually increased, and confusion and vagueness are guarded against, all the usual errors can be avoided. The names of simple ideas will be clear, because they will mean only what has been perceived in given circumstances. The names of complex ideas will be precise, because they will include only the simple ideas that have been perceived in combination with one another. To show others what one's words mean, one has only to place them in the situation in which one invented the words. Condillac called this procedure the method by which nature gives us ideas—an appeal to the one authority recognized by everyone.[49]

To this general plan Condillac added more specific directions for forming clear ideas. Simple ideas are easily made because they come immediately from the senses. Since they refer to simple perceptions—which are in fact in the mind exactly as they appear—they cannot have imaginary entities as their object. Not even children are confused by the names of sensations or of simple

48. Ibid., p. 112.
49. Ibid., pp. 106–07, 110–11.

operations of the mind, for they know exactly what they mean by
"red" or "sweet" and by "yes," "no," "I want," "I don't want."
The names of simple ideas can be exactly determined provided we
do not make the mistake of believing either that sensations are
in the objects or that the same objects produce in each of us the
same sensations.[50] The trouble arises with complex ideas, which
are the work of the mind. "If they are defective, it is because we
have made them badly. The only way to correct them is to remake
them. We must therefore take the materials of our knowledge
[i.e. simple ideas] and put them to work as if they had never been
used before."[51]

There are two kinds of complex notions, with a set of rules for
each.[52] Notions of substances[53] are formed after external models,
and "archetypal" notions are combinations of simple ideas which
the mind puts together on its own, such as notions about morals,

50. Ibid., pp. 107–08. The second of these two points requires some
elaboration since it appears to negate Condillac's earlier assertion that the
names of simple ideas can be communicated to another person by putting
him in the same circumstances as those which caused the invention of the
name. If it cannot be presumed that the second person will experience the
same sensation as the first person in the same circumstances, what, exactly,
is communicated? Condillac asserts that it does not make any difference
that what one person calls "blue" appears the same to him as what others
call "green." He understands just as well what is meant by "the grass is
green," "the sky is blue," as if he had the same sensations in the presence
of grass and sky as others have, because all these phrases mean is that "the
sky and grass come to our knowledge under appearances which enter into
our mind by sight, and which we name 'blue,' 'green.' "

51. Ibid., p. 108.

52. Cf. Locke, An Essay concerning Human Understanding (II.12.4–6),
1, 215–16.

53. Condillac uses the term "substance" to refer to the material elements
of the universe—gold, iron, etc. Since we can only know the properties of
these elements, and cannot know them as they are in themselves, he defines substance as "a name given to a thing which we do not know in
itself" (Dictionnaire des synonymes, in Œuvres phil., 3, 521). Evidently he
wished to repudiate any claim to a knowledge of substances in the Aristotelian or scholastic sense of the word, although his use of it is different
enough to make the repudiation superfluous.

jurisprudence, and the arts. Notions of substances must not be
made by combining simple ideas arbitrarily. If they are to be
clear and precise, they must be patterned accurately after the
models furnished by nature. The simple ideas brought together
in a complex notion of substance must also coexist in nature.
Somewhat more complicated are ideas which are abstracted from
substances. An abstraction is an idea to which we give our attention by ceasing to think of the other ideas which coexist with it.
Thus we can abstract the idea of matter from the more complex
idea of body. And if we cease to think of the mobility, divisibility,
and impenetrability of matter in order to reflect only on its in-
definite extension, we shall form the idea of pure space, which is
still more simple than that of matter. It is the same with all abstractions, whereby it appears that the names of the most abstract
ideas are as easy to determine as those of the substances themselves.

The procedure for archetypal notions is quite different. They
may be formed without any models. "Legislators had no models
when they brought together for the first time certain simple ideas
from which they composed laws, and when they spoke of many
human actions before having considered whether any examples of
them existed. Models for the arts were not to be found except in the
minds of the first inventors. . . . Human actions occur in an infinite
variety of combinations and it is often in our interest to have
ideas of them before we have seen models."[54] The clarity and distinctness of archetypal notions, then, depends on internal consistency and on the clarity and distinctness of the simple ideas
which make them up. Condillac summed up the difference between
the two kinds of complex notions:

> There is this difference between the notions of substances
> and archetypal notions, that we regard the latter as models
> to which we refer exterior things, and that the former are only
> copies of what we perceive outside us. For the first to be true,
> the combinations in our mind must conform to what we

54. *Essai*, in *Œuvres phil.*, *I*, 109–10.

observe in the things; for the second to be true it is sufficient
if the combinations outside us *can* be such as they are in our
minds. The notion of justice would be true even if there
were no just action to be found, because its truth consists in
a collection of ideas which does not depend on what happens
outside us. The notion of iron is true only so far as it conforms to the metal, because the metal must be its model.[55]

It will be noted that Condillac's criterion for the truth of a notion
of substance appears to support a correspondence theory of truth,
which his epistemology would not allow. To determine whether our
notion of iron corresponds to the metal, we would need to be able
to transcend our perceptions and compare our ideas of iron with
the iron itself, an act which Condillac denies we can perform. The
apparent inconsistency is only a result of carelessness of expression—a vice Condillac sometimes slipped into in spite of his warn-
ings against it. He really meant not that our notion of a substance
must conform to the substance but, rather, that it must be a copy
"of what we perceive outside us." Now we perceive, according to
Condillac, only simple ideas; notions (complex ideas) are products
of our minds. Thus his criterion of the truth of a notion of substance
merely requires us to check on whether that notion is in fact made
up of the simple ideas we perceive—the simple ideas, all the simple
ideas, and nothing but the simple ideas. Basically, this is quite as
much a coherence theory of truth as that of archetypal notions.

All this has been only a preliminary to method rather than
method itself. But once we have purged our minds of all vague
and careless ideas and expressions and built up a stock of clear
and distinct ideas with which to work, we can turn to the business
of discovering truth. There is only one method for discovering
truth, according to Condillac, and that method is "analysis."
"Analysis," like "nature," "reason," and "geometry," was a magic
word for the Enlightenment. It was borrowed from the method of
scientific discovery, and in particular from Newton. Voltaire and

55. Ibid., p. 110.

d'Alembert, as well as Condillac, championed it as the necessary corrective to the seventeenth-century habit of reasoning about fundamentally unintelligible mysteries.[56] In general, of course, analysis means to break something down into its parts in order to understand what it is and how it operates. As such, it is a useful and effective procedure in most kinds of investigation. But Condillac wanted it to mean something more than that. He wanted to find an absolute methodological principle, a formula which could be uniformly applied to all problems of metaphysics and morals, and which would make philosophical investigation an exact science. His chief illustration of analysis was, as always, drawn from mathematics. But the exactness of mathematics depends upon quantitative relationships, and when Condillac tried to show how a quantitative analysis could be applied to philosophic questions, he became either vague or trivial, as, for example, in his suggestion that any two complex notions can be perfectly compared because we can analyze them into their simple ideas and then count the number of simple ideas in each.[57]

Although Condillac had not fully worked out his methodology in the *Essai,* he did make some unsystematized suggestions based on his observations of the process of thinking. If analysis is the secret of discovery, the association of ideas is the secret of analysis.[58] Therefore, to investigate a topic we should bring to mind all the ideas we have on that topic and think about them from the point of view having the greatest association with the ideas we seek. Then we shall make discoveries almost without effort. This approach represents a new consciousness of subjective processes (the rationalists were not so aware of the role of conscious attention in productive thinking), but it does not constitute the great

56. See Ernst Cassirer, *The Philosophy of the Enlightenment,* trans. Fritz C. A. Koelln and James P. Pettegrove (Princeton, 1951), pp. 7–13.

57. *Essai,* in *Œuvres phil., 1,* 39. Grimm pointed out, with much sarcasm, that Condillac never succeeded in applying his methods. See *Correspondance littéraire, 11,* 56–57.

58. *Essai,* in *Œuvres phil., 1,* 114.

methodological discovery that Condillac had intended. His own dissatisfaction may be inferred from his unceasing preoccupation with problems of method, from the *Traité des systèmes,* published just three years after the *Essai,* to the posthumously published *La Langue des calculs,* written at the very end of his life.

Behind Condillac's statement of method, incomplete though it is, are some revealing assumptions and attitudes. While there is no need to belabor further the admiration for Newtonian science which dictated the attempt to imitate Newton's methods, more subtle implications are to be found in what Condillac has to say about method, implications about the meaning of truth and about that troublesome and complicated shibboleth, "nature."

Again and again Condillac emphasized that the method he advocated was "natural"—or, more specifically, the method by which nature teaches us.[59] And yet his model of the newly created mature man acquiring ideas, which is surely more artificial than natural, makes us wonder what the word "natural" means to him. His is a naturalism quite unlike a romantic naturalism rejoicing in chance and eccentricity, or even a scientific naturalism with its scrupulous concern for the way things in fact happen. For Condillac the source of error lies in the haphazard way we learn things as children—in other words, the way we in fact learn. Condillac presents a sort of idealistic naturalism in which the natural state of something is almost akin to Platonic forms or Aristotelian final causation. The natural is the pristine, the way things ought to be or once were before being marred by accidental changes, and the way things still are underneath the encrustations. An uncut diamond is unnatural because the natural, the original, the pristine diamond is the polished gem hidden inside. Hence the aim of Condillac's naturalism is always to get down to the hidden purity of things.[60] There is a kind of fall suggested here, an original sin

59. *La Logique,* in *Œuvres phil.,* 2, 372–73.

60. For an account of the same phenomenon with respect to religious truths, see Lovejoy's discussion of "rationalistic primitivism" in "The Parallel of Deism and Classicism," *Essays in the History of Ideas,* pp. 86–88.

which corrupted man's original innocence and purity, but the exact nature of the fall is hard to define. It is of course unlike the Christian Fall caused by eating the fruit of the tree of knowledge of good and evil. It is also unlike Rousseau's notion of a fall from the natural state to the corrupt civilized state, although the latter is more akin to Condillac's idea than is the Christian. For Rousseau, however, it was the natural virtue of man which was lost through the fall, whereas for Condillac man seems to have lost the natural capacity for clear and precise reasoning. This capacity suggests but is not quite the same as man's "natural reason," which is an idea belonging to the advocates of natural religion, who, as romantic rationalists, so to speak, held something akin to the doctrine of innate ideas but gave it a sentimental or ethical turn. Natural reason, as they understood it, was never cold or abstract. It was somewhere between the Quaker's Inner Light and the Cartesian's innate ideas—a sort of moral recognition of certain fundamental truths about the nature of God. But for Condillac, strict sensationalist as he was, no such natural reason was possible. What man lost through his fall from Condillac's rather abstract state of nature was a kind of purity of experience in which the clarity of his ideas was not muddied by the diversity and carelessness of experiences unrelated to the demands of his body—demands which enforced clear thinking and accurate learning with a life and death sanction, or at least a pleasure-pain sanction.[61] Truth, in this view, becomes subject in a backdoor sort of way to a pragmatic test. If an idea works—that is, if it secures pleasure and avoids pain—it must be true, not because truth is so defined, but because of an underlying assumption that there is a correspondence between the external and internal worlds, that there is a regularity or uniformity in nature, and, above all, that man and the natural world do belong together. Just as for Descartes God cannot deceive, so for Condillac nature cannot deceive. This never-failing confidence in nature was a thread running through all Condillac's works from the *Essai* to the *Langue des calculs.*

61. Cf. *La Logique*, in *Œuvres phil.*, 2, 373–74.

In a way, Condillac's entire intellectual career was programmed in the *Essai sur l'origine des connaissances humaines,* for it contains in germ nearly every idea to appear in his subsequent works. In the *Traité des systèmes* he expanded the criticism of the seventeenth-century rationalists contained in the introductory chapters of the *Essai,* and made a more thorough attempt to develop a methodology on the model of mathematical physics. The *Traité des sensations* is a more rigorous development of the sensationalist psychology first broached in the *Essai,* and of course the newly created man with the blank mind was the prototype of the famous statue-man of the *Traité des sensations.* The volumes written for the Prince of Parma, preceded by a "preliminary Discourse" on the theory of education, grew out of a few casual statements in the *Essai* on the "natural" method of learning. His *Grammaire, Logique,* and *Langue des calculs* were foreshadowed in the section on language. Moreover, his many-volumed ancient and modern history also reflects the thoughts contained in his historical account of the growth of language, and his *Art d'écrire* represents the aesthetic doctrines first presented in the same section. It may be said, then, that by 1746, at the age of 32, Condillac had already staked out the areas of thought he was to spend his life exploring, and that, furthermore, he had already conceived the fundamental ideas and ways of thought which were to dominate his mind. There are no dramatic reversals of opinion in Condillac's life. Even the treatise on commerce and government, published four years before his death, although reflecting a new interest, represents an old technique—the analysis and clarification of language according to the model of science.

The role of the *Essai* in Condillac's development makes perfectly good sense in the light of his statements about the importance and function of metaphysics. Metaphysics, as he conceived it, is supposed to be preliminary to all other studies and sciences. Metaphysics clears the mind and defines the ideas with which science will build the world. And that is just what Condillac meant the *Essai* to do. It is indeed a new concept of metaphysics, in which metaphysics is no longer the study of "reality" but a prolegomenon to the creation of systems of thought. The metaphysician serves man by investigating the source and nature of human knowledge and prescribing the techniques of thought based on that investigation. Metaphysics has ceased to be the summit toward which thinking gropes, and has become instead the marker on the trail— the archetype, perhaps, of the linguistic analysis of the twentieth century. Condillac's venture into metaphysics *en géomètre,* then, was the prolegomenon to his critical analysis of the major rationalist systems and to his construction of the principles upon which he believed true systems of thought could be built.

3. True Systems and False Systems

System:

A body of knowledge with mutually dependent parts, which is derived from a single principle, so that a good system is simply a principle successfully expanded. I know that many people take this word in bad part, believing that every system is a gratuitous hypothesis or something worse, like the dreams of metaphysicians. Nevertheless, this universe is nothing but a system, that is to say, a multitude of phenomena which, being related to one another as causes and effects, all spring from a first law.

Each part of it having the least complexity is a system: man himself is a system. If, then, we renounce systems, how can we explore anything deeply? I agree that in general philosophers are wrong. They invent systems, but systems should not be invented. We should discover those which the author of nature has made.[1]

In the *Traité des systèmes* (1749) Condillac expanded the methodological quest of his early years. Continuing his search for a geometric metaphysics he analyzed the writings of the major philosophers who fell short of his standard of mathematical clarity and precision. Ironically, two of the metaphysicians attacked by Condillac on these grounds were great creative mathematicians—Descartes and Leibniz.[2] In spite of their mathematical achievements, Condillac

---

1. *Dictionnaire des synonymes,* in *Œuvres phil. de Condillac, 3,* 511–12.
2. Perhaps professional mathematicians—those who know the subject best—expect less of mathematics than do the amateurs. Cf. Carl J. Friedrich, *The Age of the Baroque, 1610–1660* (New York, 1952), p. 121: "But like Bacon and Spinoza, [Hobbes] was prevented by his mathematical ineptitude from appreciating the philosophical limits of any mathematics of the infinite. Unlike Kepler, Descartes, and Pascal, whose mathematical

classified them, as well as Spinoza, Malebranche, and the forgotten author of a treatise on "physical premotion" (Père Boursier), with magicians and astrologers—as examples of the abuse of speculative systems. Philosophers and savages go astray for the same reason: they rely on vague ideas expressed by ill-defined words. This is the substance of all the critical arguments in the *Traité des systèmes*.

Condillac wasted little time on Descartes, since he felt that Locke had successfully destroyed Cartesian metaphysics in his attack on the doctrine of innate ideas.[3] He had a higher opinion of Malebranche, calling him "one of the finest minds of the last century."[4] But even Malebranche, though "of all the Cartesians, he best perceived the causes of our errors,"[5] failed to understand the activities of the mind because he insisted on treating them metaphorically, by analogy with the activities of matter.

If Malebranche misused words in one way, by taking metaphors literally, Spinoza misused them in another, by building his system on words that are meaningless, a vice common to philosophers: "Although they had no idea of what is called 'substance,' they invented the word 'essence' to mean that which constitutes 'substance,' and, in order that no one suspect this term of being itself empty of meaning, they further invented that of 'attribute' to mean that which constitutes essence. . . . Thus it is that a labyrinth of words serves to conceal the profound ignorance of the metaphysicians."[6]

Finally, Leibniz failed, according to Condillac, because he tried

---

genius made them realize the strictly formal nature of the mathematical insight, which in turn made them recognize the residual substantive problems of existence, Hobbes overestimated the cognitional value of mathematical insights."

3. Indeed, Condillac felt that Locke "did the opinion of innate ideas too much honor by the number and the solidity of the reflections he opposed to it. So much was not needed to destroy so vain a shadow." *Traité des systèmes*, in *Œuvres phil.*, 1, 143.

4. Ibid., p. 150.

5. *Essai*, in *Œuvres phil.*, 1, 3.

6. *Traité des systèmes*, in *Œuvres phil.*, 1, 172.

to explain phenomena he did not understand by principles that he understood no better. For example, he explained that a substance is extended only because it is the aggregate of several unextended substances—an explanation that, Condillac suggests, adds nothing to our knowledge of either substance or extension. Furthermore, Leibniz' monads were inadequate as building-blocks of the universe, because he was never able to explain clearly what they are, what the "force" of one is, or what it means to say that they have perceptions.[7]

It appears, then, that philosophers and metaphysicians are as foolish and undiscriminating as the vulgar who get their interpretations of the universe from astrologers and magicians. Why should this be so? Why do men—layman and philosopher alike—fall into such gross errors? The heart of the matter, according to Condillac, is a false idea of the origin and organization of knowledge. The doctrine of innate ideas, the belief that ideas precede sensations, is the most pernicious of these false notions. "They regarded sensation as something which comes after ideas and which modifies them; an error which made them invent systems as bizarre as they are unintelligible."[8] Failing to realize that all knowledge comes through the senses, the misguided philosophers do not understand how further knowledge is to be gained. Since there seem to be certain general propositions about which all are agreed and whose origin no one remembers, they erroneously assume that these propositions must be a kind of Ur-knowledge, innate and unlearned and, above all, the source of all new knowledge.[9] This misconception gave birth to the false organization of knowledge into systems derived from the so-called first principles, which are in reality nothing more than abstractions or abridged expressions of a collection of particulars learned through experience. A proposition which contains nothing but knowledge already learned cannot of itself yield new knowledge; rather, new knowledge must be sought in

7. Ibid., pp. 159–64.
8. *Essai,* in *Œuvres phil.,* 1, 8.
9. Ibid., p. 25.

the real source of the original proposition—namely, experience.[10]

The system-builders Condillac condemned shared an excess of imagination which was not balanced by the power of analysis. Their overactive imaginations caused them to see associations between ideas where none exist and to endow abstract notions with sensible forms. Their lack of a critical faculty prevented them from analyzing their ideas to determine the true relationships among them, or from going back to the origin of their ideas to perceive their true causes. "The surest means of being on guard against the systems [of the philosophers] is to find out how they created them. This is the touchstone of error and truth: go back to the origin of both, see how they entered the mind, and you will distinguish them perfectly. It is a method which the philosophers I condemn are little acquainted with."[11]

But the *Traité des systèmes,* contrary to what some of its critics have said,[12] was not simply destructive. Condillac was laying the groundwork for a program of his own. The concluding chapters of the *Traité des systèmes,* in which Condillac developed his methodological principles, are more successful and more satisfying than the corresponding section of the *Essai.* In part this is because the context of the later work provided a wider scope, a fuller opportunity for systematic methodological construction. The *Essai* had dealt with language, with ideas as the tools of thought, and with the elementary mechanism of the mind. Naturally, therefore, Condillac's methodological suggestions tended to concentrate on the correct use of these elements and to remain at a fundamental level. In his first book Condillac considered method abstractly and did not explore the concrete possibilities of building scientific systems with his clear and distinct ideas, once they have been acquired. In the *Traité des*

10. *Traité des systèmes,* in *Œuvres phil., 1,* 195.

11. Ibid., p. 206.

12. See, for example, J. P. Damiron, "Condillac. Son *Traité des systèmes,"* *Académie des Sciences Morales et Politiques: Séances et Travaux,* 60 (1862), 5–28, and 61 (1862), 5–31; Lyell Adams, "Condillac and the Principle of Identity," *New Englander, 35* (July 1876), 458.

systèmes, on the other hand, he challenged the metaphysicians not only on the grounds of inadequate ideas and imprecise language but also on the grounds of a falsely conceived organization of knowledge. He therefore became concerned, in the constructive part of the *Traité des systèmes,* with more than just pointing the way toward the discovery of truth through the formulation of clear ideas and precise language. He was concerned with the building of a true system, and he attempted to answer such questions as: What *is* a system of knowledge? What are its limits? What is its foundation? And what kinds of systems are there? He embarked, then, for the first time, on a concrete methodological essay designed to show how he would organize the discrete data of experience, the clear ideas of sensation and reflection, into meaningful systems explaining particular areas of experience.

Condillac's program for the development of true systems of knowledge was part of a project which took several forms in the seventeenth and eighteenth centuries, the project of finding a unity in the sciences which would tie them together into a comprehensive whole. The belief that all knowledge possesses, or can legitimately be given, unity is a theme which recurs in the thought of a variety of philosophers, including those who rejected what they called *l'esprit de système.* The notion of a unity in the sciences, is merely the subjective expression of the notion of order or system in nature. Anyone who deals with the first notion is implicitly dealing with the second and must ultimately answer the question of the correspondence of the unity he finds in human knowledge to an objective order in the universe. He must either claim that there is such a correspondence which justifies his particular organization of the sciences, or he must admit that the unity he finds in knowledge is not found in the objective world of nature but is imposed upon it by man, whether freely and consciously as a matter of convenience, or as the inevitable consequence of the structure of his mind (which, of course, also implies a kind of order existing in nature, even if it is restricted to man's nature).

It will be noted that the words I am using almost interchangeably—"unity," "order," "system," "classification," "organization"—are not synonymous. Nevertheless, in this context their meanings tend to overlap, and it is scarcely possible to use one of the terms without implying some or all of the others. The idea of unity in the sciences means that, at bottom, all the sciences are one science. This may mean that all the sciences really share a common subject matter which the different sciences approach differently, or it may mean that they all share a common method which they apply to different subject matters. In either case it is implied that there is an order in nature, whether material or structural, which lies behind the unity, and if there is such an order, it may be said that nature in some sense comprises a system, or set of systems, rather than a mere aggregate of unrelated phenomena. Moreover, if some kind of order exists in nature which justifies the unity of the sciences, it suggests that this unity need not remain on the theoretical level as a mere assertion but that it may be implemented on the practical level by the actual organization of knowledge into a system which corresponds to the system of nature. One of the most obvious and most commonly advocated techniques of organization is some kind of scheme of classification by which the particular sciences are grouped according to method, subject matter, structure, or other criteria. Such a scheme of classification, in turn, implies that the phenomena of nature themselves may be legitimately classified into groups possessing a coherence which the classification of knowledge reflects. Thus each of these problems is really reducible to one problem: Is there an order in nature, and if so, can the mind of man come to know that order and incorporate it into the structure of his science?

Condillac's place in the history of the systematization of science can perhaps be illuminated by classifying the several types of unity according to their governing ideas.[13] The attempts to unify knowl-

13. I have relied for much of the information in this section on Robert McRae, *The Problem of the Unity of the Sciences: Bacon to Kant* (Toronto, 1961). The particular classification which follows, however, is my own. McRae's book contains a valuable discussion of Condillac's logic and its relationship to the unity of the sciences.

edge in the seventeenth and eighteenth centuries may be classified into four major types. The first type was the metaphysical system-building program characterized by such philosophers as Descartes and Leibniz. The fundamental notion behind this program was that a total and absolute metaphysical system could be deduced from first principles. Underlying this was the assumption that all things are reducible to a few simple substances, or even to one simple substance, which provides the inherent unity behind the apparent and misleading diversity of phenomena. It was against the idea of this grand project that all other attempts to systematize knowledge were directed. The idea of a metaphysical system was unacceptable to such men as Bacon, Diderot, d'Alembert, Kant, and Condillac, because it supposed that the essential stuff of the universe, the substance of all things, is responsive to man's inquiries—a notion which they one and all rejected.

Bacon proposed instead a physical system of knowledge, based on the notion that there is a unity in nature contained in basic matter and its relationships which produces diversity by being repeated in different contexts. This kind of system, although as objective as the metaphysical type in the sense that it imputes unity to external reality, nevertheless rests upon a different foundation, because it puts limits on the reach of the system it proposes to build. The realm of essences, whatever they may be, and the realm of the spirit are both placed outside the bounds of knowledge, the first as unintelligible, the second as belonging exclusively within the jurisdiction of revealed religion. What Bacon proposed was a scheme for the organization of scientific knowledge based upon observable phenomena in which the underlying material unity may be perceived.[14]

14. See F. H. Anderson, *The Philosophy of Francis Bacon* (Chicago, 1948), esp. pp. 70–79, 144–64. I am placing Bacon after the Cartesians et al., and in apparent reaction to them, in defiance of chronology, on the grounds that the spirit and intent of the philosophical systems which Bacon *was* attacking—i.e. the scholastic, the Aristotelian, and the Platonic —were akin to the spirit and intent of the seventeenth-century meta-

By the eighteenth century one may detect a certain loss of confidence in the possibility of finding an objective unity in the nature of things, whether viewed physically or metaphysically. This is the same process which I have noted earlier in another connection[15]—a shift in interest from the objective world to the subjective, from the absolute to the relative, from the consideration of things as they are in themselves to the consideration of things as they are reflected in man's mind or as they relate to his needs and viewpoint. The *Encyclopédie* of Diderot and d'Alembert was, at bottom, a project for the unification or systematization of knowledge, but its authors conceived this unity as an essentially arbitrary scheme of classification imposed, for utilitarian reasons, upon an intrinsically ununified mass of material. Starting from a particular point of view, adopted for convenience depending upon the purpose he has in mind, man can organize scientific knowledge into a classificatory scheme which will enable him to make use of it.

Equally subjective, but by no means arbitrary, was the systematic scheme proposed by Kant, who also found the source of unity in the human mind. To begin to do justice to Kant's schematization would require a more thoroughgoing treatment of his philosophy than would be pertinent here. However, it can be briefly characterized as a new attempt to find a real or absolute unity —that is, a unity which is not simply imposed but which has a real existence—in the structure of human knowledge. Unable to return to the external or objective absolutes of the seventeenth-century metaphysical world-view, Kant nevertheless found a set of unifying absolutes in the nature of reason itself. Reason, which for Kant was not accidental or arbitrary or merely utilitarian, provides

---

physical systems, and that, conversely, the spirit and intent of the Baconian system of thought were congenial to, and often taken up by, those who *did* explicitly reject the systems of Descartes and his fellow metaphysicians. The classificatory scheme of the *Encyclopédie* was avowedly derived from Bacon, and Condillac often compared Bacon favorably to Descartes.

15. See above, pp. 39–40.

a logical and teleological structure which constitutes the unity of
the sciences into a single whole.

Aspects of all these types of unity—the physical, the metaphysical, the utilitarian, and the rational—may be found in Condillac's idea of the true system. Like Bacon, he believed that
nature herself possessed a unity which transcends the diversity of
experience. He shared with Leibniz a conviction that the structure
of external reality is fundamentally a logical one. He anticipated
Kant in his attribution of ordering principles to the nature of
reason. He joined Diderot and d'Alembert in their attack upon
l'esprit de système and agreed with them that our understanding
of the nature of things is relative to our needs. The reconciliation
of these diverse elements is to be found in Condillac's idealiza-
tion of what was for him the nearest approach to a true system that
man had yet devised—the Newtonian system of the universe.

Condillac believed that the universe is in fact organized into
a vast, rational, interconnected system, but he also believed that it is
impossible for man ever to comprehend that system in its totality
or to comprehend its parts in relation to the whole:

> Placed, as we are, on an atom which revolves in a corner of the
> universe, who would believe that philosophers had proposed
> to demonstrate in physics the first elements of things, to
> explain the generation of all phenomena, and to develop
> the mechanism of the entire world? To imagine that we can
> ever have enough observations to make a general system is to
> hope too much from the advancement of physics. The more
> materials experience furnishes us, the more we will feel what
> is lacking for so vast a construction. There will always remain
> phenomena to be discovered. Some are too far from us to be
> observed. Others depend on a mechanism which eludes us.
> We lack the means to penetrate to the sources of things.
> Now this ignorance leaves us impotent to go back to the
> true causes which produce the small number of phenomena
> that we know and to link them into a single system. For,

everything being connected, the explanation of the things that we observe depends on an infinity of others, which we shall never be able to observe.[16]

If we cannot discern the system of nature as a whole, we can discern some of the parts of the system. These parts, moreover, do not simply exist as separate pieces of data whose relationships we cannot perceive without the transcendental knowledge which is forever denied us. On the contrary, they form, as it were, sub-systems, groups of related phenomena whose behavioral laws, although not their ultimate causes, are discoverable. These sub-systems make up the legitimate objects of man's inquiry.

A valid system has certain distinguishing characteristics, the most significant of which is its logical structure. Every system which explains a set of phenomena, whether it be the phenomena of material motion or the phenomena of man's mental faculties, may be reduced to a single identical proposition—that is, to a proposition in which an expression is said to be equal to itself. Condillac has taken the form of the algebraic equation and extended its applicability to cover all knowledge. How, it may be asked, does Condillac avoid the charge that his valid system is nothing but a tautology? For that matter, how does he avoid being accused by his own statement that a proposition which contains nothing but knowledge already learned cannot of itself yield new knowledge? How, in other words, can he regard an identical proposition as instructive? How can a proposition which is reducible to the statement, "the same is the same,"[17] give us information about the behavior of phenomena? The answer lies in the limited capacity of the human mind. We can only acquire a complex notion or comprehend a system by building it up step by step from the partial ideas which constitute it. Moreover, even when we have built up a complex notion or a system, we still cannot hold all of its constituent ideas simultaneously in our

16. *Traité des systèmes,* in *Œuvres phil.,* 1, 197. Italics mine.
17. *De L'Art de raisonner,* in *Œuvres phil.,* 1, 621.

minds. If we could grasp an entire system at once, perceiving distinctly each part of it and all the relations of the parts, we would not need to form any propositions at all; or, rather, we would intuit the entire system as an identical proposition. Such is the nature of God's knowledge. "Each truth is for him like 'two and two make four.' He sees them all in a single truth, and doubtless nothing is so frivolous in his eyes as this science with which we inflate our pride."[18] Condillac seems to be saying that, if we had the capacity to grasp it, all knowledge *is*, at bottom, only a tautology, but that since we cannot so grasp it, we must acquire our information by the process of analyzing the elements of the equation into a series of propositions whose truth is verified by its ultimate reducibility to an identity. Thus, a statement which is a tautology to God is a genuinely instructive discovery to us. Condillac confirms this paradox with a somewhat more down-to-earth example: "A child who learns to count thinks he has made a discovery the first time he notices that two and two make four. He is not mistaken. For him it is a discovery."[19] For the adult, however, it is an identity which tells him nothing he did not already know. Condillac finds his logic of identical-instructive propositions to be equally applicable to descriptive statements referring to observable phenomena. "An identical proposition is one in which the same idea is affirmed of itself, and consequently every truth is an identical proposition. In fact, this proposition, 'gold is yellow, heavy, fusible, etc.,' is true only because I have formed a complex idea of gold which includes all these qualities. If, consequently, we substitute the complex idea for the name of the thing, we shall have this proposition, 'that which is yellow, heavy, fusible is yellow, heavy, fusible.'"[20] Just as every true proposition is an identity, so every system, which is logically nothing but a related sequence of true propositions, is also fundamentally "only a single and same idea."[21]

18. *L'Art de penser*, in *Œuvres phil.*, *1*, 748.
19. Ibid.
20. Ibid.
21. Ibid., p. 749.

Such a system is Condillac's own development of the faculties of the mind from sensation, which is reducible to the proposition, "sensations are sensations."[22] Condillac's system of the faculties is constituted of "a series of propositions instructive in relation to us, but altogether identical in themselves."[23]

Another such system is Newton's system of universal motion. Unfortunately, Condillac never revealed, in so many words, what he regarded to be the basic identical proposition of this system, but we may infer it to be "a balance is a balance." In a handbook written to instruct the Prince of Parma in the art of reasoning, Condillac used the Newtonian system as the best model. He related the phenomena of planetary motion to the behavior of the various simple machines of classical mechanics, and argued finally that both the behavior of the planets and the behavior of the machines are reducible to the principle of the balance: "Now our universe is only a great balance. The sun, fastened on the shortest arm, is in equilibrium with the planets placed at different distances, and all these bodies move on a point of suspension or fulcrum, which we call the common center of gravity. . . . We have risen from knowledge to knowledge only because we have passed from identical proposition to identical proposition."[24]

Leibniz' conception of the universe as a preestablished harmony is built upon a similar logical structure, which is theoretically comprehensible to an infinite intelligence in a single intuition. For Leibniz all truths, including all individual facts which we can only know a posteriori (such as historical events), are known to God a priori.[25] This is so because the subject of any proposition contains or implies all predicates of the proposition, so that a total knowledge of the subject "Julius Caesar," for example, contains or implies all descriptive statements about Julius Caesar, such as

22. Ibid. See below, pp. 172–73, for the step by step demonstration of this system. See also, *De L'Art de raisonner*, in *Œuvres phil.*, *1*, 629.

23. *L'Art de penser*, in *Œuvres phil.*, *1*, 749.

24. *De L'Art de raisonner*, in *Œuvres phil.*, *1*, 676.

25. See Louis Couturat, *La Logique de Leibniz* (Paris, 1901), pp. 215–21.

the statement that he decided to cross the Rubicon. Our finite
human intelligence only comes to know that Caesar decided to
cross the Rubicon because of a posteriori evidence that he did so.
But since his decision is a particular element in the totality of
that which is Julius Caesar, and Julius Caesar, in turn, is a particular element in the totality of the cosmos, God's knowledge of
Caesar's decision is an a priori knowledge contained in his perfect
knowledge of that totality.[26] Logically, this is quite different from
an assertion that God, in his omniscience, foresaw Caesar's act.
This would be a variety of a posteriori knowledge logically
equivalent to man's own knowledge of Caesar's act, because it
implies only that God could look into the future as into a crystal
ball and observe the act in advance of its happening, observe it, in
other words, as an empirical phenomenon. But in Leibniz' understanding the world is not really a world of independent phenomena,
or groups of phenomena, to be observed. On the contrary, the
phenomena are simply the particular instances or elements of a
single coherent whole. As Couturat puts it, Leibniz' nature "is
penetrated with logic, or better, it is a living logic."[27]

Leibniz' notion that God has an a priori knowledge of all facts
is essentially the same as Condillac's notion that God's knowledge of
all facts is contained in a single identical proposition. For Condillac
a total knowledge of a single complex notion contains all the simple
ideas that make up that notion, which is much the same as saying
that the subject of a statement contains all predicates that can be
made of it. Thus an analysis of the complex notion "Julius Caesar"
reveals, among other things, that one of the elements contained in
the notion is a decision to cross the Rubicon. It follows that the
statement "Julius Caesar is he who decided, at a given moment in
time, to cross the Rubicon," is reducible to the identical proposition, "Julius Caesar is Julius Caesar." Moreover, a total knowledge

26. See Frederick Copleston, *A History of Philosophy* (6 vols. West-
minster, Md., 2d ed., 1950), 4, 281–82.
27. Couturat, *La Logique de Leibniz*, p. 257.

of the complex notion of "the universe" would contain all the simple ideas that make it up, which means all phenomena and their relationships and ultimate causes. It could be said, therefore, that the statement, "the universe is a universe in which a man called Julius Caesar decided, at a given moment in time, to cross the Rubicon," is ultimately reducible to the identical proposition, "the universe is the universe." Such, presumably, is the propositional form of God's infinite knowledge.

Condillac could not have known the whole of Leibniz' logical system. The only work of Leibniz which we know Condillac to have read, from his corrosive attack on it in the *Traité des systèmes,* is the *Monadology,* which based the preestablished harmony not so much on logic as on the idea of the monads as the basic stuff of the universe. Moreover, even if Condillac were acquainted with the other writings of Leibniz which had been published by 1749, he could only have gleaned a partial understanding of his philosophy. The full emergence of the structure of Leibniz' thought had to wait for the posthumous publication of several of his works in the 1760s[28] and, even more, on the examination of letters and other documents carried out by Louis Couturat at the turn of this century. The independence of Condillac's development of a similar view of universal harmony suggests, perhaps even more strongly than would imitation, his deep affinity, in spite of his empiricist commitments, to the rationalist tradition represented by Leibniz and carried on and transformed by Kant. Condillac could not remain content with the mere observation of phenomena that the philosophy of empiricism dictated. He always felt that underlying

28. Condillac could have read additional works of Leibniz while expanding his own ideas in the *Cours d'études,* the *Logique,* and the *Langue des calculs.* However, there is no evidence that he did so. In any event, the works of Leibniz published in the 1760s still did not reveal the extent to which logical ideas permeated his thought, and Condillac's *Traité* of 1749 contained already the basis for all his later ideas, so that further acquaintance with the work of Leibniz still would not account for Condillac's predisposition to see the world in terms of the logic of analysis.

and informing the phenomena there is a single, rational, coherent, God-created system which man most nearly understands when he thinks analytically.

Nevertheless, Condillac insisted that man's approach to an understanding of the system of nature must always be a limited one, must always proceed by the discovery of partial systems. Descartes failed because he did not recognize this limitation. He thought he required only matter and motion to create the universe, but the result was a system which was merely ingenious. Newton, on the other hand, wiser and more modest than Descartes, "did not seek to form the world, but was content to observe it," and the result was a model system which successfully explains a particular portion of the mechanism of the universe.[29] The structure of the Newtonian system reveals what a true system should look like. First of all, it must rest on a true principle, which is nothing other than a "fact verified by experience." And, as one might have guessed, Condillac's example par excellence of a true principle was Newton's law of the attraction of bodies on which the system of universal motion rests. Not a hypothesis, then, or a supposition or an a priori assumption but an empirically discovered and empirically verified fact must lie at the base of every valid system. Equally important is its internal organization. Every part of the system must be mutually connected in a causal relationship; abstract logical connection is not enough, although the chain of causal relationships must be expressible as a sequence of identical propositions.[30]

Condillac recognized the existence of two types of systems—those which describe and explain effects brought about by natural causes,

29. *Traité des systèmes*, in *Œuvres phil.*, *1*, 200. Condillac found it necessary to warn the more ardent Newtonians against falling into the same error by trying to explain all phenomena by the principle of attraction. True to his methodological principles in this case, Condillac argued that only those phenomena whose connection with the principle of attraction had been empirically verified could legitimately be explained by it. To go beyond that was mere fantasy. Cf. *De L'Art de raisonner*, in *Œuvres phil.*, *1*, 678.

30. *Traité des systèmes*, in *Œuvres phil.*, *1*, 206–07.

and those which seek to prescribe ways to bring about effects desired by man. Descriptive systems include mathematics, astronomy, physics, and, oddly enough, the fine arts, which Condillac found to be "less our work than nature's."[31] It is taste, rather than principle, that produces a work of art, and a systematic study of art proceeds by observing existing works, and is intended to explain how these works came to be, rather than to prescribe ways to make more of them. Politics and the mechanic arts represent the type of prescriptive system. The magistrate is a sort of mechanic who seeks to understand, by an empirical study of the character, customs and mores of the people, how to regulate the artificial body which is a nation. He must be prepared to change his system in response to changed external circumstances—population growth, increased social complexity, cultural or moral decadence, and so on.[32] Likewise, a mechanic can do nothing to operate his levers, pulleys, and wheels until he has observed the workings of nature.[33]

In fact, no system can be created—or, rather, discovered—until the workings of nature have been observed. The observation of phenomena and the ordering and analysis of the ideas we acquire of them are elementary lessons taught us by nature. "While yet children, we acquired knowledge by a series of observations and analyses. . . . This knowledge is a collection of ideas, and this collection is a well-ordered system, that is to say, a sequence of exact ideas that analysis has put into the order existing among the things themselves."[34] Before we could collect our ideas into a well-ordered system, however, it was necessary for us to distribute our ideas—which, to begin with, were ideas of individual objects—into classes of different degrees of generality. This, too, was taught us by nature, as we observed first, for example, individual trees, then classed them all under the general name, "tree," and finally distinguished the several species of tree according to comparative

31. Ibid., p. 215.
32. Ibid., pp. 208–09.
33. Ibid., p. 214.
34. *La Logique,* in *Œuvres phil.,* 2, 378–79.

size, structure, fruit, and so on. This process of classification is the first step toward grasping the systems of nature—in this case, the system of vegetable life. There is a difficulty, however. Condillac reminds us that these classes into which we distribute our ideas have no real counterparts in nature. "Everything is distinct in nature."[35] Only individuals exist; classes are our own creation. This points back to the world of the strict empiricist—a world made up of discrete and unrelated (at least as far as we can tell) phenomena—and causes one to wonder what happened to Condillac's vision of an ordered world, of the reality of systems in nature.

This question might be dealt with by pointing out that Condillac was talking about two different things—namely, cause-effect relationships, on the one hand, and classes, on the other—and in denying the real existence of the latter, he was not denying that of the former. After all, it might be said, Condillac was a nominalist, so of course he believed that classes, which are general ideas or abstractions, are only names used to signify a group of similar individuals and that they have no ontological status of their own. There is, then, no inconsistency between his assertion that there are systems in nature and his assertion that there are no classes in nature. Nevertheless, a comparative analysis of his position in each case may serve to illuminate both, because both reflect the problems inherent in the views of a man who has been converted to empiricism while remaining attached, more deeply than he knew, to the rationalist's faith in an ordered and knowable cosmos.

"It is not according to the nature of things that we distinguish classes, it is according to our manner of conceiving."[36] The order that we attribute to natural phenomena, then, is of our own devising and reflects the structure of our minds rather than the structure of nature. But what is the source or cause of our manner of conceiving? "Since our needs are the motive for this distribution, it is for them that it is made. The classes therefore form a system in

35. Ibid., p. 381.
36. Ibid., p. 380.

which all the parts are naturally connected, because all our needs are linked to one another, and this system . . . conforms to the use we want to make of things."[37] Our manner of conceiving, then, is determined by purely utilitarian considerations. This might mean that we must regard the systems we create as having no ascertainable correspondence to things as they are in themselves, since their creation has depended not upon external reality but upon internal necessity. Condillac, however, did not accept this conclusion, and he found his safeguard against such a solipsism in nature, of which we and our needs form an integral part. Our needs, he says, themselves form a system; that is to say, they comprise one of the infinity of subsystems which go to make up that vast system which is the universe. In this vast system—it is an article of faith for Condillac—everything is connected; all the parts, all the subsystems, are mutually dependent. It follows therefore that our grasp of these subsystems, although limited and partial, and arising in the first instance from the dictates of our own nature, nevertheless has some kind of parallel or correspondence to the objective organization of things. It need not be the case that we perceive things or order them in exactly the same way as they are in themselves. Such an exact correspondence is not probable, owing to the limited nature of our knowledge, and it is in any case not verifiable. We can, however, be sure that the world we create in our minds is not a mere fantasy but a genuine reflection of reality. That is, we can be sure of this as long as we stick to the methods of observation, analysis, and classification that arise out of our needs. It is the utilitarian consideration itself that turns out to be, for Condillac, the best test of truth, because it is the way nature taught us, it is the result of that part of us which ties us to the world we want to know. It is when we depart from the system of our own needs, when we build systems that no longer serve our needs and therefore are not subject to the utilitarian test, that we run the risk of error. It is, in short, when reason thinks itself

37. Ibid.

to be autonomous that it ceases to be reliable. When it knows itself to be a part of and dependent upon nature, it is in touch with reality.

All this is closely related to the basic epistemological theory of representative perception. We do not perceive objects; we perceive only our own ideas. And yet the consistency of our experience suggests that our ideas consistently represent objects to us, even if the precise relationship between the objects and our ideas of them remains a mystery. The farther removed we get from the perception of ideas (which are always perceived as individuals), the more tenuous this relationship becomes. Nevertheless, it is necessary for our welfare, even for our survival, that we extend our thought beyond the limits of individual perceptions. Indeed, we cannot help it; our manner of conceiving compels us to classify and generalize. Fortunately, we have available to us the test of experience—nature's own device—to verify our belief that our classes, generalizations, and systems in some sense represent the real organization of natural phenomena. Just as the consistency of our experience with individual ideas justifies us in believing that they represent real objects, so the consistency of our experience with general ideas and ideas organized into causal systems justifies us in believing that they too represent reality, provided that we never lose sight of the undetermined character of this representation and the incompleteness of our systems.

What Condillac was getting at, as he developed these ideas into a formal methodology, was nothing other than the actual method of science—limited, incomplete, but, within its limitations, certain. Whatever criticism may be leveled at some of Condillac's own attempts to apply his method,[38] it must be said of him that he presented a lucid and cogent description of the nature and limitations of scientific explanation. In this respect Condillac achieved in his later works, the *Art de raisonner* and the *Logique,* as well as in the *Traité des systèmes,* the task he had set, but did not really

38. See below, p. 84.

carry out, in the *Essai*. In the early book, for example, one looks in vain for an empirical check, which Condillac came to insist on in the *Traité des systèmes* at every step in forming a system. The principle on which any system is built must be an empirically determined fact, and every element that goes to make it up must be checked against experience, against the empirical test of observation and experiment. Condillac emphasized the need for observation and experiment throughout the *Traité des systèmes*, even though mathematics was his model of clear ideas and sound method. Paradoxically, Condillac was freer to stress the role of empiricism in the *Traité des systèmes*, which was devoted to the principles of mathematical analysis, than he was in the *Essai*, which was written to explain and demonstrate the empiricist epistemology. In the *Traité* he was taking for granted, as a working scientist does, the validity of experience, the real (or practical) correspondence of idea to thing, which he could not do in the *Essai*, because there he was engaged in precisely those questions of epistemology and metaphysics that undermined the certainty of experience, although not our need to rely on it, *faute de mieux*. In the *Essai* he was left with nothing but the internal certainty or coherence of mathematics to point to as a pattern of truth. In the *Traité des systèmes* he simply ignored the corrosive implications of his own epistemological skepticism and based his method instead on that interesting combination of attitudes which scientists so often reveal: pragmatism with respect to details, and faith with respect to an overall pattern.

A disputed issue in the early development of scientific method was the nature and use of hypotheses. In reaction against excessive speculation, many thinkers—Bacon, for example—rejected hypotheses out of hand. Condillac, however, did not share this extreme view. Hypotheses have a legitimate use in the discovery of truth, according to Condillac, but they are dangerous if not treated with care, and they often lead the unwary astray. A common error, for example, is to turn a hypothesis into a principle. A system is then erected on the foundation of this hypothetical principle, and if the parts of the system can be made to hang together logically, it is assumed to be a valid system and to prove, retroactively, as it were, the truth of the hypothesis. This Condillac condemned as mere rationalistic ingenuity. A hypothesis used correctly, leading to the formation of good systems, is a sort of scouting technique. In this manner, hypotheses can suggest lines of inquiry, possibilities for fruitful experiment or observation. A hypothesis, then, is a guide for a trial and error process which seeks not only to discover facts as yet unknown but also to check on the hypothesis itself. Now for this process to be truly productive, and for proper control over the hypothesis, Condillac suggested certain rules. First, it must be possible to exhaust all suppositions. In other words, it is not enough to make one hypothesis and to try to verify it by seeing if a coherent explanation can be built on it. The same must be done with all possible relevant hypotheses. Second, we must have ideas as clear and as complete as the ideas of mathematics. And last, we must never suppose that we can form ideas about things we have not observed on the model of things we have observed. In short, hypotheses cannot stand alone. They must be incorporated into a sound empirical method.

Condillac was harsh in his condemnation of philosophers who neglect the facts because they think they have the key to the explanation of all phenomena, whatever they may happen to be: "I have heard of one of those natural philosophers who, congratulating himself on having a principle which explained all the phenomena of chemistry, dared to tell his ideas to a trained chemist. The latter, having been good-natured enough to listen to him, told him that there was only one difficulty. The facts were quite otherwise than he supposed. 'Very well,' replied the natural philosopher, 'tell me what they are so that I may explain them.'"[39]

In the last analysis, however, the validity of a hypothesis must be tested by its usefulness. That is, if a hypothesis effectively explains a set of phenomena, makes its practical workings evident

39. *Traité des systèmes,* in *Œuvres phil.,* *I,* 199.

to us, and, above all, shows us how to profit from our knowledge, then we ought to use it even if it rests on shaky theoretical foundations, provided that we do not claim for the hypothesis more than is due it. In other words, we may use such a tenuous hypothesis just so long as it profits us to do so, but we must never claim that it is a true principle.[40]

Akin to his pragmatic attitude toward the use of hypotheses was Condillac's notion of the nature and meaning of scientific explanation. The true scientist, according to Condillac, does not seek to penetrate to the inner, unobservable nature of things, but limits himself to making systematic and descriptive statements about the observable behavior of phenomena. While his statements are descriptive in the sense that they merely report how the phenomena in question regularly behave, they do not explain why they behave that way; they are systematic in the sense that they apply not to a single occurrence only but to a whole class of phenomena. These systematic descriptions sometimes reach such a level of generality that they may be called laws or concepts, but they still refer to nothing but observable phenomena. To clarify his meaning and to make a case for the Newtonians, Condillac contrasted the Newtonian concept of "attraction" with the Cartesian "impulsion." For Newton the concept of attraction merely referred to the phenomena of motion which he observed; it was a convenient way of summing up the data under a single head. "The Cartesians reproach the Newtonians with having no idea of attraction. They are right, but there is no basis for their judgment that impulsion is any more intelligible."[41] The difference between them is that Newton did not claim to know what attraction "really" is, and his system did not depend upon such spurious knowledge. The Cartesians, on the other hand, claim that their concept of impulsion is a true first principle, that it reveals something of the inner nature of moving bodies, that it explains not how but why they move.

40. Ibid., p. 201.

41. Ibid., p. 200. Cf. Voltaire, *Lettres philosophiques*, XV, in *Œuvres complètes*, 22, 139.

However, as Condillac made clear, it is not the function of a scientific law to be a principle in that sense. Its function is to explain phenomena, and the best law is that which explains the most phenomena.[42] But, of course, this explanation must be empirically verified, not merely logically coherent or theoretically elegant. Thus Condillac relied for his criteria of the "truth" of a scientific law not on an impossible discovery of its correspondence to the nature of things but on its workability, its practical value, its comprehensiveness. In turn, his satisfaction with criteria of this kind reveals his faith in the idea that nature is all of a piece and that if something works for us, satisfies our needs, fits our manner of conceiving, it must be a true revelation of nature.

There seem to be two lines of thought running through Condillac's methodology—the logic of analysis based upon the principle of identity, and the demand for empirical verification through observation and experiment. These two very different principles fit together because of our incomplete knowledge of the universe, requiring us to proceed empirically where an infinite mind could operate analytically. In *De L'Art de raisonner* and *La Logique* Condillac admitted that the logic of identity, while the only test of the absolute truth of a proposition, is of limited practical application. Nevertheless, the status of this logic allows it to serve as an ideal to be approached as closely as possible in all reasoning, and as a warning against too great a confidence in our demonstrations where they fall short of it. Thus the system of reasoning which Condillac developed was a kind of compromise between his vision of the perfect logic of the cosmos, on the one hand, and his recognition of the practical limits of the human understanding, on the other.

In *De L'Art de raisonner* Condillac outlined three types of evidence, each with its own method of verification, its own function, and its own limitations. The first is the evidence of reason, which is just another term for the logic of identity. Since for

42. *Traité des systèmes*, in *Œuvres phil., I,* 211–12.

Condillac every true statement is an identity, the surest way to prove the truth of a statement would be to determine whether its subject and predicate are indeed identical. Where the identity or lack of identity is not self-evident, one follows the procedure of a mathematician dealing with an equation. One substitutes equivalent terms for one of the elements of the statement until the identity or nonidentity of the elements becomes self-evident. Now this is a procedure which depends upon how much we know about the elements of the statement. It can only be followed completely when we know what Condillac called the true or first essence of the elements in question—i.e. the first principle which governs all the properties of the element.[43] In mathematics this is entirely possible because the principle of all numbers is the notion of unity by which all numbers may be compared. Outside mathematics the requirement is more difficult—so much more difficult that Condillac hedged. He implied that there were other areas in which the evidence of reason could be used in a pure form, but he never specified one.

Nevertheless, the evidence of reason can be partially applied to cases where, while we do not know the true essence of a thing, we do know what Condillac called the "second essence." The second essence is not a principle which governs all the properties of a thing; it is itself only a property, but it appears to have a special priority over the other properties such that it somehow explains them. For example, extension is only a property of body, not its true essence, which is unknown to us. But all the other observable properties of body are functions of extension and may be explained in terms of extension. In the same way, sensation is the second essence of the mind. (It will be noted that Condillac modified Descartes' dualism into extended substance and sensing substance, but unlike Descartes, he did not regard these distinguishing characteristics as providing us with an insight into the nature of Being.) In these cases we can demonstrate by reason only those

43. *De L'Art de raisonner,* in *Œuvres phil.,* 1, 628.

relationships which are reducible to the second essence. As an example, Condillac ran through a series of identical statements, beginning with "the mind [is a substance which] has sensations" and ending with "the mind [is a substance which] reflects." By the substitution of terms it is manifest, then, that reflection is merely a form of sensation. Condillac also called upon the evidence of reason to demonstrate the nonidentity of mind and body, because, he argued, no matter how one varies the terms, one can never reach an identity between "an extended substance" and "a sensing substance."[44]

Reasoning about second essences, however, requires the use of the other two kinds of evidence to provide our knowledge of the second essences. It is not by the evidence of reason that we know that body is extended or that the mind has sensations. It is by the evidence of fact and feeling, respectively. (Condillac classified these separately, but in principle they are the same. Feeling is really interior fact.) The evidence of fact is based upon observation of phenomena. Condillac defined a fact very simply as "everything we perceive. . . . It is a fact that bodies are extended; it is another that they are colored, although we do not know why they appear to us as extended and colored."[45] That is, a fact is a phenomenon or appearance. We do not know, and it does not matter, whether things as they are in themselves resemble things as they appear to us. The evidence of feeling likewise refers to phenomena, in this case to what we experience as taking place within our minds: sensation, attention, remembering, comparing, and so on. Both

44. Ibid., p. 629. There is still a third type of knowledge of things, that in which we know neither the first nor the second essence but can only list a series of properties whose relationship is totally mysterious to us. Such is the case with our knowledge of particular substances, like gold, where we can say that it is hard, yellow, fusible, etc., yet we do not know why it has these qualities and other metals have other qualities. None of the distinguishing qualities of gold, so far as we know, has the priority over the others that a second essence has. In this case we cannot reason about gold; we can only describe it. See ibid., pp. 628–29.

45. Ibid., p. 636.

these types of evidence are subject to error. Our perception may deceive us into thinking that the distance of an object from us is less than it is, or that a square building is round.[46] Likewise, we may be mistaken in our judgment of our internal experiences. We may, for example, attribute to ourselves lofty motives for an act when in fact we are motivated by something quite different; or we may suppose that we have made a choice freely when in fact we have been determined in the choice by an external cause.[47] Thus one must know how to observe with respect to both external and internal phenomena. One must know how to correct errors, to challenge assumptions, to isolate phenomena by experiment in order to clarify confused perceptions, and so on.

Most of our systematic knowledge is built by a sound combination of the evidence of fact and the evidence of reason. Newton's system is the prime example. His information came from observing phenomena. The system he built out of the observed phenomena is demonstrable by reasoning. The result is a well-constructed system resting upon a principle which, regarded from the point of view of its acquisition, is a "fact verified by experience," and regarded from the point of view of its demonstration, is an identity. Thus Condillac's twofold logic is a description of the mechanism by which we build—or, rather, discover—true systems. The evidence of reason is a reflection of the logical structure that all true systems possess, and the evidence of fact is a reflection of our limitations in knowing these systems, limitations which require us to discover the pieces of the system and fit them together step by empirical step, when an infinite mind could intuit them in a single all-embracing identity.

It seems, then, that for Condillac there is a unity in nature which man's science can reflect only imperfectly. Human knowledge may indeed be given a methodological unity that reveals the logical structure of the cosmos in which all its parts participate. It is

46. Cf. *Essai*, in *Œuvres phil.*, *1*, 9; and *La Logique*, in *Œuvres phil.*, *2*, 373.

47. *De L'Art de raisonner*, in *Œuvres phil.*, *1*, 631.

therefore quite legitimate to speak of a unity of the sciences and equally legitimate to seek to organize our knowledge into interconnected explanatory systems, provided that we never fail to recognize that the true unity of things is contained in that one logical proposition which is God's knowledge and which is forever beyond our grasp.

4. The Statue-Man

You will understand how easily we are led to make systems if you consider that nature itself has made a system of our faculties, of our needs, and of things related to us. It is in accordance with this system that we think; it is in accordance with this system that our opinions, whatever they may be, are produced and combined.[1]

Sensations give birth to the whole system of man, a complete system all of whose parts are linked and mutually sustaining. It is a sequence of truths: the first observations prepare the way for those that follow, the last confirm those that preceded them.[2]

In many respects the *Essai sur l'origine des connaissances humaines* can be considered a first draft of Condillac's most famous and most important work, the *Traité des sensations*. The intervening *Traité des systèmes* outlined the kind of rigorously logical model that successful inquiry ought to establish, thus providing the methodological guidelines for the *Traité des sensations*. In the *Essai* he had traced the development of the human mind through all its stages, from the most elementary state of consciousness to the highest faculty of reason, but the *Essai* contained ambiguities and weaknesses which left Condillac fundamentally dissatisfied, or so one may assume from the fact that eight years later he tried again to "recreate the entire human understanding."

In the first place, Condillac failed to achieve a truly rigorous development of sensationalism because he left ambiguous the role of reflection in forming the understanding. In the second place,

1. *Traité des systèmes*, in *Œuvres phil. de Condillac*, 1, 216.
2. *Extrait raisonné du Traité des sensations*, in *Œuvres phil.*, 1, 325 (hereafter cited as *Extrait raisonné*).

his exclusive concern with the inner processes of the mind had caused him to leave in doubt the existence of external material reality. Diderot hinted that Condillac had come dangerously close to the idealism of Berkeley.[3] The difficulty was that Condillac, like Locke, treated sensations sometimes as images of external reality and sometimes as only an interior state of being. Moreover, whenever he tried to clarify his position, he appeared to assert an idealist position. "Whether we ascend, to speak metaphorically, into the heavens, whether we go down into the abyss, we never leave ourselves; and we never perceive anything but our own thought."[4] This was the sentence that had most shocked Diderot,[5] for to say that all we know are our own ideas is only one step away from saying that nothing exists except our own ideas; and even those who were not thoroughgoing materialists were unprepared to accept a philosophy which denied the reality and permanence of the physical universe—i.e. of the universe as known to the scientist. The *Essai*, then, left Condillac two major pieces of unfinished business: to develop the full range of psychic life out of simple sensation, and to relate the psychic life to the external world.

This program required a closer analysis of the contribution of tactile to visual perception than Condillac had given in the *Essai*, where he had treated the subject superficially and inaccurately.[6] Condillac's interest in the relationship of the senses to one another was nothing new in the eighteenth century. From Berkeley's *New Theory of Vision* (1709) to Diderot's *Lettre sur les aveugles* (1749)

3. *Lettre sur les aveugles*, in *Œuvres*, *I*, 305.

4. *Essai*, in *Œuvres phil.*, *I*, 6.

5. Diderot was perhaps too easily alarmed. Condillac's observation was at bottom merely a refutation of "naïve realism," a refutation concurred in by every philosopher of note since Descartes. However, Diderot's uneasiness and Condillac's concern to put his mind to rest—not by pointing out the limited implications of his original statement but by establishing that the external world exists after all—testifies to the insecurity felt about that external world once direct philosophical contact with it had been broken.

6. As Condillac himself admitted; see *Extrait raisonné*, in *Œuvres phil.*, *I*, 328.

there was manifested a concern with the problem which Cassirer saw as central to eighteenth-century epistemology and psychology: "Is the experience derived from one field of sense perception a sufficient basis on which to construct another field of perception that is of qualitatively different content and of specifically different structure?"[7] Would, for example, a person born blind, who has learned to distinguish objects by touch, be able to recognize the same objects by visual perception alone if his sight were suddenly restored? This problem is of decisive significance for an epistemology based on sensation, because it lays bare a still deeper question: Can the primary data perceived by the senses produce by themselves the coherent image of a physical world that we have in our consciousness, or is some organizing faculty required to complete the process? Locke had tacitly admitted an independent organizing faculty in the mind; Condillac's aim was to eliminate it and to derive all the activities of the mind and all the contents of consciousness from simple sensation alone. For that reason he had to find an answer to this crucial question that would be consistent with his aim and at the same time could account for all the evidence of experience.

The statue-man, hero of the *Traité des sensations,* was Condillac's guide to a thoroughgoing sensationalist psychology and to a solution for the problem of knowledge. By imaginatively re-creating the hypothetical experiences of the statue as its senses were unlocked one by one, Condillac explored the functioning of the senses and the growth of the mental life. To make more compelling his contention that all the operations of the mind derive in an unfolding sequence from sensation, he first endowed the statue with only the least informative of the senses, the sense of smell, and on this humble basis he constructed hypothetically the germ of all the mental and emotional faculties. If, he argued, it can be thus shown that the high mental powers of reason and reflection are derivable from mere consciousness of odors, and without the aid of innate ideas or autonomous faculties, then surely the exclusively sensational

7. Cassirer, *The Philosophy of the Enlightenment,* p. 108.

origin of the human understanding must be granted. Using a method of imaginative identification,[8] he went on to examine the relationship of the senses to one another and demonstrated the crucial role of touch and movement in the awareness of self and the discovery of the outside world. Finally, Condillac "observed" the statue, now blessed with five senses and all the physical activities and needs of man, as he learned to provide for his survival and comfort. Motivated by the experience of pleasure and pain and guided by the mechanism of the association of ideas, the statue-man acquired practical knowledge, formed abstract ideas, and even made moral and aesthetic judgments. In other words, he exhibited the full mental capacity of a man, limited only by his lack of language and the absence of all human contact—a limitation that Condillac had evidently concluded was not nearly so crippling as he had indicated in the *Essai*.[9]

If the *Traité des sensations* is more important for understanding Condillac than the *Essai sur l'origine*, it is not simply because it corrected what he had come to feel were errors and filled in the gaps left by the *Essai*. Behind the *Traité des sensations* was an expanded purpose, one that was more suggestive of the problems of eighteenth-century philosophy and specifically richer in implications for a philosophy of man. Whereas the *Essai* had only attempted to answer some questions left unanswered by Locke regarding the origins of knowledge, the *Traité* accounted, explicitly or implicitly, for the whole man: reason, will, passions, personal identity, and moral character. Many of the ideas in the *Traité des*

8. Condillac invited the reader to participate in this identification in order to understand the argument. "I give notice that it is very important to put oneself in the place of the statue that we are going to observe. We must begin to exist with it, have only a single sense when it has only one; acquire only the ideas that it acquires, contract only the habits that it contracts. In a word, it is necessary to become what it is." "Avis important au lecteur," *Traité des sensations*, in *Œuvres phil.*, I, 221.

9. See Condillac's admission that he was wrong in the *Essai* and that he had "given too much to signs," in a letter to Maupertuis, 25 June 1752, *Œuvres phil.*, 2, 536.

sensations are fundamentally the same as those to be found in the *Essai,* but the *Traité* contains Condillac's total image of man, and the implications of that image open up some of the most compelling intellectual and moral problems of the Age of Enlightenment.

While there was much that was significant and original in the *Traité des sensations,* the statue-man himself was not an original idea. Indeed, Grimm accused Condillac of stealing it from Diderot's *Lettre sur les sourds et muets,* which had appeared three years before the *Traité.*[10] Grimm was unjust, for the idea of the statue, or something like it, was almost a cliché among his contemporaries, and Condillac, though not crediting Diderot with the idea, did not claim it for his own. In a dedicatory preface he attributed it to Mlle. Ferrand,[11] and, repeating this assertion in answer to Grimm's charge, he added that Diderot had known all along that he had such a project afoot.[12] Moreover, a similar notion had been used by Buffon and would be taken up a short time later by Bonnet.[13] Although Condillac's statue possessed the individuality of his own detached, logical cast of mind (Grimm complained that Condillac had drowned Buffon's statue in a barrel of cold water),[14] it seems evident that he had merely picked up an idea that was current coin at the time.

10. Grimm, *Correspondance littéraire,* 2, 442–43.

11. *Traité des sensations,* in *Œuvres phil., 1,* 222. Georges LeRoy, the most thorough of editors, has admitted that there is almost no information about Mlle. Ferrand *(Œuvres phil., 1,* 222, n. 5). She had evidently died two or three years before the publication of the *Traité des sensations,* and Condillac took the opportunity to pay tribute to her memory in terms that suggest a rather warm intellectual friendship. Other than this we have only Grimm's gratuitously offensive comment that she "was a person of little wit and a disagreeable manner, but who knew geometry, and who left a bequest to M. de Condillac in her will." *Correspondance littéraire,* 2, 204.

12. "Réponse à un reproche," *Œuvres phil., 1,* 318–19.

13. G. L. de Buffon, *Histoire naturelle de l'homme,* in his *Œuvres philosophiques,* ed. Jean Piveteau et al. (Paris, 1954), pp. 309–12; Charles Bonnet, *Essai analytique sur les facultés de l'âme,* in his *Œuvres d'histoire naturelle et de philosophie* (10 vols. Neuchâtel, 1779–83), 6, 6–7. Bonnet claimed that he had arrived at the idea independently of Condillac.

14. Grimm, *Correspondance littéraire,* 3, 112.

Besides the charge of plagiarism, Condillac was open to the criticism that he had violated his own methodological principles. In the *Traité des systèmes* he had expounded the importance of beginning with principles which are facts verified by experience, yet in the *Traité des sensations* he seemed to be using a fiction as an analytic technique. Not only was the statue-experiment itself imaginary, but surely the principle on which it was based was precisely the kind of unverifiable hypothesis that Condillac had earlier condemned.[15] Where is the empirical data for the idea that sensation in a pure state is the primary element of experience? Was this not an a priori assumption about the nature of experience, an abstraction and not a fact?[16] If so, the whole statue experiment was false to the spirit of the scientific method that Condillac advocated. In answer to this criticism Condillac might have pointed out that the fundamental terms and concepts of Newtonian physics, such as mass, momentum, and force, were also abstractions, representing a world no man ever saw, touched, heard, or smelled. Far from being a contradiction of his earlier work, the *Traité des sensations* was a carefully worked out exercise in his own methodology. The statue was meant to be a sort of friction-

15. *Traité des systèmes,* in *Œuvres phil.,* 1, 121–22. Charges of this kind were made most often in the nineteenth century; see Victor Cousin, *Histoire générale de la philosophie depuis les temps les plus anciens jusqu'au XIXe siècle* (11th ed. Paris, 1884), pp. 501–11. Cousin's work first appeared in 1828.

16. Asserted by a critical disciple of Condillac, Maine de Biran, writing in 1805. See Gabriel Madinier, *Conscience et mouvement* (Paris, 1938), p. 2, and LeRoy, Introduction, *Œuvres phil. de Condillac, 1,* xxxiii. Of all Condillac's contemporaries, only the persistently hostile Grimm made this point, and even he criticized Condillac's handling of the statue, as full of "arbitrary and impossible suppositions," rather than the idea of the statue itself. He preferred Buffon's version, but he seems to have been most struck by its poetic rather than its scientific superiority: "The precise philosopher [Condillac] does not fare well beside the philosopher of genius. The first movement of M. de Buffon's statue is to reach out his hand to take the sun. What an idea! What poetry! For philosophers in their conjectures, like poets in their imitations, have only one oracle to consult—that of nature." *Correspondance littéraire, 2,* 442–43.

less machine—an ideal model from which all extraneous or inter-
fering elements had been eliminated so that the relevant factors
might be approached and studied in isolation. In this ideal model
pure sensation was the psychological equivalent of momentum or
force—i.e. a fundamental unit of experience abstracted out of
the complex jumble of data that concrete experience presents to us.
The analysis of the statue, in short, was a consciously conceived
study in psychological mechanics. As such, it was quite in keeping
with the assumptions of his age. The informal metaphysics of the
Enlightenment tended toward a mechanical philosophy which saw
nothing artificial in likening man to an animated statue, even as
the universe was likened to a watch. Diderot imagined the brain
to be like a bell rung by the nerves acting as vibrating strings,[17]
and of course La Mettrie had extended Descartes' concept of the
animal-machine to man himself. In addition, Condillac shared the
conviction of his age that the way to get at the truth of anything
is to analyze it. Since a real experimental dissection of psychic
experience was not possible, a hypothetical analysis would have
to serve. The thought-experiment of the statue must have seemed
to him a legitimate means of overcoming difficulties that were
merely circumstantial. In short, he had problems to solve and he
needed an analytic technique. This one was suggested—by Mlle.
Ferrand, Diderot, Buffon, or all three; it suited the spirit of the
times and his own temperament, so he used it. And, be it said, he
used it with more thoroughness and attention to detail than any
of his rivals could claim, for Condillac appreciated the value of
precision in a good experiment.

> Nature gives us organs in order to show us by means of
> pleasure what to seek, and by means of pain what to avoid.
> But there it stops; and it leaves to experience the task of
> making us contract habits, and of finishing the work which
> it has begun.

17. *Lettre sur les sourds et muets,* in *Œuvres,* 1, 367; and *Le Rêve de
d'Alembert,* in *Œuvres,* 2, 113.

This is a new view, and it shows the simplicity of the ways of the author of nature. Is it not cause for wonder that it was only necessary to make man sensible to pleasure and pain to generate ideas, desires, habits, and talents of every kind in him?[18]

Here we have the heart of the argument of the *Traité des sensations*. Condillac's "new view" was nothing less than a doctrine of the physiological origins of personality, or more precisely, the doctrine that man is the product of the reactions of his sense organs to the stimuli provided by the physical environment.[19] In 1754 this could hardly be described as a "new view." It was new for Condillac— he had not reached such a position when he wrote the *Essai*—and it was new in relation to Locke, for whom man still possessed a spiritual faculty, reason, which exists independently of the senses, although it cannot function without the data they provide. Nevertheless, it is an idea which can be found in the seventeenth century: in Hobbes, for example, who regarded man as made up solely of matter in motion. More recently and closer to home, in 1748 La Mettrie had published *L'Homme machine,* in which he sought to demonstrate that man is as purely physical a being as an animal or a plant and is totally dependent upon physical conditions operating through his senses. Moreover, it appears that Diderot was also moving in the direction of a totally physical understanding of man. In his *Lettre sur les aveugles* he put forth the notion that man's ideas are relative to his senses and would be different if he were deprived of one or more of the usual five. A physiological doctrine of man, then, was not new. It probably was not even uncommon, al-

18. Condillac, *Traité des sensations*, in *Œuvres phil., 1*, 222.

19. Thus, from another point of view—from the outside—it is also a doctrine of the environmental origins of personality in that individual character will be shaped by experience, by the particular stimuli which provoke the physiological reflexes. However, what Condillac is concerned to establish in the *Traité des sensations* is the nature of what man brings to experience, and it appears that all he brings is sensitivity to pleasure and pain.

though it is difficult to say just how widespread it was in mid-century, before the full-blown materialist systems of Helvétius and d'Holbach had appeared. What can be said is that there was an increasing tendency to find physical explanations of man's nature and activities satisfying, although such explanations were not necessarily accepted as part of a thoroughgoing materialism.

Certainly Condillac did not intend to advocate a materialist theory of man or the universe just because he felt he could explain man in physiological terms. He made a distinction between the *senses,* which belong to the body, and *sensation,* which is a function of the mind, and it is sensation to which we owe all our mental development: "The principal object of this work is to show how all our knowledge and all our faculties come from the senses, or, to speak more precisely, from sensations; for in reality, the senses are only the occasional cause. They do not feel, it is the mind alone which feels through the agency of the organs; and it is from the sensations that modify it that the mind draws all its knowledge and all its faculties."[20] Although this qualification was undoubtedly important in Condillac's mind, its effectiveness in modifying the direction of his thought may be questioned. It seems to me that the distinction, coming as it does after an assertion that knowledge and faculties come from the senses (he did not have to say this at all, if he did not mean it), can only be a technical, not an essential, distinction. It is as if he was merely pointing out that the administrative center of the understanding is the mind. In any case, I do not think this *ex post facto* distinction[21] can weaken the force or the implications of the primacy of pleasure and pain, which Condillac presented as inescapably physiological categories producing physiological reflexes from which the statue learns:

> If nature gives it an agreeable sensation, we may imagine that the statue is able to enjoy it by keeping the parts of its

20. *Extrait raisonné,* in *Œuvres phil., 1,* 323.
21. This observation was made in the *Extrait raisonné,* which was written to accompany the *Traité des animaux,* in which Condillac felt impelled to defend himself against charges of materialism.

body in the same position, so that it would appear that such a sensation would tend to maintain repose rather than to produce movement.

But if it is natural for the statue to give itself up to a sensation which pleases it and to enjoy it in repose, it is equally natural for it to shrink from a sensation which hurts it. It is true that *it does not know how to shrink from such a sensation, but in the beginning it does not have to know; it is sufficient to obey nature. As a result of its organization, its muscles, contracted by pain, move its limbs, and it moves automatically, without yet knowing that it moves.*[22]

The instinctive reaction to the fundamental physical experiences of pleasure and pain is the root, the true source, of the development of the mind in both its aspects, the understanding and the will. The key to the understanding is attention, and the key to the will is desire. Both attention and desire are merely "sensations differently transformed." Both are directly caused by pleasure and pain. It is pleasure or pain that causes that intensity of feeling by which a particular sensation dominates the consciousness of the statue, and this domination is attention. Besides, as Condillac had already demonstrated in the *Essai sur l'origine des connaissances humaines,* all the faculties of the understanding evolve out of attention. Desire presupposes the development of at least some of the faculties of the understanding, because desire means that the statue has "the idea of something better than the present state and the power to judge the difference between two succeeding states."[23] But, of course, desire is specifically the wish to escape a present pain or to experience again a remembered pleasure. The faculties of the will—passion, love, hate, hope, fear—evolve out of desire through the accumulation of experience in precisely the same way as the faculties of the understanding evolve out of attention.

A demonstration of the genetic priority of sensation, which had

22. *Traité des sensations,* in *Œuvres phil., 1,* 255. Italics mine.
23. Ibid., p. 232.

so eluded Condillac in the *Essai,* was made possible by the statue analysis. There Condillac had been still too much under the influence of Locke to think about the human mind from the point of view of its activities. Although he recognized that Locke had confined himself to an essentially static analysis of the contents of the mind rather than a re-creation of its activities, Condillac, in the *Essai,* did not completely carry out the Baconian project himself. It is true that he talked about mental activities and their development, but he patterned his analysis too closely after Locke's to break free of its limitations. With the statue, Condillac declared his independence of Locke and embarked on a genuinely developmental reconstruction of the faculties. His decision to include the will in his analysis (the *Essai* had concerned only the understanding) not only made for greater comprehensiveness but also provided the means for filling in some gaps in the evolution of reason. The relationship between reason and the will, and between the will and the passions, that Condillac developed is symptomatic of the paradox of the Age of Reason, in which reason unexpectedly turned upon itself and, by its own rigorous application, struck at the very foundations on which it rested—an intellectual development of baffling circularity and continuing relevance.

The more closely one looks at the development of the idea of reason in the Enlightenment, the more tangled it appears. The faith in reason for which the age is noted was in many respects a legacy from the past, a legacy that was increasingly threatened by intellectual developments within the very century which, by reputation, exalted reason more than any other. In the Aristotelian tradition, enshrined in scholasticism, reason was man's distinctive attribute. While all forms of life possessed a vegetative soul, and all animals a sensitive soul, man possessed a rational soul as well.[24] According to Aristotle himself, it was by virtue of his rational soul that man participated in the divine and the eternal.[25] In the Middle Ages,

24. See Heikki Kirkinen, *Les Origines de la conception moderne de l'homme-machine* (Helsinki, 1960), pp. 58–66.
25. See W. D. Ross, *Aristotle* (5th ed. London, 1953), pp. 121–22.

of course, reason was below revelation. Man could not attain through reason to those truths which were most significant; these were known to him only through the acts of divine revelation. Nevertheless, reason remained man's highest *natural* faculty— unique, autonomous, the God-given instrument of truth about the natural world and even a little beyond. In the Thomistic system the existence of God, for example, although not the Trinitarian nature of God, was knowable through reason alone.[26] So far as it went, then, reason was exalted and trusted in the thirteenth century as well as in the eighteenth.

The Continental rationalism of the seventeenth century pre- served one very important feature of the philosophy it replaced. Rationalism assumed the existence of an ordered Reality that is accessible to reason. It is the function and power of reason to penetrate beyond the transitory phenomena—mere appearances as they are—to the reality beyond. This is true of rationalism what- ever the nature of that reality turns out to be—thought and exten- sion, *Deus sive Natura,* or a preestablished harmony of monads. Sometimes, as in Spinoza, reason or rationality remains more a moral goal to be striven for than the actual dominant faculty of man. But even so, Spinoza sometimes implies that rationality is a realizable goal. Certainly, like Descartes, he held a view of human nature in which the passions are imperfect or confused ideas; it is the function of the understanding to clarify them and to assert the natural (in the sense of ideal) dominance of reason over the passions. In this tradition, then, reason remains man's highest faculty, superior to the passions, independent of experience, capable of comprehending the eternal stuff of which the universe is made.

The autonomous reason had acquired a special significance for the image of man with the replacement of the Aristotelian universe of substances and qualities by the universe of matter-in-motion. In the development of Continental rationalism, reason represented that faculty of mind which is self-generating and which exempts

26. See Copleston, *History of Philosophy,* 2, 318–21.

man from the mechanistic or deterministic world that rationalism tended to create by its devotion to the inexorable logic of cause and effect. Thus there are two closely related problems involved: the problem of man's rationality and the problem of man's freedom. The problem of the autonomy of reason may be defined as involving the relationship of reason to the whole of man's nature. It raises such questions as: Is reason a separate and independent faculty, with its own laws, the same for all men? Or is reason in some way dependent upon sense experience or subject to the needs and passions of men and therefore relative, either to individual men and their unique experiences or to the universal but nonrational physiological structure of man? This was essentially a debate between rationalism and empiricism. The problem of man's freedom in the more general sense, on the other hand, may be defined in terms of man's relationship to the external world and to its laws. Is man a free and autonomous being who can will and act spontaneously according to freely made choices? Or is man so subject to the mechanical laws of nature that he is no more free to choose his goals and his actions than a falling stone is free to fall or not to fall? This was essentially a debate within rationalism itself, although it was not necessarily confined to those who called themselves rationalists; that is, to the extent that it was a problem for any given thinker, that thinker was making rationalist assumptions about the nature of the universe. It is inevitable that any discussion of these two issues will overlap, but for purposes of analysis it may be fruitful to concentrate attention on each debate, and Condillac's place in it, in turn.[27]

Although it was not at first obvious, the whole thrust of empiricism was to undercut the autonomy of reason by making it sense-dependent. In the Cartesian system, since thought is the essence of mind, the processes of reason are capable of development without reference to sense experience. The potentially self-sufficient character of reason is revealed in the mind-body relation-

27. The debate about man's freedom will be taken up in Chap. 5.

ship, in which sense data are distinguished from innate ideas and rational deductions precisely by their deficiencies. Only pure thought is clear and distinct. Moreover, the passions are seen as disturbances of man's essentially rational makeup, which he suffers as a result of possessing a body.[28] The body, then, intrudes its needs, desires, and inadequacies into a being that would, without them, be purely rational. For Locke, on the contrary, pure thought divorced from experience does not exist. Not even the innate faculty of reflection with which he endowed the mind can function until it is activated by sensory experience. Nevertheless, reflection in Locke's system remains to some degree autonomous, because it has the inherent capacity to take the simple ideas provided by the senses and to work them up into complex ideas. In other words, the mind has an innate and autonomous power to reason about experience.

Locke's psychology of uneasiness and the ethics related to it also indicate the partial displacement of reason in early empiricism. "Uneasiness," the sense of discontent and the most basic and unfocused expression of desire, is at the root of all actions and therefore at the root of will, which is the determination to act.[29] Reason is employed in the service of will, to choose the best means to put the uneasiness to rest and, at a higher level of development, to weigh a present pain against a future reward or a present pleasure against a future punishment.[30] This is a reversal of the rationalist ideal of putting the will in the service of reason. In Descartes, for example, the will is the source of error in the sense that it extends beyond the understanding; that is, it is possible to will to make judgments about any object whether the limited understanding grasps it or not. Error can be avoided only if the will waits upon the understanding, and one refrains from making judgments when

28. Descartes, *Les Passions de l'âme* (Pt. I, Art. XLVII), in *Œuvres, 11,* 364–66.

29. Locke, *An Essay concerning Human Understanding* (II.21.29ff.), *1,* 330ff.

30. Ibid. (II.21.48ff.), pp. 344ff.

one does not see clearly and distinctly.[31] Moreover, the function of the will as the agent of the soul is to control the effects of passion by choosing, on behalf of a rationally conceived good, not to act at the behest of the passions. According to Descartes, the will is most free when it is most moved by grace and knowledge toward the right choice rather than when it serves the passions or is indifferent to the alternatives presented.[32]

Descartes' rationalist ethics and the psychology tailored to fit it presuppose an absolute good apprehended by reason. Locke, on the other hand, could not appeal to such a transcendent good but was obliged to derive his ethical criteria from experience. Inevitably, derivation from experience suggests a relative good and evil, interpreted in terms of pleasure and pain. In ethics, then, as well as in psychology, reason has surrendered its priority to the senses and to the will as agent of the senses. Nevertheless, although the reach of reason has been severely curtailed by Locke, its activity remains free.

Along with objective order in the universe, the rationalist position required an internal order—a substantial, unified, and continuing self. Inevitably, then, the displacement of autonomous reason was paralleled in philosophy by the disintegration of the substantial self. In Descartes the self had epistemological priority and a high ontological status. The existence of the self is a reality which is detected by intuitive and immediate awareness. It requires neither the mediation of logic through inference nor the mediation of the senses through perception. The statement, "I think, therefore I am," defines both the discovery of the self and its nature.[33] The self—i.e. the mind or the soul—is a thing that thinks and, in

31. Descartes, *Méditations*, IV, in *Œuvres, 9, 46.*

32. Ibid.; cf. his *Principes de la philosophie* (Pt. I, chap. 35), in *Œuvres, 9,* B 40.

33. Although the *cogito* is put in the form of a logical proposition, it should be understood not as such but, rather, as a descriptive statement about the fundamental intuition of the self. That is to say, Descartes was not asserting that we deduce our existence from our intuition of thought; he was rather making an existential claim that we know ourselves as think-

thinking, knows itself, and from that knowledge can build the universe.

Locke also held that the existence of the self is immediately apprehended by intuition, but placed as it is in a different epistemological context, the self loses something of its autonomy. To begin with, Locke had discarded the problem of what constitutes the self or personal identity; this is a metaphysical issue that lies outside the scope of the *Essay concerning Human Understanding*. He was instead concerned to discover what gives us the *idea* of personal identity. But in discussion the idea and the reality inevitably overlap and indeed become confused. *"Self* is that conscious thinking thing,—whatever substance made up of, (whether spiritual or material, simple or compounded, it matters not)— which is sensible or conscious of pleasure and pain, capable of happiness or misery, and so is concerned for itself, as far as that consciousness extends."[34] This is the crux of the change from Descartes' view: personal identity or self rests on consciousness, not on substance. I think that I exist, therefore I exist, and I exist only insofar as I think that I exist. But what happens to the self when consciousness is interrupted, as, for example, in insanity? To clarify this point Locke introduced the legal concept of accountability as the criterion of personal identity. John sane and John mad are not the same person if identity of consciousness is lost, for John sane cannot be held responsible, in that case, for actions committed by John mad. Where consciousness does not extend, there is no identity.[35] Locke has unobtrusively slipped from an

---

ing and being in one moment of intuition. See Copleston, *History of Philosophy, 4,* 91ff.

34. Locke, *Essay concerning Human Understanding* (II.27.17), *1,* 458–59.

35. Ibid. (II.27.20), p. 461. In the Second Meditation, Descartes also asserted that the logical consequence of the *cogito* is that when I do not think, I do not exist, but this was in the still very limited context of the foundations of epistemology. In the Sixth Meditation, having moved from the order of knowing to the order of being, Descartes makes clear the

assertion that consciousness of identity gives us the *idea* of self to the implication that consciousness of identity *equals* self. The self still holds its epistemological priority, but its metaphysical autonomy has been badly undermined.

It remained for Berkeley to suggest and Hume to make clear the devastating consequences of a consistent empiricism in the destruction of the worlds of both rationality and common sense. Berkeley drew more radical conclusions from the phenomenological analysis of the idea of material substance than Locke could have foreseen, but he saved the rational order of things by maintaining a theory of spiritual substance, and, above all, by placing his radically subjective epistemology within a theocentric metaphysical context. Hume, however, accomplished what Berkeley held back from. He extended phenomenological analysis to the idea of spiritual substance. The result was the total breakdown of external objective order, autonomous reason, and continuous self. Hume analyzed causality into a mental habit, the self into a bundle of perceptions, and reduced reason to slavery to the passions. Only the realm of mathematical demonstration, depending entirely as it does on the meaning given its terms and having no factual content, is within the scope of pure reasoning.

It is perhaps indicative of the inevitability of the direction taken by post-Lockean empiricism that Condillac's concern with a science of human nature has so much in common with Hume's. Although Hume's principal philosophical works preceded Condillac's by a few years, they do not seem to have been known to him, even indirectly. (Condillac knew Berkeley's only through Voltaire's account in the *Eléments de la philosophie de Newton.*) On his own initiative Condillac saw that empiricism required an analysis of the mind itself and not merely of the ideas we have of external substances and relations. The differences—and they are many—between Condillac

---

metaphysical continuity of the substantial self, whose essence is thought, and which therefore always thinks. *Méditations*, II, in *Œuvres*, 9, 21; *Méditations*, VI, in *Œuvres*, 9, 62; cf. *Réponse aux objections*, in *Œuvres*, 9, 190.

and Hume stem in large part from Condillac's cryptorationalism
and from his constant anxiety lest he stray beyond the limits of
Christian orthodoxy. This anxiety led him in the end to cheat on
the demands of his professed empiricism in a flight back to the
a priori.

Taking off from Locke's psychology of uneasiness, Condillac
found in desire the moving force behind the development of the
entire human mind. Where Locke had found desire at the root of
the will, Condillac saw it as the spring of both the will and the
understanding.[36] Moreover, he found a constant interaction between the will and the understanding, in which the will emerges
as the dominant faculty. Some of this had been hinted at in the
Essai, where the importance of pleasure and pain in the development of the understanding is explained. But in the *Traité des
sensations* the whole process is laid before the reader. The first
experiences and the first ideas are sensations. In a series of sensations some will be painful or at least less pleasant than others.
This results in uneasiness. The memory of the more pleasant state
converts mere uneasiness into desire—that is, the conscious direction of the attention toward that state which will relieve the uneasiness; and desire not only forms the basis of the activities of
the will—hate, love, fear, and so on—but also stimulates and
directs the developments of the activities of the understanding
beyond mere perception and rudimentary memory to the highest
reaches of reason.[37] While it is true that the understanding provides
the ideas of things toward which the will moves, the will selects
the ideas that the understanding fixes upon and thinks about. It is
need physically felt, not logic rationally grasped, that determines
the association of ideas, which the *Essai* had already established as
the fundamental principle of reason. It follows therefore that need,
not logic, is the foundation of reason.

Condillac's reduction of reason was paralleled by his analysis
of the self, or rather his analysis of how we get the idea of the self.

36. *Extrait raisonné,* in *Œuvres phil.,* I, 325.
37. *Traité des sensations,* in *Œuvres phil.,* I, 228ff.

For after subjecting the idea of the self to a near-Humean atomization, Condillac restored the reality of the self virtually by fiat. The self, Condillac argued, is not intuitively known, nor can it be inferred at the first moment of the statue's consciousness. The self is not discoverable until change has occurred. "What we understand by this word ['I'] seems to me applicable only to a being who notices that in the present moment he is no longer what he has been. So long as there is no change, he exists without any reflection upon himself; but as soon as he changes, he judges that he is the same as he formerly was in another state, and he says 'I.'"[38] Condillac, then, rejected Locke's assertion that one cannot perceive without knowing that one perceives.[39] In fact, Condillac's statue does not learn to distinguish between himself and what he perceives until he has been endowed with touch and movement. The other four senses do not convey to him the idea of the outside world, so that when he first becomes aware of himself through change, it is as identical with his sensations. At this stage the self *is* its modifications; there is nothing outside the self, and the self is nothing but sensation. "Its 'I' is only the collection of the sensations which it experiences, and those which memory recalls to it."[40]

There is another stage in the discovery of the self—the discovery of the not-self. This awakening comes only through the sense of touch, which reveals to the statue its physical dimensions, at once enriching the content of the self and giving it limits. There is something beyond the self, and the self is more than sensation. It is, or is involved closely with, a body, and it *has* sensations— quite a different proposition from merely being sensations. It is an entity in a world of entities.

Condillac's *via negativa* to the awareness of personal identity is, I think, an ingenious and original argument. In psychological insight it foreshadows twentieth-century conjectures that an infant's

38. Ibid., p. 238.
39. He had changed his position on this since the *Essai*. See *Essai*, in *Œuvres phil.*, *1*, 11ff.
40. *Traité des sensations*, in *Œuvres phil.*, *1*, 239.

self-awareness is first made conscious by his discovery—usually painful—that his being is not coextensive with his universe. But like Hume's analysis, it does not raise the self above the level of a collection of sensations. A personal identity established in part by awareness of what it is not and in part by judgments extending beyond the phenomena is very tenuous indeed. Nevertheless, the self, spiritual and substantial and unified, must be saved, because that which is called the self from a psychological point of view is nothing less than the soul when looked at from a metaphysical or theological point of view. Condillac therefore annexed the "collection of sensations" to a soul and declared that the soul is spiritual substance, unified and immortal, in its essence capable of direct knowledge without the mediation of the senses, but doomed by original sin to total dependence upon the body.[41] This assertion is not defended,[42] nor is it integrated into the rest of Condillac's system, either methodologically or substantively. The orthodox immortal soul is simply tacked on to a philosophy that would seem to be uncongenial to it.[43]

As noted earlier, Condillac had set himself a twofold task in the *Traité des sensations:* to develop the full range of psychic life

41. *Essai,* in *Œuvres phil.,* 1, 7–8; *Traité des animaux,* in *Œuvres phil., 1,* 371.

42. Except by one casual objection to Locke's statement that for all we know God might have endowed matter with thought, to which Condillac replied that since the subject of thought must be one, and matter is a multiplicity, the subject of thought is spiritual substance *(Essai,* in *Œuvres phil., 1, 7).* But this is a deductive argument, depending precisely on those traditional metaphysical concepts and assumptions that Condillac repudiated. His methodological principles ought not to have allowed him to make assertions about "substances" or about what the subject of thought must be, or to distinguish dogmatically between matter and spirit. As Diderot might have said (and did say, to another, similar line of reasoning): "Metaphysico-theological balderdash!" ("Entretien entre d'Alembert et Diderot," *Œuvres, 2,* 116). Condillac's half-conscious assumption of a metaphysical dualism, among other things, makes him a Cartesian *malgré lui.*

43. Condillac's real religious beliefs are not easy to pin down. See below, pp. 137–43, for a discussion of the problem.

out of simple sensation, and to relate the psychic life to the external world. The link between these two projects was his discovery of the "master-sense, touch."[44] Condillac's discussion of the momentous role played by the sense of touch in human experience, a reversal of opinion which he attributed to Mlle. Ferrand,[45] demonstrates that the reductive analysis he applied to the psychology of knowledge had pushed his philosophy toward a still more radical subjectivism. He tried to maintain his hold on the material world through touch, but the logic of his own system precluded certainty. Whatever Condillac intended, the *Traité des sensations* turned out to be more Berkeleyan than the *Essai* had been.

The central theme of Condillac's psychological and epistemological exploration in the *Traité des sensations* is the problem of perceptual order, a problem that must be dealt with in any philosophy purporting to derive all knowledge from sensation. For it is an incontestable fact that we are conscious of an external physical order, in which objects have physical dimensions, occupy space, and exist in definite and measurable spatial relationships to one another. It is, moreover, an order in which the different kinds of sense data fit together into a coherent structure seemingly perceived as a whole. We perceive a rose. We do not have to synthesize discrete flashes of perception—a sweetness, a redness, a softness—into something that we then call a rose. On the contrary, mental effort enters in only when we attempt to break the rose down into these separate sense data. Our immediate perception—at least as far as we are aware—is of a whole rose possessing these qualities and existing at a particular place in the garden, and we perceive this all at once, without thought. Moreover, this immediate perception of structure and relationship is not confined to isolated objects but is true of our entire field of perception at all times. As Cassirer puts it, "the cardinal question of all theory of knowledge

44. *Traité des sensations,* in *Œuvres phil.,* I, 285.
45. Ibid., p. 221.

is that of the meaning of this order, while the cardinal question of all genetic psychology is that of its derivation."[46]

Although the problem of perceptual order holds true for all the senses, it is especially acute for the sense of sight, because it is especially difficult to disentangle what we immediately perceive by sight and what we learn to perceive by sight. It is on precisely this question that Condillac changed his mind between 1746 and 1754. In the *Essai* he had asserted, against the opinions of Molyneux,[47] Locke, and Berkeley, as well as against the evidence of a famous experiment,[48] that we can perceive shape, depth, size, and distance with vision alone. At most we might need to reflect on what we see in order to form ideas of surfaces, figures, and the like, but the important point is that we need no other sense than sight to observe everything that in our actual experience we are accustomed to observe.[49]

The *Traité des sensations* marks Condillac's abandonment of the idea of the self-sufficiency of vision, as the statue-analysis made for a considerable refinement of his study of sensation. In considering the senses of smell, taste, hearing, and sight, Condillac found that none of them, alone or in combination, would reveal to the statue the existence of anything outside himself. For that matter, his knowledge of himself would be limited to mental phenomena. He would know nothing of his own body. Nothing in the nature of visual or aural phenomena, much less the phenomena of taste and smell, carries with it the implication of an external origin. By themselves (i.e. without the sense of touch) they must appear to the statue simply as random modifications of his own being. Even

46. Cassirer, *Philosophy of the Enlightenment*, p. 110.

47. William Molyneux (1656–98), English philosopher, astronomer, and politician, a friend of Locke, and author of *Dioptrica nova* (1692).

48. A boy who had been blind since birth had his sight restored by a London surgeon, Dr. Cheselden, in 1729. He was then asked to identify by sight certain objects which he was familiar with by touch. He could not do so. Reported in Voltaire, *Eléments de la philosophie de Newton* (Pt. II, chap. 7), in *Œuvres*, 22, 469–70.

49. *Essai*, in *Œuvres phil.*, 1, 58–59.

the sensations of touch, if unaccompanied by movement, would not furnish evidence of an external, material world. But when movement is added, awareness of space and of otherness follows as a necessary consequence of the impenetrability of matter. If the statue's hand meets an object, it is stopped; his hand has encountered an obstacle and can move no further. From this elemental fact the statue judges that there are at least two objects in the world, himself and the obstacle, and that there is such a thing as space in which he can move freely before he reaches the obstacle.[50] For the first time he has had an experience which he not only need not but cannot interpret as merely a change in the state of his own being. Exteriority has become a part of his consciousness through touch, and all his other sensations take on a new dimension as he learns to incorporate his tactile and kinesthetic knowledge into all aspects of experience.

Condillac has, in effect, presented the old doctrine of primary and secondary qualities in a new form, a form which makes the traditional distinction between them still more marked. The subjectivity of the secondary qualities—color, sound, taste, odor—is emphasized by the fact that, experienced alone, they would provide no knowledge of an objective world. Only the discovery of the primary qualities, the discovery of a world of extended space and extended objects, reveals the existence of anything other than subjective mind.

It is in Condillac's analysis of the way we learn to perceive

50. *Traité des sensations*, in *Œuvres phil.*, *1*, 254–57. This is the theory developed for the revised edition of 1778. Most of the revisions in the 1778 edition are stylistic and insignificant. This passage is one of the exceptions. In the 1754 edition Condillac explained the discovery of matter and otherness (as well as the discovery of the statue's own body and its physical boundaries) by the experience of double contact, which would occur if the statue's hand touched another part of his body, and the contrast between the sensation of double contact with that of single contact when his hand touched an external object. (See ibid., p. 255, note a.) The 1778 edition expanded and clarified the earlier version by adding the passage about the impenetrability of external objects, but the principle remained the same as in the earlier edition.

that Cassirer's distinction between the meaning of the perceptual order and its derivation becomes blurred. For Condillac the two questions become the same, as the answer to the second provides the answer to the first. Condillac explained the meaning of the order by tracing its derivation, and we see the stages of learning the order paralleled by corresponding stages of reality in perception. Genetic analysis—the favorite technique of the French Enlightenment—has here been given an almost cosmic validity, for in this case not only does it account for the existence of perceptual order within us; it also defines the ultimate meaning and transcendent value of that order.

A hidden assumption in genetic analysis is that getting back to the primitive is equivalent to getting back to the real. It is not surprising to find, then, that for Condillac absolute reality is the primary experience of undifferentiated sensation as a mode of being.[51] In the entirely passive experience of modifications of his own being, in which there is not even a recognition of the different kinds of sensation produced by the different senses, the statue knows reality. This is unequivocal, unchallengeable, and immediate data. Its reality is not weakened by judgments based on habit or ideas built upon ignorance. It is, in the true geometric spirit, the least common denominator of experience. It can be reduced no further.

The next stage in learning to perceive is the discovery of the different sense organs and the realization that experience comes in five forms. Condillac maintained that this seemingly obvious fact must be learned. "Our statue would most certainly believe that odors and sounds come to it by its eyes, if, giving it sight, hearing and smell at one and the same time, we posit that these three senses be always exercised together, so that with each color seen it smells a particular odor and hears a particular sound, and that it smells and hears nothing when it sees nothing."[52] Through experiments made possible by touch and movement, the statue discovers

51. Ibid., p. 254; cf. *Essai,* in *Œuvres phil., 1,* 50.
52. *Traité des sensations,* in *Œuvres phil., 1,* 288.

the parts of its body. Sensations no longer seem at this stage to be modifications of the mind; instead they are located in the organs of the body: sound is in the ear, light and color are in the eye, and so on.[53] The attribution of sensation to specific organs is itself not a sensation but a judgment, and in making judgments, we lose a little of the reality of pure sensation. This new five-way order, located in different parts of the body, is not absolute; it is a derivative reality, dependent upon the nature of our sensory apparatus. If we had fewer or more or different sense organs, sensation would take on another shape and meaning for us.[54]

Finally, the statue learns to attribute sensations to external objects, and in doing so, leaves reality behind altogether. Having discovered the external world through touch, the statue then learns that if he moves a flower toward his nose, the odor becomes more intense; he learns that what he sees depends on where he directs his gaze; and so with all the senses. He comes to judge that sensations are not in him but in the object. Habit renders the judgment automatic, and soon it becomes confused with the sensation and indistinguishable from it. He no longer merely thinks the odor is in the flower; he smells it there. The internal order of five kinds of sensation has now been completely projected onto the external world.[55]

The overpowering effect of habitual judgments on our perceptions is particularly revealed in the tactile-visual relationship. First, we learn from touch that objects have shape and that they are placed at various distances from us until they recede into the horizon. Guided by this knowledge, our eyes learn to analyze shapes into their separate parts and to see the relationship of the parts. We learn that light and shadows and relative size are clues to depth and distance. Then, incorporating our judgments into our perception, we "see" depth and distance; or as Condillac, with his

---

53. Ibid., pp. 275, 277, 279.
54. Ibid., p. 224. This was also Diderot's argument in the *Lettre sur les aveugles*.
55. Ibid., pp. 275ff.

persistent concern for clarity of language, puts it, we do not "see" these things; we "observe" them.[56] The attempt to distinguish between what we perceive and what we judge raises anew the epistemological question of the meaning of the perceptual order. I have already suggested that for Condillac this is not a different question from that of the derivation of perceptual order. That both meaning and derivation have changed for him since 1746 may be demonstrated by considering his argument in the *Essai* that we see shape without the aid of touch:

> I go on to the moment when this man is capable of reflecting on what strikes his sight. The whole will certainly not appear to him as a point. He perceives, therefore, an extension in length, breadth, and depth. If he analyzes this extension, he will form ideas of surface, line, point, and all kinds of figures, ideas that will be like those he has acquired by touch. For by whatever sense extension comes to our knowledge, it cannot be represented in two different ways. Whether I see or touch a circle and a rule, the idea of the one can represent only a curved line, and that of the other only a straight line. This man, born blind, will therefore distinguish by sight the globe from the cube, because he will recognize the same ideas that he had formed of them by touch.[57]

Although the *Essai* had a subjectivist orientation, it is clear that Condillac assumed a real external order giving rise through sensation to ideas that represent and correspond to those external objects. Therefore he deduced the derivation of perceptual order from what he believed to be its meaning.

In the *Traité des sensations*, however, he discarded his assumptions about the external world, and concentrated on the derivation of our image of it. In doing so, he abandoned the intellectualism of the *Essai*, in which perceptions are ideas and are immediately formed by sensation. When the perceptual order is broken down

56. Ibid., pp. 280–81.
57. *Essai*, in *Œuvres phil.*, *I*, 57.

into its most fundamental elements—raw sense data—it is not expressed in ideas or images. These are late developments requiring a complicated, if rapid, process of analysis, synthesis, and abstraction. The reversal of order emphasizes the intensified subjectivity of the *Traité des sensations*. Condillac now drew the meaning of the perceptual order from its derivation and found that its derivation reveals much more about ourselves than about the external world. The sense of touch suggests that there is an external world, but does not establish it: "Touch is no more credible than the other senses. Since we recognize that sounds, tastes, odors, and colors do not exist in objects, it must be equally true that extension does not exist in them either."[58] Like Berkeley, then, Condillac ultimately declined to give primary qualities a privileged status, but unlike Berkeley, he refused to conclude that ideas and minds are the only reality. He remained uncommitted on this point: "I do not say that there is no extension; I only say that we can only perceive it in our own sensation. Whence it follows that we do not see objects in themselves. Perhaps they are extended, and even flavorful, sonorous, colored, odoriferous. Perhaps they are nothing of the kind. I maintain neither the one opinion, nor the other."[59]

Perhaps Condillac's psychology of knowledge can be summed up by using it to answer the question: Given empiricism, what, if anything, does man bring to experience? Explicitly, Condillac would admit two things to be native to man: a particular sensory organization and a set of physiological needs driving him to develop all the potentiality of that organization.[60] Although he had so atomized sensation that much less is attributed to it immediately than in the *Essai,* much more is attributed to it derivatively. Both developments

58. *Traité des sensations,* in *Œuvres phil., 1,* 306.
59. Ibid., n. 1.
60. Of course, he also endowed man with a substantial soul, but this was extrinsic to his theory. Man's soul, as Condillac analyzed it, plays no part whatever in the development of his capacities and knowledge. He could get along quite as well without one. Therefore, although Condillac's conservatism in this matter ought not to be overlooked, the soul cannot really be treated as part of his theory.

have the effect of making man seem more mechanical. On the one
hand, sensation is nothing more than a chaotic mass of undifferentiated data. On the other hand, this very chaos, stimulated
by the most elemental needs, is enough to account for the richest
intellectual and emotional experiences man knows. Ultimately, the
most sophisticated piece of scientific reasoning, the most ethereal
of religious or romantic sentiments, is nothing but "sensation,
differently transformed."

Man brings one more element to experience in Condillac's system, and that is memory. He tried to explain memory, too, as a
sensation differently transformed, but his explanation is nothing
more than a trick of words. To define memory as a remembered
sensation[61] is by no means the same thing as reducing it to sensation or accounting for it in terms of sensation. In attempting a
reduction of terms, Condillac merely created a false equation:
memory equals sensation plus memory. The argument that memory
is produced by attention[62] also falls short of his purpose, because
it is not immediately obvious why even the most transfixed attention to an object should cause the sensation produced by that object
to remain in the consciousness after the object has departed from
the field of perception.[63] He is left, therefore, with a mysterious

61. *Extrait raisonné*, in *Œuvres phil.*, 1, 326.
62. *Traité des sensations*, in *Œuvres phil.*, 1, 225.
63. In the *Essai* he had tried to clarify the relationship between imaginary
and actual sensation by saying that they result from the same internal physiological process, whether it is a vibration of the brain fibers, the circulation of animal spirits, or "any other cause." But since he conceded that the
physiological mechanism by which sensation is registered in the mind is
unknown, this clarification is somewhat weakened. Moreover, it explains
neither how we can distinguish between actual and remembered sensations,
nor why the physiological mechanism should be triggered off at all in the
absence of the object represented by the sensation. (*Œuvres phil.*, 1, 16, and
n. 1.) In the *Traité des sensations* he reaffirmed his uncertainty about the
basis of memory. "When an idea is recalled by the statue, it is not, then, because it is preserved either in the body or the mind. It is because this movement, which is the physical and occasional cause of the idea, is reproduced
in the brain. But this is not the place to hazard conjectures on the mechanism of memory." (Ibid., p. 231.)

and irreducible psychic fact, and one of enormous importance for his psychological system. Memory is as indispensable to the development of man as sensation itself. It makes learning possible; it is the basis of self-awareness; in the form of habit it dominates all aspects of human life. Without pleasure and pain, said Condillac—that is, without physical need—man would remain in a state of lethargy, a vegetable.[64] It is equally true, in the system he created, that without memory man would remain a vegetable.[65]

The doctrines of the *Traité des sensations* reveal the influence of the statue's intrinsic passivity. Something has happened to the operations of the mind since the *Essai*. They have been in some way emasculated, deprived of their initiating force. In the *Essai*, to remember, to imagine, to judge, were acts of the mind, ways in which the mind organized sense data and converted sensation into thought. In the *Traité* these and the other operations have become almost properties of sensation itself, rather than capacities of the mind. They are ways in which sensations are present to the mind, in different combinations and sequences, and the mind contributes little more than the ability to register their presence. For example, in the *Essai* attention, even though caused by the affinity of a particular object to our needs, is still defined as our activity: "to be attentive to a thing is to be more conscious of the perceptions that

64. *Extrait raisonné*, in *Œuvres phil.*, *1*, 324.
65. Condillac had a habit of dropping the most astonishing remarks in footnotes. With reference to the problem of memory, he casually asserted a position that completely restores to man the kind of mysterious and autonomous faculty, intuitively apprehended, that the *Traité des sensations* was written to abolish: "There is in us a principle of our actions that we feel but cannot define. We call it force. We are equally active with regard to everything this force produces, whether within us or outside us. For example, we are active when we are reflecting or when we are making our body move." (*Traité des sensations*, in *Œuvres phil.*, *1*, 226, col. a, n. 1.) I do not know what to make of this statement. It could not have been dictated by the necessities of convention, either his own or society's, as were his assertions about the soul. I can only suggest that in spite of his contention that transformed sensation explains everything about man, Condillac felt on some level of consciousness that it does not.

it gives rise to than of those that others produce while acting on our
senses at the same time."[66] In the *Traité* attention is not so much
the action of the mind toward a thing, as sensation itself present in a
particular way. Sensation *becomes* attention by dominating the consciousness. "Thus a sensation is attention either because it is alone
or because it is more vivid than all the others."[67]

For Condillac man is quite literally a creature of pleasure and
pain. Man has become what he is as a consequence of pleasure and
pain, without which he would have been lifeless:

> As many as are our needs, so many are our different en-
> joyments, and as many as are the degrees in our needs, so
> many are the degrees in our enjoyment. In this lies the germ
> of all we are, the source of our happiness and of our un-
> happiness. . . .
>
> The history of our statue's faculties makes the growth of
> all these things clear. When it was limited to fundamental
> feeling, one uniform sensation comprised its whole existence,
> its whole knowledge, its whole pleasure. In giving it suc-
> cessively new modes of being and new senses, we saw it form
> desires, learn from experience to regulate and satisfy them,
> and proceed to new needs, to new knowledge, to new pleasures.
> The statue is therefore nothing but the sum of all it has ac-
> quired. Why would it not be the same with man?[68]

On the level of metaphysics, man is a mystery,[69] and on the level
of the supernatural, man is an immortal soul, but on the level of
the natural and the scientific, man is what he has acquired and
nothing more. And in the hierarchy of authorities which Condillac
shared with his century, it was the natural and scientific explanation
that commanded assent.

66. *Essai*, in *Œuvres phil.*, 1, 11–12.
67. *Extrait raisonné*, in *Œuvres phil.*, 1, 326.
68. *Traité des sensations*, in *Œuvres phil.*, 1, 314.
69. Ibid., p. 64. That is, in the traditional sense of metaphysics; we can
study the operations of the mind, but we cannot know man's "nature" in the
sense of essence. See *Essai*, in *Œuvres phil.*, 1, 4.

5. Man's Uniqueness and God's Order

> It would be of small interest to know what animals are, if
> this were not a means for knowing better what we ourselves
> are. It is from this point of view that speculation on such a
> subject is permissible. "If animals did not exist," says M. de
> Buffon, "the nature of man would be even more incomprehen-
> sible than it is." But it must not be supposed that by com-
> paring ourselves with them we can come to understand the
> nature of our being. We can only discover its faculties, and the
> method of comparison can be a technique for submitting
> them to observation.[1]

In the *Traité des sensations* Condillac had created a subjective,
almost a solipsistic, world. He had explored the growth of man's
mental life and constructed an epistemology on introspective principles. He had, in effect, set man apart from the rest of the universe
and observed him in isolation, considering external phenomena only
as encountered in the sensations of the statue-man. The implications
of his thought-experiment—solipsistic from the point of view of
the statue, mechanistic from the point of view of the observer—
forced him to extend his vision and to define man's various relationships in the world beyond himself: his relation to nature, to God,
and to other men. The metaphysical and moral problems posed by
these relationships were of profound concern to an age which
had so decisively cut loose from the philosophical moorings of its
Christian past. The dominant theme running through discussions of
such problems in the mid-eighteenth century was materialism, not
because it was the dominant conviction—it was not—but because
it was the most challenging and aggressive possibility.

Let us put this in a broader perspective. In the period 1680 to

1. *Traité des animaux*, in *Œuvres phil. de Condillac, 1*, 339.

1715, Hazard's generation of the *crise de conscience*,[2] philosophical controversy was dominated by Christianity. Although the Christian faith had already lost its position as the universally accepted common ground of European thought, it remained central in the sense that every man had to define his relationship to it, had to declare himself a defender, a reconciler, or an opponent. In much the same way, the members of the next generation had to come to terms with materialism, because the critical principles with which their fathers had so vigorously attacked Christianity led unmistakably in that direction. These critical principles rested upon a naturalism which carried through the entire century. Naturalism may be defined as the belief that nature is all-embracing, that nothing exists apart from it, that all man's endeavors—in science, in morality, in religion, in social organization—must rest upon the principles of nature. In these general terms naturalism is compatible with a bewildering variety of philosophies, depending upon the meaning attached to the word "nature." By and large, the philosophes derived their image of nature from Newtonian physics, so that for them "nature" tended to mean the operation of mechanical laws upon material bodies. Therefore their naturalism suggested the doctrines of "materialism," the belief that nothing exists except matter, and "mechanism," the belief that all causation is mechanical causation and that all activity is subject to the laws of causation.[3] Thus a philosophe could only with difficulty escape the

2. Paul Hazard, *La Crise de la conscience européenne* (Paris, 1935).

3. Although materialism and mechanism are not identical or even mutually dependent doctrines, they tended to go together in the eighteenth-century concept of natural processes. Within the mechanist-materialist school of thought there occurred a development from the Cartesian concept of animal life as unconscious automaton to a concept of vital mechanism, in which matter is endowed with the property of self-determining purposive motion. (See Aram Vartanian, *La Mettrie's L'Homme Machine: A Study in the Origins of an Idea* [Princeton, 1960], pp. 18ff.) This development, highly significant though it was, left unsolved the philosophical problems raised by mechanistic materialism, which I am discussing here. It merely placed the operations of mechanical causation within the organism, instead of leaving them to act upon it from without.

choice between embracing mechanistic materialism, with all its fearsome consequences of nihilism and irrationalism, and repudiating it and risk compromising his hold on scientific naturalism.

The challenge of materialism crystallizes the chief dilemma of the Age of Enlightenment. The philosophes were caught between contradictory intellectual commitments: on the one hand, they wanted to integrate man fully into the order of nature, to explain man and all his works in terms of mechanical laws just as they explained the phenomena of physics; on the other hand, as residuary legatees of the Western humanist tradition, they were concerned to preserve man's uniqueness as a rational and moral being. This intellectual dilemma could be viewed with equanimity by a philosopher who kept himself above the battle, but not by a philosophe, because the former could keep his philosophical conclusions separate from his life, while the latter could not. Hume, for example, was a radical skeptic in his study, but he could go about the activities of daily life in full expectation that the laws of causality would hold up. The philosophes, however, were distinguished as a group by their desire to act on their philosophical convictions—to bring philosophy to bear on problems of man and society and to initiate reforms on the basis of reason. An inherent contradiction between thought and action, between philosophy and life, could not therefore be tolerated. If their philosophy seemed to suggest that man is not rational or not free, their whole *raison d'être* would be called into question. It was of the utmost importance, then, to seek a way out of the dilemma posed by their thoroughgoing naturalism.

Condillac was dragged into the materialist controversy by his *Traité des sensations*. Had he not been implicitly accused of materialism, it seems unlikely that he would have either perceived the dilemma or been concerned to resolve it. For Condillac was in many ways an anomaly in his circle. Ever more a philosopher than a philosophe, he lacked the passion and the intellectual daring that characterized the latter group. He was conventional, even timid, in his outlook. Most of all, he had no firm dedication to the reform of society, the regeneration of man, or anything else. Apart from a tepid fidelity to the Catholic faith and a project (one can scarcely call it a mission) to geometrize metaphysics, Condillac was without commitments. His defense of man's uniqueness and spirituality in the *Traité des animaux* was much more a function of a wish to preserve his orthodoxy than of a passion for utopia. But before examining the *Traité des animaux,* it would be well to analyze the pertinent particular problems implicit in the general problem of materialism.

Although it had not been apparent at first, the replacement of the Christian-Aristotelian cosmos by the mechanistic universe of the New Science meant chaos in the moral as well as in the epistemological sphere. The anthropomorphic cosmos of Christian Aristotelianism was a moral and metaphyscial structure, imbued with qualities, purposes, and a built-in hierarchy of values. The philosophes wanted, above all, to avoid metaphysics (in the traditional sense of the term). They wanted to base their social and ethical theories on the scientific study of nature, not on metaphysical speculations about "essences" and final causes, nor on theological speculations about the supernatural. The hidden assumption, inherited from certain tendencies of seventeenth-century rationalism, was that nature itself constitutes a kind of self-evident metaphysics. The phenomena of nature point beyond themselves to an order or harmony permeating the universe from which judgments of meaning and value can be inferred. The vogue for "natural" religion and "natural" theology, basing their claims on "natural" reason, stems from this assumption. Condillac's generation was beginning to have misgivings about it.

To begin with, there was the question of order. Is there really order in the universe? If so, what kind of order is it? Is it a rational and moral order or merely the order of blind material necessity? How can an impersonal and mechanistic universe have rational and moral purpose? Indeed, even the evidence of natural phenomena, which had at first looked so harmonious, began to appear ominously discordant. Voltaire saw, in the Lisbon earthquake,[4] and Diderot, in his consideration of the world of the blind man, testimony not only to the moral indifference of nature but also to its lack of order and rationality. There is too much cruelty, too much waste and destruction, too many monstrous and anomalous occurrences, to suppose design in nature. Natural order cannot mean anything but the material necessity of efficient causation. The mid-eighteenth century saw the rediscovery of evil in the universe, but in the context of nature rather than of religion—a difference which proved to be critical. The Christian world-view had taken evil for granted, had accepted it as a consequence of the Fall. Evil had been man's free choice, and he as well as the whole natural order had to suffer from that choice. If there was pain, anguish, and discord in the world, it was because man freely gave the powers of darkness and disharmony a foothold. God allowed it but did not cause it; moreover, God provided redemption at great cost to himself. Sin and evil were no scandal to the orthodox Christian. But one important aspect of the seventeenth-century rebellion against Christian orthodoxy was precisely the rejection of the Christian concept of sin. Deists, for example, wanted to minimize or explain away evil in the universe. They rejected original sin and the torments of hell. They found such concepts degrading to man and unworthy of God, whose universe must be an expression of his own order and harmony. The harmony of the physical workings of the Newtonian universe must be paralleled by a like harmony in its moral workings. But the generation born after 1700, no longer dewy-eyed from the fresh discovery of universal laws, took a harder look at nature and saw much evil. Lacking a religious explanation for and redemption from that evil, they could only be shocked and disillusioned. The rise of atheism in the middle decades of the century is surely to be explained in large

4. For an interesting discussion of Voltaire's role in the downfall of Leibnizian optimism, see Theodore Besterman, "Voltaire et le désastre de Lisbonne: ou, La Mort de l'optimisme," *Studies on Voltaire and the Eighteenth Century,* ed. T. Besterman, 2 (1956), 7–24.

measure by this disillusionment with the serene and happy world of the deists.[5]

The mechanistic universe gave rise not only to a new problem of evil but also to new problems of morality and freedom. Man's place in the universe must be seen in a different light. If he belongs entirely within the natural order, and the philosophes claimed that he does, than he has no special destiny, he is protected by no special providence, he is in no way exempt from the workings of the natural laws. The philosophes had a moral aim in arguing man's integration into nature. They wished to free him from bondage to supernatural forces. Their goal was a naturalistic ethics which would take into account man's natural drives instead of denying their expression, as Christianity tends to do. They believed that a naturalistic ethics would rest on a surer foundation than a supernatural morality imposed from above and enforced by posthumous sanctions. Moreover, since they no longer accepted supernatural authority or believed in supernatural punishments, they had to find a new basis for morality in order to prevent the collapse of society into license. They had to show that even though man is free from external supernatural directives, there remain compelling natural reasons for him to behave in certain ways and to refrain from behaving in certain other ways. The fact that in mid-century the rise of moral nihilism paralleled the rise of atheism suggests the difficulty of finding such reasons once faith in a moral order in nature had been undermined. If man is morally free—that is, if he is free to make his own morality in an indifferent, impersonal, and meaningless universe—what is to prevent each man from making his own morality based on his private whims? The Marquis de Sade did precisely that. More

5. This discussion, and much of that which follows, is based upon material in Crocker, *An Age of Crisis,* passim. Crocker has a tendency to regard extreme thinkers, or the thoughts of representative thinkers in extreme moments, as more representative than they are. Nevertheless, if put in its proper perspective, the extreme thought of an age may be illuminating by showing up clearly certain tendencies which are implicit but unrecognized in its more central thought.

conventional answers to the problem were based on a utilitarian
ethics whose ultimate appeal is to prudence, and which has no recourse against power—no answer to the man who can get away with
indulgence of his whims, however destructive those whims may be.
The danger, then, of a naturalistic ethics was that it pointed toward
moral anarchy held in check only by social tyranny—a consequence
no philosophe could entertain with equanimity.

Parallel to the problem of moral freedom was the problem of
causal freedom. Can man, subject as he is to natural laws, make free
choices and act in such a way as to carry out those choices? Or is
man nothing but a machine, whose every act can be explained in
terms of an infinite regress of material necessities? If the latter is
the case, then morality—any morality—is meaningless and reason
itself is suspect. But if man *is* free, then does this not introduce an
unwelcome and inexplicable element of the supernatural—in the
sense of being above the mechanism of natural laws—into the
universe? The philosophe felt himself caught in a genuine dilemma
between a superstition he had rejected and a nihilism he abhorred.[6]
Although not every thinker of the French Enlightenment saw the
issues quite as baldly as I have stated them here, or concerned
himself with each aspect of the problem, the fact is that every
philosophical controversy in the period took place in the shadow of
this dilemma. In an implicit sense it was inescapable, because every
compromising statement made by a moderate philosophe (and most
of them were moderate) was open to the assaults of both more
radical and more orthodox thinkers, prepared to press every intellectual advantage. If Condillac illustrates anything at all about the

6. See, for example, Diderot's letter to Sophie Volland: "Atheism is
close to being a kind of superstition, as puerile as the other. . . . Nothing is
indifferent in an order of things which is tied together and conducted by a
general law; it seems that everything is equally important. There are no
great or small phenomena. If I believe that I love you of my free will, I
am mistaken, it is nothing of the sort. Oh, what a fine system for ingrates! I
am maddened at being entangled in a devilish philosophy that my mind
can't help approving and my heart refuting." Quoted in Lester G. Crocker,
The Embattled Philosopher (East Lansing, 1954), p. 320.

problems of Enlightenment thought, he illustrates the difficulty of maintaining a consistent position in the middle of the road.

A major battleground of the materialist controversy was the problem of man's relationship to animals, a problem which had been brought to the surface by Descartes' assertion that animals are mere insensate automata.[7] For the antimaterialist philosophe this was a crucial issue, because it laid bare the conflict between his desire to integrate man into the natural world, on the one hand, and his investment in man's moral and rational uniqueness, on the other. Condillac became involved in this problem for two reasons. First, the *Traité des sensations* gave aid and comfort to the materialist cause, because it implied, despite Condillac's disclaimer, that man's mental activity is totally reducible to its physical components. The result of this doctrine is to destroy man's uniqueness by differentiating him only quantitatively from other animals as possessing a more complex physical organization. Second, Condillac wanted to dissociate himself from the theories of Buffon, with which his book had been identified.[8] Buffon was not a materialist. He specifically endowed man with unique spiritual qualities which marked him off from the animal kingdom. But he explained the activities of animals in terms of a mechanistic materialism, and his development of man's psychological functions so emphasized the physical elements that he raised the alarm in orthodox quarters. He was condemned by the Sorbonne in 1751 and forced to submit.[9] The cautious Condillac, alarmed by Grimm's comparison of his theories to Buffon's, feared being tarred with the same brush. Besides, there was a question of personal pique involved, for Grimm made him out to be a distinctly

7. The standard general works on this controversy are Hester Hastings, *Man and Beast in French Thought in the Eighteenth Century* (Baltimore, 1936); and Leonora Cohen Rosenfield, *From Beast-Machine to Man-Machine* (New York, 1941).

8. *Traité des animaux*, in *Œuvres phil.*, 1, 339.

9. See Daniel Mornet, *Les Sciences de la nature en France, au XVIIIe siècle* (Paris, 1911), pp. 108ff.; and Smith, *A History of Modern Culture*, 2, 518–19.

second-rate Buffon.[10] In the *Traité des animaux,* therefore, Condillac established his independence from Buffon and asserted the compatibility of his philosophy with religion.

The *Traité des animaux* is the least impressive of Condillac's major works[11]—evidence, perhaps, of the intellectual tightrope he was walking. Philosophically, Condillac was an innovator, attacking or ignoring tradititional ideas in order to lay a new foundation for metaphysics. But his originality was at war with a social and religious conservatism and even a personal timidity, which would not let him acquiesce in the theological and moral consequences that his philosophical principles suggested. In order to resolve the conflict —or, rather, to deny its existence—he was forced to abandon his customary strict devotion to the method of analysis. The last part of the *Traité des animaux* is full of just those kinds of imprecise thinking that Condillac most abhorred: question-begging explanations, deductions from vague general principles, and the most banal of conventional answers to crucial questions.

As critic of the theories of Descartes and Buffon, however, Condillac was quite up to form. He suggested that Descartes had fallen in love with his system of the universe based solely on the laws of motion, and wanted to extend those laws to animate beings, making them pure mechanisms. "The more a philosopher has generalized an idea, the more he wants to generalize it. He is interested in expanding it to everything, because it seems to him that his mind expands with it, and it soon becomes in his imagination the first cause of phenomena."[12] Thus Descartes' *idée fixe* caused him to ignore the evidence of observation. Observation of animal behavior reveals that the same senses which regulate men's actions appear to regulate theirs. How can we suppose that their eyes do not really see, their ears do not really hear? Strictly speaking,

---

10. *Correspondance littéraire, 2,* 442–43.

11. Nevertheless, it is called by one student of the subject "the most important work of the century regarding the souls of beasts." Hastings, *Man and Beast in French Thought,* p. 53.

12. *Traité des animaux,* in *Œuvres phil., 1,* 340.

we cannot demonstrate that they do; but then, strictly speaking, we cannot demonstrate that other men perceive as we do either, since the only consciousness we can test by direct experience is our own, and yet we would consider it extravagant to suppose that other men lack our kind of consciousness just because we can imagine that God might create beings who can do mechanically what we do by reflection. The burden of proof is on Descartes, and he has not satisfied us. Therefore it is fair to attribute to animals something more than mechanically caused motion, to assert that they have sensations.

Buffon also claimed that the actions of animals could be explained in mechanical terms. He did not deny them sensation but limited them to a kind of sensation that is purely material or "corporeal," which operates through a sensory and motor mechanism triggered off by the *ébranlements* caused in the external senses by the actions of objects; these *ébranlements* travel to the brain and from there to the nerves, causing the appropriate movements. Man's superior status was maintained, in Buffon's theory, by possession of a dual nature. He can find in himself the corporeal sensations of an animal, but his distinguishing feature, the condition of his uniqueness, is an immaterial soul that experiences spiritual sensations and holds the corporeal half of his nature in subjection. The coexistence of these two natures is the source of man's moral and emotional conflicts.

To Condillac, Buffon's theory was simply Cartesianism in other terms, equally false and equally vulnerable.[13] The concept of "corporeal" sensation, he argued, is meaningless and unsubstantiated. Buffon had claimed that man can easily find the two kinds of sensation within himself by introspection, but Condillac reflected on his own sensations "in vain." "I do not feel, on the one hand, my body,

13. Ibid., p. 343b, n. 1. The effectiveness of Condillac's criticism may be gauged by Grimm's angry response: "It is a fine way to avenge yourself on a man you have complaints about to write a work against him and fill it full of unkind and dishonest things. . . . M. l'abbé de Condillac ought to know that when one lacks respect for others, and above all for men of esteem, one does not do them the least harm but one degrades oneself. . . . M. de Buffon puts more insight into one discourse than our abbé puts of his life into all his works." *Correspondance littéraire, 3,* 112.

and on the other, my soul; I feel my soul in my body. All my sensations seem to me only modifications of the same substance, and I do not understand what could be meant by 'corporeal sensations.'"[14] Moreover, to admit these two kinds of sensations breaks up the unity of the self and raises all sorts of unanswerable questions about the relationship of the two selves that each man must have within him. Second, Condillac rejected Buffon's mechanical explanation of animal motion. He cited the physiocrat Quesnay as an authority against the concept of *ébranlements,* and he pointed out that Buffon himself had elsewhere conceded that a machine without a soul would be incapable of sensation. Third, Condillac asserted that Buffon was trying to explain animal behavior by falling back on the vague and ill-defined words that people are accustomed to accept as explanations, such as *ébranlements,* instinct, and appetite. In fact, he cannot explain, on his principles, how animals function, how they take care of themselves, or how they can be trained to modify their natural behavior. Finally, Condillac found that Buffon contradicted himself and came very close to admitting that animals have ideas and memory and that they judge and make comparisons.[15] It would seem that Buffon, too, was walking the tightrope; and Condillac, of all people, caught him out.

In Part II of the *Traité des animaux* Condillac established his own system of animal nature. With a sneer for the professional philosophers, "who ordinarily prefer an absurdity that they invent themselves to a truth that everyone accepts," Condillac championed the popular opinion that animals are capable of acquiring at least some knowledge. His system, Condillac tells us, is not arbitrary. "It is not drawn from my imagination but from observation, and every intelligent reader, *who will commune with himself,* will recognize its soundness."[16] Like his "observations" of the statue-man, Condillac's observation of animals is purely hypothetical: witness the numerous paragraphs in the *Traité des animaux* begin-

14. *Traité des animaux,* in *Œuvres phil., 1,* 342.
15. Ibid., pp. 343–44.
16. Ibid., p. 356. Italics mine.

ning "supposons." Condillac imagined an animal in certain situations—at the first moment of birth or endangered for the first time by a falling object— decided what the animal would do or think or feel in these circumstances, and used the data gathered by this "observation" to substantiate his fundamental hypothesis about animal learning processes. It is a peculiar empiricism, revealing once again the quasi-mathematical abstractness of his method. It is less accurate to draw a triangle and determine the relationships among its sides and angles by measurement than it is to calculate those relationships by analyzing the properties of an ideal triangle existing only in one's mind. Condillac evidently considered that physical observation of a real animal would likewise lack the precision of mental calculations about an abstract, and therefore ideal, animal.

Animals, in Condillac's system, acquire their habits just as men acquire their knowledge and faculties—through experience. The newborn animal feels pleasure and pain, compares the two states, and under their impetus learns it has a body and learns to behave in certain ways to satisfy the needs of its body—that is, to procure pleasure and avoid pain. The repetition of the same acts in answer to the same needs makes those acts habitual, and the reflection that had preceded the habit and generated it is forgotten. Thus animal behavior often appears automatic or machine-like in that it unvaryingly repeats certain patterns and responses, but in fact it is not automatic. There was a time when each animal had to think through each pattern of behavior before it became a habit.[17]

Condillac then took a closer look at the development of a "system of knowledge" in animals. The first moments of an animal's life are given over to his education, although he does not know it: "When we think he is entirely absorbed in play, it is really nature playing with him in order to instruct him."[18] Nature exploits the animal's pleasures and pains for his own good, using them to teach him just as she teaches man. Animals, too, form chains of associated

17. Ibid., pp. 356–57.
18. Ibid., p. 357.

ideas based on their physical needs. They, too, develop ease and facility in running through those chains of ideas, so that the steps in the process of thinking become blurred and indistinguishable. Here Condillac essayed one of his rare attempts at explaining the physiological mechanism of thought. He suggested that a vortex of associated ideas is formed in the memory around each need, and when the need is activated, it communicates movement around the vortex to the circumference—i.e. the external organs of the body—and stimulates the appropriate action to satisfy the need.

The physiological explanation, however, must not be understood as equivalent to later notions of conditioned reflexes, which it appears to resemble. Condillac endowed animals with mental initiative and the power of invention, but defined in such a way as to make these apparently active faculties nothing more than the "sensation, differently transformed," of the *Traité des sensations:* "Animals invent, then, if 'to invent' means the same thing as to judge, to compare, to discover. They invent even if the word means to represent to oneself in advance what one is going to do. The beaver pictures the dam it wants to build; the bird, the nest it means to construct. These animals would not build these things if their imaginations did not give them models."[19] With so much mental capacity, all that prevents animals from developing further, from becoming more like the human beings whose faculties they share, is the fact that they have infinitely less power of invention than man has. Condillac stated two possible reasons for this, which, if really different, have vastly different implications. The first is a purely physical reason. Animals have fewer needs than man and therefore fewer things to learn. In learning them, the animal attains at an early age the perfection of its type and can advance no further. In other words, with fewer sources of pleasure and pain, an animal attains a state of equilibrium (as opposed to uneasiness) much more easily than man does, and is therefore not stimulated to develop potentialities it might in fact have. The other reason denies it the potentialities. Animals have less power of invention because they do not

19. Ibid., p. 358.

have the same means for expanding their ideas or putting them together in an infinite variety of new combinations. "It is not that they altogether lack intelligence, it is that their intelligence is more limited."[20] This raises a new question. What is this mysterious "intelligence"? It is not a customary word in Condillac's narrow vocabulary. In the psychology of knowledge of the *Traité des sensations,* in which every faculty is nothing but transformed sensation, individual differences are explained environmentally. The quickness of the reflective process—i.e. facility at running through sequences of ideas—depends on the variety of experiences rather than on an inborn power, since every man brings to experience a uniform capacity to feel pleasure and pain based upon universal needs. If Condillac was really consistent about this, he might only have been saying that an animal's intelligence is more limited because his needs are more limited and he therefore has fewer experiences. In that case, there would only be one reason for the difference of development between man and animal, and that is a difference of physical organization. However, it may be that the notion of "intelligence" in the *Traité des animaux* was a partial return to the more active psychology of the *Essai sur l'origine des connaissances humaines,* in which he did endow men with different degrees of facility in the association of ideas as innate differences of mental organization. If this is what he means to say, then animals are different from men both in terms of physical needs and of mental organization. But this interpretation negates the achievement of the *Traité des sensations*—the reduction of the faculties of the mind to sensation.

In all probability, Condillac found his own explanation of animal nature more satisfying than the mechanistic explanations of Descartes and Buffon because he recognized that the reduction of animal nature to mere machinery does not safeguard the spiritual status of man. Crocker has pointed out that in the eighteenth-century discussions of animal nature, those who elevated animals usually did so in order to detract from man's stature, to puncture

20. Ibid.

man's vanity over his fancied superiority, whereas those who lowered the status of animals usually meant to suggest that man does indeed stand alone as a moral, rational, and spiritual being.[21] Of course, the lines of the argument often cross one another in a more complex pattern than this. Some of the writers who elevated animals in order to denigrate man were operating within the framework of man's innate superiority. Their point was merely to shame man by comparing his often irrational, selfish, and "brutal" behavior with the sense and nobility so frequently shown by animals. There is here no question of lowering man's metaphysical status; it is rather one of challenging him to live up to that status.[22] On the other side of the issue there are those like La Mettrie and Diderot (in his rigorously materialistic moments) who saw no essential difference between animals and men, and who felt that whatever basic principle explained the behavior of one explained that of the other also. So when they lowered the status of animals to that of machines governed by muscular irritability, they intended it to follow that man's status be lowered as well.

Condillac represents still another variant on the main themes, for in making animals manlike, he certainly did not mean to make man bestial. On the contrary, he used the *Traité des animaux* to establish that his animated statue did not imply a man-machine, and he did so by demonstrating that not even animals are mechanical automata. For if animals were automata, if all their behavior could be explained mechanically, then inevitably man would follow them into the soulless, godless void. If the problem of man's uniqueness must come up, better deal with it on a high rather than a low level. Surely it must have seemed to Condillac much less damaging to religion to have to prove that animals, despite evidence to the contrary, lack immortal souls, than to be required to demonstrate that men, despite evidence to the contrary, are more than machines.

21. Crocker, *Age of Crisis,* pp. 83ff.
22. See Hastings, *Man and Beast,* pp. 68–85. The writers she discusses are obscure today but evidently had a wide circulation in the eighteenth century.

That Condillac did indeed have such metaphysical concerns on his mind when he turned his attention to the problem of animal nature is borne out by the otherwise irrelevant chapters in the *Traité des animaux* on man's discovery of God and morality. The organization of the *Traité des animaux* reflects Condillac's systematic program to restore the ancient hierarchy on a new basis and to refute those who would reduce all life, including man's, to the same squalid clay. Condillac wanted to prove, then, that animals are more than machines and that men are more than animals. And he would, at the same time, restore religion, free will, and an absolute morality, but in the new context of nature, rather than the old context of revelation. Condillac did not deny revelation, but he did not wish to depend upon it more than he could help. He wanted to show that we can get to God and morality by purely natural means, and then it can be shown that although revelation confirms and even supplements our natural knowledge, we can get along without it.

Condillac had still another personal investment in his version of animal nature, and that was the protection of his empiricist epistemology. Other systems of animal behavior emphasized instinct and distinguished between man and animal by saying that while man has reason, animals have only instinct. Condillac could not accept this theory, because instincts are too much like innate ideas. If animals somehow have imprinted in their beings—whether mechanical or mental—the knowledge necessary for their survival, why is it not likely that man has imprinted in his mind the knowledge necessary for his salvation or for his understanding of the universe? Condillac eliminated instincts from animal nature by explaining them away. An instinct, in his theory, is itself rudimentary reason, so that the distinction between animal instinct and human reason vanishes. An instinct is "habit deprived of reflection."[23] Everything an animal does—from seeking milk at its mother's breast to fleeing a natural enemy—is first learned from

23. *Traité des animaux*, in *Œuvres phil.*, *1*, 363.

experience and reflection, trial and error, pleasure and pain. When its behavior becomes automatic through repetition, the reflection is forgotten and it appears as what we call instinct. It is in reality no more instinctive than the ability of a preoccupied Parisian to walk across his city, reaching his destination without paying attention to the route. This is not instinct but habit. And if we are going to distinguish man from animals on this basis, we can say that the measure of reflection man has beyond his habits is what constitutes his reason and his superiority.

Does this mean, then, that man's superiority is purely quantitative? Or purely a matter of physical organization? What about the unique personalities of individual men, so different from the uniformity to be found among all the members of a species of animal? Condillac accounted for this by a paradox. All animals of the same species behave like one another because they do not try to copy one another to any appreciable extent. All men are different from one another because they, of all animals, are the most given to imitation. This paradox may be explained by the fact that each member of the same animal species is born with the same needs and attributes, and therefore each one contracts the same habits founded on the same principles and acquired through the same experiences. There would be uniformity among them even if they were isolated from one another. Animals cannot communicate among themselves to any appreciable degree, so that each is limited to his own experiences and each generation begins anew. There can be neither progress nor variation within a species. Men would be the same if isolated from one another and unable to communicate ideas.[24]

If men were isolated but lived in various parts of the world, different climates and circumstances would result in different experiences and would therefore produce slightly different kinds of men. But without communication, progress would be limited and individual differences would remain small. Only in society are there

24. Ibid., pp. 358–59.

obvious differences among men. In society men communicate, they copy one another, and most important, they form a mass of cumulative knowledge, so that each generation is not compelled to repeat the experiences of its predecessor. Differentiation results from the fact that each individual copies not one other man but many, appropriating the observed behavior and experiences of others as he finds expedient. Each man, therefore, will put together a different combination of borrowed traits and habits, thus creating his own distinctive personality. Progress means that each generation widens the possibilities open to the next by increasing the range of differentiation. The import of this difference between men and animals is that each animal constitutes a self-enclosed, limited, and altogether determined system of habits, while each man is a self-defining being with an infinite range of free choices before him.

The next question that comes to mind is: Why cannot animals communicate? Does this go back to a fundamental difference in intelligence or is it a result of physiology? To begin with, says Condillac, there can be no communication between different species of animals because each species is organized so differently that they have no common needs or common experiences to form the basis of communication. "Thus, although the principal ideas acquired by touch are common to all animals, each species develops a separate system of knowledge."[25] Within the same species there is a limited amount of communication, although not enough, evidently, to form the basis of progress. But inarticulate cries and bodily actions serve to express thoughts among animals who possess the same physical organization, so that the same feelings produce in each the same cries and movements. We can, by constant repetition, teach a dog to understand a limited range of articulate sounds. A parrot, on the other hand, although he can be taught to pronounce articulate sounds himself, can make no sense of them, because his exterior organization is so different from ours that our bodily actions are meaningless to him and therefore there is no means of

25. Ibid., p. 360.

teaching him. Then Condillac found himself again facing the big question: What *is* the real difference between man and beast?

> But if animals think, if they make known some of their feelings, if there are some who understand a little of our language, how then do they differ from man? Is it only a matter of more or less?
>
> I answer, that, powerless to know the nature of beings, we can judge them only by their operations. This is why it would be vain to seek a way of marking the limits of each. We shall never see between them anything but more or less. It is thus that man seems to us to differ from the angel, and the angel from God himself, but from the angel to God the distance is infinite, just as from man to the angel it is considerable, and doubtless greater still from man to beast.
>
> Nevertheless, to mark this difference we have only vague ideas and figurative expressions, "more," "less," "distance," I do not undertake to explain these things. I do not make a system of the nature of things because I do not know it; I make only a system of their operations because I believe I do know them. Now it is in their operations that they seem to differ only by more or less, not in the principle that constitutes what each of them is. And from that alone it must be concluded that they differ in their essence. That which has less certainly does not have in its nature the power to have more. The beast does not have it in his nature to become man, as the angel does not have it in his to become God.[26]

Behind the careful ambiguity of this passage lies the classic assumption of a chain of being, a continuous and unbroken gradation of the forms of life stretching from the lowest species up to God.[27] Each form has its place on the scale marked out, a place that

26. Ibid., pp. 361–62.
27. See the classic study of this concept, Arthur O. Lovejoy, *The Great Chain of Being* (Cambridge, Mass., 1936); see also Crocker, *Age of Crisis,* pp. 79–80.

both links it to and differentiates it from the creatures immediately
below and above it. Condillac can only infer the existence of such a
hierarchy, since his empirical data extend no farther than the behavior of creatures. Nevertheless, and in spite of his protest that
he does not know the nature underlying the behavior of things,
he *does* infer the scale, and with it an essential distinction between
each major step of the scale. Among his materialist contemporaries,
like La Mettrie, d'Holbach, or Diderot, the principle of continuity
is stressed far more than the idea of differentiation, with each
species on the scale (which for them, not so incidentally, stops
short of the angels and God) merely a more complexly organized
form of the one below. Condillac, however, understands the chain
of being as tentatively affirming man's unique place, rather than as
revealing his affinity to the rest of creation. For him animals turn
out to be less than man by their very nature. Even for Condillac,
however, man's natural uniqueness is definable in terms of capacities
and attributes, rather than in essential qualities. He makes no use
of the traditional assertion that man possesses a rational soul while
animals do not—a clear and qualitative distinction.

On the issue of animal soul—a touchy one for a Christian—
Condillac is forced into an extraordinary claim to knowledge of
God's specific wisdom. Conceding that animals have a kind of soul
in their system, Condillac asserted that their souls are not immortal,
because only the action of God can endow a soul with immortality,
and God had decided to grant this gift exclusively to man.[28] In
this regard, and only in this regard, is man marked by an absolute
distinction from the animal world, by the possession of a quality
which can in no sense be reduced to a quantitative difference. And
even this distinction is not inherent in man's nature but is attached
to him by divine fiat. Animals, then, are less than man in capacities
and attributes, and their quantitative deficiencies are fixed in their
very nature.

Among the deficiencies of animal nature is that an animal cannot

28. *Traité des animaux*, in *Œuvres phil.*, I, 371.

acquire the knowledge of God. While the knowledge of God is not innate, as some philosophers have claimed, it is still open to man alone, because only man is capable of the kind of reasoning and conceptualization necessary to arrive at an idea of God. Condillac's argument for the existence of God, characteristically identical to his account of the origin of our knowledge of God, is essentially the traditional cosmological proof. It is understandable that he would find this argument appealing. Along with the argument from design, which Condillac also made use of to demonstrate God's intelligence, the cosmological proof stands out as an a posteriori argument among the classical proofs. He rejected the ontological proof, Descartes' choice, because we know too little about essences for a proof based on the relationship between essence and existence to have any meaning. We can only know things by the relationship they have to us; as they are in themselves, they are beyond our reach. What is satisfying about the cosmological proof is that it proceeds from our experience to God. Since it is based on God's relationship to us, it is both more reliable as proof and more meaningful in what it tells us about God than the ontological argument can be. We do not have in our minds a notion of an infinitely perfect being: these are just words. An argument based on such empty words neither proves God nor tells us anything comprehensible about him. Our idea of God is really a complex notion, made up of a certain number of partial ideas, and the questions to ask are how we get those ideas and on what basis they can be combined. The genesis of our idea of God, in other words, is the key to its validity and its meaning.

When man first began to reflect on the experience of pleasure and pain, he realized that he was totally dependent on external things for the quality of his existence at any given moment. His happiness or unhappiness was contingent on the sun and the rain, the fertility of the soil, the friendliness or hostility of animals. "This knowledge humbles man before all that is."[29] It was natural

29. Ibid., p. 366.

that he should deify the objects on which he felt so dependent, to make them gods who could be propitiated and persuaded to look on him with favor. Incapable of metaphysical subtleties, early man never doubted the power, intelligence, and liberty of his gods. Primitive polytheism proves how real is man's sense of dependence, how inescapable a fact of his existence. It is ironical that only when he has learned to advance beyond polytheism, to reason from his contingency to a single First Cause who determines not merely the quality of existence but existence itself, only, in short, when he is ready to know God, does it occur to him to doubt God. Atheists cannot deny man's dependence, and so they are compelled to admit a First Cause. But they argue from his contingency to an impersonal and blind first cause, a mere necessity without design or intelligence. It has become necessary to prove the intelligence and liberty of God, which primitive man accepted without question.

Unlike some of his contemporaries, Condillac was still much more impressed by harmony than by disorder in the universe.

> Can one see the order in the parts of the universe, their mutual dependence, and the way so many different things make up such a durable whole, and remain convinced that the universe is caused by a principle that has no knowledge of what it produces, that, without design, without sight, nevertheless relates each being to particular ends subordinated to a general end? If the object is too vast, cast your eyes on the vilest insect. What delicacy! What beauty! ... What foresight in the choice of offensive and defensive weapons! What wisdom in the means provided for its subsistence![30]

The expression of rational order in the universe is a self-evident refutation of the atheist's claim that man's contingency proves his insignificance in a meaningless universe. For if God's intelligence did not embrace the cosmos "at a glance, if something escaped him, were it only for an instant, disorder would destroy his work."[31]

30. Ibid., p. 368.
31. Ibid.

Condillac thus allowed to God a more significant and active role than was becoming customary by mid-century. God did not, it appears, merely start the machinery going and then, retiring to a discreet distance, leave it to its own well-oiled devices. On the contrary, God's presence and concern are vital, in Condillac's eyes, to the continued maintenance of the cosmic order. To be sure, God does not intrude himself upon the scene with miraculous interventions, nor is he required periodically to repair defects in the original work, as Newton himself would have it.[32] It is enough that God act as Supreme Monitor, eternally sustaining the harmony of the universe by the sweep, the vigilance, and the moral authority of his gaze.

Given God's all-embracing intelligence and his independence of any prior cause or principle, it is easy to deduce his liberty and, indeed, all the other traditional attributes of God. They are contained in the basic qualities of power, intelligence, and liberty. "This being, as intelligent, discerns good and evil, judges merit and demerit, appreciates everything. As free, he is self-determining and acts in accordance with what he knows. Thus, from his intelligence and his liberty are born his kindness, justice, and mercy, in a word, his providence."[33]

In his discussion of the attributes of God, Condillac alluded to another charge leveled against his philosophy: that it leads to determinism. The *Traité des animaux,* he felt, was not the place to discuss the problem of free will, but in fact he had already discussed it in an appendix he had just written for the *Traité des sensations* —the *Dissertation sur la liberté.*

Condillac's understanding of free will was the common-sense view that man is free to make choices between possible alternatives and to act upon these choices. He justified his position by an appeal to experience—or, rather, to a hypothetical demonstration that the

32. See Edwin A. Burtt, *The Metaphysical Foundations of Modern Physical Science* (London, 1925), pp. 291–97.
33. *Traité des animaux,* in Œuvres phil., 1, 368–69.

phenomenon in question could have evolved from experience, whether or not it did so in fact being of lesser concern. He did not consider the problem from the point of view of either theological or scientific determinism—that is, determinism by forces external to man, whether they are the laws of nature or the will of God. He acknowledged man's dependence on external things as objects of desire and sources of pleasure and pain. This dependence defines the area of choice within which man's freedom operates. Such definition does not negate freedom; it merely limits its range.

The source of freedom, for Condillac, is in desire itself. (The statue-man, reanimated for the occasion, provides the data for his theory.) As man accumulates experience, he finds in himself a multiplicity of desires corresponding to the variety of sources of pleasure and pain that he discovers. Moreover, he discovers the possibility of error and repentance when he realizes that a particular choice of action has cost him a pleasure he might otherwise have had, or resulted in a pain he could have avoided. From these experiences he learns to deliberate, to consider what course of action will give him the maximum of pleasure and the minimum of pain. Thus he will choose to resist some desires in order to satisfy others. For example, he might have a desire to eat a large quantity of delicious fruit, but experience has taught him that this will result in a severe stomach ache. Therefore, in deference to his desire to avoid the pain of the stomach ache, he will resist his desire for the pleasure of eating the fruit. Sometimes, when in the grip of a violent passion, he will lose the power to deliberate, and where there is no deliberation, there is no choice of action and therefore no freedom. But normally he has the power to deliberate on the basis of acquired knowledge and consequently has the power to yield or not to yield to a particular desire. This is what Condillac means by freedom, and it would not exist if there were never a conflict among desires. If man could experience only one desire at a time, his actions would be wholly determined by the movement of passions in his soul and he would have no freedom. His freedom is to be found in the tension among his desires as—like factions in the body politic—they contend for supremacy.[34]

While Condillac may have believed in man's freedom, his philosophy pointed in the opposite direction. There is a link missing between his psychological analysis in the *Traité des sensations* and his argument for man's power of deliberation in the *Dissertation sur la liberté.* He does not tell us how man takes control of his mental apparatus, how he emerges from passive submission and reaction to changing sensations to a state of free, self-determining autonomy. In the *Essai* he had postulated language as the missing link, but then in the *Essai* he had endowed man with the activity of reflection as a birthright. In the *Traité des sensations,* however, he had allowed his statue to progress much further without language than he had thought possible in the earlier book. In his expanded analysis of the faculties as transformed sensation, he discovered a greater potentiality in passivity, in mechanical processes, than the Lockean psychology of the *Essai* had permitted. Language, in the *Traité des sensations,* is therefore necessary only for the acquisition of theoretical knowledge, for building systems of abstract ideas. For practical knowledge, for the knowledge necessary to survive, to seek pleasure and avoid pain, language is dispensable.[35]

The statue-man, deprived of language and yet able to take care of himself, never makes the transition from passivity to activity. The processes by which he learns to look after his needs, including those by which he selects among his desires, can be, and are, described in mechanical terms as things that happen to him rather than things that he does. The key to his behavior is the association of ideas, and without language he cannot control the mechanism of association. The feeling of hunger brings to his mind the picture of the fruit that has relieved his hunger in the past, and which had first attracted him through the sensations of color and odor. The image of the fruit is automatically associated with the tree on which

34. *Dissertation sur la liberté,* in *Œuvres phil., 1,* 317.
35. *Traité des sensations,* in *Œuvres phil., 1,* 296–97.

he had found it, and that image with the location of the tree. The
idea of its location inspires him to go there and to repeat the act
of eating, which he had originally discovered as a random response
to sensory stimulation.[36]

The development of conflicting desires that Condillac finds at the
root of freedom can also be explained, in his own terms, mechanically, eliminating the power of deliberation. At one time, urged on
by the pleasure of taste, the statue eats too much of the fruit. The
result is a severe stomach ache. At first he does not connect the two,
but if he continues to overeat, always with the same doleful result,
he will soon have in his mind two associations with the fruit—
relief of hunger and the pleasure of taste, on the one hand, and the
pain of a stomach ache, on the other. His future "decisions" about
whether to eat the fruit or not will be determined by the relative
strength at any given time of these two associations. When the
memory of the pain is recent, he will resist the desire to eat in
deference to the more vivid desire to avoid the pain. When the
memory of the pain fades and the sensation of hunger grows,
he will again eat of the fruit. In neither case has he deliberated. He
has merely been moved to action by the strongest desire. The
advocates of a fully mechanical explanation of man[37] account for
all of man's actions by precisely this kind of determinism, and there
is nothing in Condillac's system to refute them. His assertion that
man acquires freedom through the multiplicity of his desires is
merely an assertion. He is not entitled to it if his philosophy is to
be consistent.

Whatever objections one might make to the statue-man as a free
being, man's freedom is basic to Condillac's final defense of man's
uniqueness in the *Traité des animaux*. As we have seen, the metaphysical difference between man and animal is problematic. Both
have spiritual souls. If man's is immortal, it is because God has

36. Ibid., pp. 299ff.
37. E.g. Helvétius, La Mettrie, d'Holbach; Diderot accepted their arguments for a time, then rebelled in violent, humanistic outrage against them.
See Crocker, *Age of Crisis,* pp. 117ff.

so decreed, not because immortality is native to the essence of man's soul, while the souls of animals are by *their* nature doomed to mortality. As Condillac explained it, in a brief excursion into theodicy, God owed man immortality in order to recompense him in the next life for injustice in this, but since he lays no moral demands on animals, they suffer no injustice and need no redress.[38] With regard to natural capacities, man's superiority is even more equivocal. His more advanced development Condillac attributed to a different physical organization, but he then later declared that since God would surely not have imprisoned a soul with human capacities in the confines of an animal body, we are assured of a genuine difference.[39] There is little comfort for either humanist or Christian in arguments such as these, but Condillac had not exhausted his resources. The real source of man's uniqueness lies in his moral nature—a position Condillac defended, for the most part, without those jarring flights into the supernatural with which he was accustomed to save the day when all else failed.

Man's unique discovery of the principles of morality is a function of his superior intelligence and his power of deliberation. Hence it is a derivative distinction, rather than an innate one, but it is none the less significant, for it not only provides the occasion for man's immortality, it also transforms man by enlarging and enriching the nature of pleasure and pain.

Characteristically, Condillac explained man's discovery of morality in terms of natural experience. As man develops the techniques of pursuing pleasure and avoiding pain, he comes to see the benefits of mutual aid. Men can gain a higher ratio of pleasure to pain if they join together in cooperative effort than if each man pursues his own advantage in isolation from or in competition with

38. *Traité des animaux*, in *Œuvres phil.*, I, 371.

39. "Lettre de M. l'abbé de Condillac à l'auteur des 'Lettres à un Américain,' " *Œuvres phil.*, I, 385. This is an answer, published in the *Mercure de France* of April 1756, to criticisms of the *Traité des animaux* by the Abbé de Lignac in *Suite des "Lettres à un Américain" sur les IVᵉ et Vᵉ volumes de "l'Histoire naturelle" de M. de Buffon, et sur le "Traité des animaux" de M. l'abbé de Condillac* (4 vols. Hamburg, 1756).

other men. On this utilitarian basis society is established, and
with it the conventions by which men agree to resist some desires
for the sake of gratifying others. These conventions are the beginning of morality: "In these conventions men would believe they
saw only their own work, if they were not capable of rising to a
knowledge of God. But they soon recognize their legislator in this
supreme being who, disposing of everything, is the sole dispenser
of good and evil. If it is by him that they exist and are preserved,
they see that it is he whom they obey when they give themselves
laws. They find them, so to speak, written in their nature."[40] Of
course, when Condillac said men find the laws of God "written in
their nature," he had in mind not a revival of innate ideas but,
rather, that man's nature is such that he must inevitably, by following his natural hedonistic impulses, discover those laws. He was
reasserting, on naturalistic foundations, an absolute God-given
moral law. He was holding out against the drift of his age toward
moral relativism, just as he held out against materialism. And just
as his physical analysis of man seemed to flirt with materialism, so
the utilitarian basis of his moral doctrine seems to hint at relativism.
But it appears that the genesis of the idea of morality does not
exhaust its meaning. Pleasure and pain are the means by which man
comes to know the moral law; they are not its sanctions or the
source of its authority. Condillac came to his final moral theory
neither by a scheme of reduction nor by a call for the deus ex
machina. Experience and utilitarian considerations got him just so
far, and then off he soared into the purest rationalism—free, for
once, from the strained and self-conscious demiempiricism with
which he so obviously never felt at home. He deduced the natural
law from the attributes of God, which in turn he had deduced from
the rational order of the universe, which he declared to be self-
evident.

It is by virtue of his destined moral nature that man differs
most radically from animals, for it is this that makes him an

40. *Traité des animaux*, in *Œuvres phil.*, 1, 370.

open-ended system, self-defining and unlimited, whereas the animal is a self-enclosed and finite system, quickly achieving the perfection of his type. Animals, as we have seen, have few needs. They are easy to satisfy and content to spend most of their time in a state of lethargy, going into action only when pain threatens. Man, however, in becoming moral finds a new dimension of pleasure and pain. He no longer seeks mere physical pleasure or flees only from physical pain. He experiences pleasure when he is moved to a virtuous act, and he suffers when he is inclined to a vicious one. Driven by the restless activity of his soul, never content with animal-like lethargy, always in search of new desires, man explores these new pleasures and pains and finds that they add a delicacy and refinement, a care for means and a love of balance, to the pursuit of physical pleasures, which in turn opens up the riches of intellectual and aesthetic pleasures. His life then comes to be dominated by moral, intellectual, and aesthetic pleasures, so much more rich and varied than physical pleasure, which remains earthbound and sluggish, tied to the limited system of needs that man shares with the animal. "In a word, moral [qualities], which in origin are only accessory to the passions, become in man's hands the most important."[41] Intellectual superiority, the power of deliberation, the knowledge of God, and the perception of moral qualities in a rational universe—these are man's unique and distinguishing characteristics. The animal, deprived of reason, unable to deliberate, in bondage to a system of habitual behavior, with no obligations and no rewards, is by nature and not by accident separated from man by an unbridgeable gulf.

In the end, after many false starts and dubious claims, Condillac found his way to an understanding of man which preserves his unique place in the universe—so necessary to a religious outlook— without doing grave violence to the naturalist predilections of the eighteenth century. Still, the exact character of Condillac's religious position is not easy to determine. He was at least a deist. Whether

41. Ibid., p. 373.

he was more than that, whether he was genuinely Christian in his convictions, is a hard question, and to answer it we must analyze and weigh evidence that is something less than consistent.

He was, of course, a priest; but like so many younger sons, he evidently had been compelled to enter holy orders by family pressure. A priest without vocation, he is supposed to have celebrated Mass only once in his life, presumably at the time of his ordination.[42] Yet he always wore the cassock and he maintained a chapel on his estate at Flux, where every Sunday and feastday services were held, which the staff of the estate were required to attend, Condillac himself providing "the example with the precept."[43] When he was dying, he called for a priest and claimed that he died in the Catholic faith.[44]

In his writings Condillac never missed a chance to protest his orthodoxy, especially in the context of theories that might cast doubt upon it; but his protestations follow, by and large, the pattern of the conventional disclaimers that most of his contemporaries felt obliged to set forth from time to time to appease the royal censors and the Sorbonne theologians. For example, in the *Essai sur l'origine des connaissances humaines* there is a conflict between Condillac's conjectures on the origin of language and the biblical account of the creation of man. The Book of Genesis implies that Adam and Eve were created with an innate language, or were at least taught it directly by God at the time of their creation. But Condillac speculated about the natural origins of language and sought to describe how language first appeared and how it evolved historically from gestures and inarticulate cries to articulation and grammatical structure. He took the sting out of his departure from revealed truth by blandly denying the truth of his own account. Undoubtedly, he said, man learned language the way Scripture tells us he did, but the business of a philosopher is to concern himself

42. Baguenault de Puchesse, *Condillac,* p. 9.

43. Ibid., p. 21.

44. Ibid., p. 23. Condillac's practice of piety rests on family tradition, so one may question its reliability. It is, nevertheless, believable.

with natural rather than supernatural means, whichever was actually employed. As a philosopher, he will attempt to determine how man would have learned language, had he not been so endowed by direct supernatural action.[45] In much the same vein Condillac explained that he was concerned with the soul in its natural state, after the Fall and before death, when it is totally dependent upon the body; he did not deal with its supernatural essence, which does not need sensory experience to know and reflect upon things.[46]

It is scarcely credible that Condillac honestly regarded his own naturalistic explanation of the origin of language as mere fantasy and thought that the truth of the matter lay elsewhere. At the same time, more was intended than a conventional and hypocritical show of piety. For what Condillac has done in his disingenuous disclaimer is to establish a sharp cleavage between the natural and the supernatural realms, so that if explanations in terms of the supernatural are not invalidated by natural explanations, the reverse is also true. In short, Condillac was unobtrusively declaring the independence of the philosopher—independence from the given data of revelation, from the apparatus of theology, and from the whole context of the supernatural—on the grounds that they do not apply to the natural world and that the philosopher's business is exclusively with the natural world. The supernatural must not be permitted to intrude upon or set limits to his inquiries. The two modes of explanation, then, exist side by side without touching one another. The separation is even more conspicuous in Condillac's assertion that the soul operates under different laws in its "natural" state from those governing its supernatural state. Therefore the soul, too, is a legitimate object for naturalistic dissection.

Condillac was by no means the first to insist upon an autonomous realm for natural philosophy, nor was he the most forthright. A

45. *Essai*, in *Œuvres phil.*, *1*, 60, 60a, n. 1. Cf. Rousseau, *Discours sur l'origine de l'inégalité*, in *Œuvres*, *1*, 226; and Voltaire, *Traité de métaphysique*, in *Œuvres complètes*, 22, 213, where similar conventions are adopted.

46. *Essai*, in *Œuvres phil.*, *1*, 7.

century and a half before Condillac's day, Galileo and Bacon had both unequivocally asserted that science was a secular enterprise to which ecclesiastical authorities and theological systems were simply irrelevant. With this pronouncement they heralded a new era, but even they had some lonely predecessors, like Pietro Pompanazzi early in the sixteenth century, whose pleas for a free science fell largely on uncomprehending ears.[47]

By the eighteenth century such a view had become quite common. That it was not universal may be explained by its assumption that both supernatural and natural explanations may be simultaneously true within their own systems, which somehow do not touch.[48] They reflect different ways of looking at the same problems: the process of history, the nature of man and his destiny, the origin and structure of the universe, and so on. In other words, two standards of truth are involved here—one which is tested by evidence and observation, and one which is tested by authority, whether the external authority of institutionalized revelation or the internal authority of a personal and private revelation. Not everyone in the eighteenth century, on any side of the religious issue, could accept this dichotomy. In the first place, of course, there were those orthodox souls who would not accept limits on the range of theological explanation. For them theology was still queen of the sciences and the source of all true understanding. Science and philosophy must conform to the traditional Christian interpretation of things, on earth as well as in heaven. Less straitlaced religionists sought a kind of integration between science and theology, in which each would complement the other. Theology would set certain limits to the scientist's activity and explain what he could not. Science, on the other hand, could adumbrate what revelation merely suggested, could demonstrate the truth of re-

47. Franklin L. Baumer, *Religion and the Rise of Skepticism* (New York, 1960), pp. 113–15.

48. That is, it contains this assumption when it is sincerely held and does not merely function as a screen behind which religion may be disregarded totally as outmoded and disproven.

ligious claims, could correct theology where it had wandered into fantasy and extravagance, and could furnish moral inspiration as the study of God's handiwork. A whole school of British physico-theologians devoted themselves to reconciling science and religion in this manner.[49] Still another view—and one which most of the philosophes held to a greater or less degree—involved the flat rejection of theological claims to truth. There could be only one standard of truth, and that was the empirical test of natural science. The supernatural explanations of traditional religion were simply false—the products of ignorance, misunderstanding, or even willful fraud. Condillac's position, however, had the great merit of permitting him to remain on relatively good terms with moderate orthodoxy (although not always with those rigorist bulldogs, the Jesuits), while pursuing an independent course in his natural philosophy. Only in the defensive *Traité des animaux* did Condillac get his intellectual wires crossed and mix theological arguments with natural explanations—as, for example, in his solution to the question of animal souls and immortality.

Perhaps the most striking thing about Condillac's religious references is their irrelevance to everything else in his philosophy. They could all be, and most of them are, relegated to footnotes. They make no difference to his system, which would be the same without them. Only the deistic arguments of the *Traité des animaux* are integral, because without the moral and rational structure they bring to it, his atomistic universe would fall apart. But heaven and hell, the immortal soul, the Fall of man, the whole Christian revelation, in fact, seem superfluous. It does not support or explain or enrich anything in Condillac's philosophy. Whether he really believed in the Christian revelation, or whether it was a mere convention which he dared not openly reject, is probably impossible to ascertain, but some tentative suggestions may be made. I think it more likely than not that he really accepted, with little passion and with some mental reservations, the Catholic position and simply

49. For example, John Ray and William Derham, discussed in Willey, *The Eighteenth Century Background,* pp. 34–42.

kept it isolated from his philosophy, with which it was not compatible. I doubt that he let himself recognize the corrosive implications of his philosophical criticism for the religion he continued to embrace. His empiricism was incompatible with the metaphysics on which Catholic theology had always rested; his psychology made unnecessary any belief in the fundamental spirituality of man; and his assumption that anything worth explaining can be accounted for by natural means made theological explanations superfluous. But Condillac remained a Christian and a Catholic. How he did it, by what intellectual or psychological machinery he managed not to let his left hand know what his right hand was doing, may be explained by two elements in his makeup: his conventional and retiring spirit, and his formalistic, unemotional temperament. Controversy and rebellion were deeply threatening to Condillac. He could wage a quiet war of words with dead philosophers whose day had already passed, but if it came to a clash with living authority, Condillac's submissive nature stood ready to yield—and to yield inwardly, not merely with a show of acquiescence. Condillac's submissiveness went deeper than lip-service. Moreover, his detached, unemotional temperament permitted him to accept the forms of faith in a passionless manner. His nature did not demand the kind of conviction that shakes the spirit in order to give assent, nor did he have the kind of burning integrity that forces a man to pursue every doubt, to exhaust every alternative, to profess no faith which is not felt as a deep part of his being, and to defy at all costs any authority who would make him violate that integrity. Condillac did not demand so much from himself, did not think so much of himself as to set himself against the decent order of established religion and a stable society. He must have had some mental reservations, but there were ways to deal with these. (There are always ways to deal with these.) He could regard the areas where his views unmistakably departed from traditional Catholic teaching as peripheral, not central, to the faith. He could even feel that the future was on his side, that the Church would change her teaching in time. But meanwhile, if the Church's authority were exerted, he would submit—that is, be silent and wait. Condillac has had much company, over the ages, in this attitude. It is not the kind of attitude that breeds heroes or martyrs, but it fairly represents the sort of accommodation that most men must make between their consciences and some authority or other in order to sustain life, sanity, and a coherent culture.

In any case—whether or not this hypothetical reconstruction of Condillac's religious attitude is correct—the sharp separation between his religious claims and his philosophy reveals a trend which gathers momentum in the nineteenth century and is conspicuously dominant in the twentieth. It is a historical fact that the claim that science and religion can coexist in mutual independence has nearly always masked (not necessarily consciously) a de facto relegation of religious explanatory systems to a level of existential insignificance. It is of the very essence of a religious view of the world to demand total integration into the lives of its adherents—intellectually, emotionally, morally, and culturally. When this integration has been broken up, the religion loses its vitality, its moral authority, and its relevance. This is apparent enough in Condillac's own position. The fact is that his Catholicism made no difference to his life, his mind, or his moral character. A Catholic in a Catholic society, he would have been the same man had chance made him a skeptic in a skeptical society, a Calvinist in a Calvinistic society, or a Moslem in an Islamic society. And this is a measure not only of Condillac himself but of what was happening—of what had happened—to Christianity's relation to the culture of Europe.

6. The Perfection of Language and the Search for the Primitive

> We who consider ourselves informed often need to go to the most ignorant peoples, to learn from them the origin of our knowledge; for we need this origin above all; we are ignorant of it because it has been a long time since we were disciples of nature.[1]

> Primitive languages, although limited, were better made than ours, and they had the advantage of showing clearly the origin and development of acquired knowledge.[2]

Condillac's interest in the methodology of science and philosophy led to a lifelong concern with the problem of language and with related aspects of human expression. The desirability of a genetic and structural analysis of all forms of expression follows from the conviction that the value of any inquiry depends on the approximation of its method to that of mathematical analysis, and that mathematics is essentially a language. In order to show how language could be made precise, Condillac had first to show how it had become careless, which led him to explore its origin and development. The resulting theory that both the language and the art forms of primitive times sprang from the same impulses and at first were not distinguishable from one another elicited an aesthetic theory of some originality in an age still dominated by the classical conception of art as imitation of *la belle nature*. Finally, as the crown of his linguistic speculations, he tried to work out a system of logic, based on mathematics, which would be a perfect form of expression. The sections on language, method, and art in the *Essai*

1. *La Langue des calculs*, in *Œuvres phil. de Condillac*, 2, 427.
2. Ibid., p. 464.

sur l'origine des connaissances humaines, several volumes of the *Cours d'études* (the *Grammaire,* the *Art de penser,* the *Art d'écrire,* with the *Dissertation sur l'harmonie du style* subjoined to it, and the *Art de raisonner),* the *Logique,* the *Dictionnaire des synonymes,* and the unfinished and posthumously published *Langue des calculs* all testify to the extent and persistence of Condillac's interest in the subject.

Speculation about language was one of the many new, or at least young, subjects to arouse the curiosity of the Enlightenment. The debased coinage of scholastic and conventional language—Bacon's Idols of the Market-Place—had provoked a number of seventeenth-century writers, many of them scientists, into considering the problem of communication. In England, Cave Beck, John Wilkins, and Seth Ward, as well as Newton and Boyle, expressed interest in the possibility of a brand new mintage, of stable value and universal currency. Newton, Wilkins, and Beck drew up extensive plans for a universal philosophical language (and were satirized for their pains in *Gulliver's Travels),* and on the Continent Descartes and Leibniz devoted some effort toward the same end.[3] Behind this new interest, of course, lay the needs and philosophy of the New Science. Medieval Latin, the only universally understood language available, was inadequate to the task of expressing scientific concepts with the desired precision. It not only lacked the proper vocabulary, but it was mired deep in the scholastic tradition and breathed a spirit which seventeenth-century scientists found sterile.

The changing character of philosophy also played a role in stimulating interest in language. As we have seen, the Enlightenment was the beneficiary of a shift in seventeenth-century philosophy from speculation about the objects of thought to speculation about the mechanics of thought. This change is apparent in the many works devoted to exploring the functioning of the senses, the analysis of mental operations, and the formation and constitution of ideas. The epistemological problem, with its ramifications,

---

3. See R. W. V. Elliott, "Isaac Newton's Of an Universall Language," *Modern Language Review,* 3 (1957), 1–18.

was a key factor behind the fundamental subjectivism of such speculation, but even more specifically, the interest in language reflects the inherent nominalism of the empirical philosophy. What the realist had believed to be things, the nominalist thought were only names. Consequently, the nominalist tended to limit himself to the study of names rather than pursue the things, which he felt would always turn out to be mirages.

For various reasons, then, practical and philosophical, critical and constructive, problems of language and meaning had become living issues by the end of the seventeenth century. The eighteenth century continued to discuss these issues and added another of its own—language as a natural phenomenon. Speculation about the historical origin of language was scarcely possible until two traditions had been discarded or modified. The scriptural tradition and the rationalist tradition both precluded, or at least inhibited, such speculation. According to the Bible, man was directly and supernaturally endowed with language (specifically Hebrew, traditionally believed to be the oldest form of speech) at the moment of his creation. Not only did Adam have the prerogative of naming the animals that shared his paradise, but he was provided with a companion and helpmate, and as Bishop Warburton disarmingly pointed out, without language there would have been no means of enjoying such companionship.[4] Moreover, God gave Adam religious knowledge, which would have been beyond his understanding had he lacked words in which to express it. To consider the natural origin of language, then, required a willingness to abandon the biblical account, and this disposition was rare before 1700, at least in public.[5] Indeed, even in mid-century many writers, includ-

---

4. William Warburton, *The Divine Legation of Moses Demonstrated* (10th ed. 3 vols. London, 1846), 2, 376. This popular and influential work was first published in 1737.

5. But one is not surprised to find Richard Simon engaging in speculations about the origin of language, in *Histoire critique du vieux testament* (Amsterdam, 1685), pp. 84ff. However, he was more interested in the later stages of its development than in the steps leading to its birth, so he contributed little of substance to eighteenth-century theories. It is much

ing Condillac, felt constrained to use the story in Genesis as a screen behind which to put forth their own naturalistic theories, while remaining immune from censure.

The rationalist tradition also inhibited discussion of the origin of language, not because it presented an explicit and dogmatic theory of its own, but because of its general understanding of the nature of human reason. Man's possession of innate ideas, his ability to make varied sounds, and his impulse toward social intercourse, all produced, naturally, self-consciously, and rapidly, a spoken language. Language, in this view, is itself an innate capacity, the inevitable expression of man's innate reason. So directly does language correspond to rationality that for Descartes the fact that animals do not have language was sufficient proof that they have no reason whatever.[6] Bossuet and Buffon concurred. It was not necessary, then, to re-create the circumstances in which language first occurred or to suppose a long period of gradual development. Man came, man thought, man spoke. The only problem language posed for the rationalist was the problem of clarity and exact definition. As a phenomenon, it is given in the nature of man.[7]

If Condillac's interest in the origin of language reflects the empiricist side of his philosophy, his method of inquiry reflects his rationalism. He was convinced that man becomes man only through experience. Man is what he has acquired. He has acquired

---

more surprising that a Church Father, Gregory of Nyssa, seems to have accepted the natural origin of language, for which Warburton soundly criticized him in a footnote, saving, although barely, his own orthodoxy (*Divine Legation*, 2, 375, n. 2). Before Simon, and apart from Gregory, speculation on this subject seems to have been limited to a handful of ancients, like Lucretius and Horace, who included it in discussions of the origins of society. See F. B. Kaye, "Mandeville on the Origin of Language," *Modern Language Notes*, 39 (1924), 136–42; see also Otto Jespersen, *Language, Its Nature, Development and Origin* (London, 1922), pp. 19ff.

6. Descartes, *Discours de la méthode*, V, in *Œuvres*, 6, 58.

7. See Paul Kuehner, *Theories on the Origin and Formation of Language in the Eighteenth Century in France* (Philadelphia, 1944), pp. 13ff.

reason and language, and therefore the origins of both are appropriate objects of inquiry. Language is the gradual, sporadic, undetermined outgrowth of experience. Art, another product of
experience, originated as the most primitive forms of spoken and
written language, from which ordinary prose and phonetic script
were more sophisticated offshoots. Even logic is rooted in experience, because the way to a valid logic is to "observe what nature
teaches us."[8] "What nature teaches us"—in this innocent phrase
we have left the concrete world of empirical data behind and are
on the high road to rationalism. Experience is equivalent to nature,
and nature for Condillac is regular, mechanical, mathematical, and
to be understood by applying to it the method of reductive analysis
—a method which, in Condillac's hands, always turns out to have
a remarkable kinship to rational intuition. One need not read much
of Condillac's linguistic speculation before discovering that, as
always, he may profess empiricism in his theories but has smuggled
rationalism into his methodology—the hiding place of more than
one man's unacknowledged metaphysics.

Eighteenth-century speculation on the origin of language deserves a more exhaustive treatment than has yet been given it or
than can be given it here. Its novelty as a field of inquiry in the
Enlightenment would alone justify such a study, but beyond that it
affords an unusually fruitful entry into the nature of eighteenth-
century thought, touching as it does upon a whole catalogue of
characteristic intellectual problems: the search for the primitive,
the priority of reason or the passions in human nature, the supposed universality of human nature, the meaning and value of
human society, the role of convention in man's development, and
so on. Moreover, the conditions of such speculation in the eighteenth century—i.e. its purpose and method—are especially help-
ful in tracing particular theories of language to the philosophical
background from which they sprang. In most cases, especially
before 1760, speculation about language was entered into not for

8. *La Logique*, in *Œuvres phil.*, 2, 374.

its own sake but incidentally to some larger question.[9] Furthermore, the method employed was nearly always exclusively a priori.[10] In attempting to reconstruct what must have happened on the basis of certain assumptions about the nature of man, Enlightenment thinkers tell us much more about their assumptions than about the origin of language.

Few writers before Condillac had any notion that man originated language by natural means, and fewer still tried to imagine how he did it. There were perhaps half a dozen between Lucretius and Leibniz who said something about the natural origin of language, but only two before Condillac who speculated seriously about it: William Warburton, the latitudinarian Bishop of Gloucester, and Bernard de Mandeville, the cynical author of the *Fable of the Bees*.[11] Condillac acknowledged his debt to Warburton. Indeed, a substantial part of his discussion was taken from him directly, sometimes with quotation marks and sometimes without.[12] And he could easily have come across the work of Mandeville, whose ideas closely resemble Condillac's.[13]

After the appearance in 1746 of Condillac's *Essai sur l'origine*

9. In the 1760s there began to appear treatises devoted to the exclusive study of the origin and formation of language. Apparently interest in the subject for its own sake had been stimulated by the growth of speculation about it for the sake of other inquiry.

10. This is not to be wondered at even apart from the unrecognized a priorism of so much of Enlightenment thought, for by its very nature the origin of language as an empirical study is lost to us. Certain quasi-empirical techniques have been developed in the twentieth century, based on the data derived from the study of contemporary primitive peoples and changes in the internal structure of language, but in the eighteenth century none of this was available. See Jespersen, *Language,* pp. 416ff.

11. See Kaye, *MLN, 39,* 136–42. Kaye does not seem to know about Warburton, but he is my source for the "half dozen": Horace, Diodorus Siculus, Vitruvius, Gregory of Nyssa, Simon, and Vico.

12. The sections on the origin of language in Book IV of Warburton's *The Divine Legation of Moses Demonstrated* were translated by Léonard de Malpeines as *Essai sur les hiéroglyphes des Egyptiens* (2 vols. Paris, 1744).

13. Kaye, *MLN, 39,* 140–41.

des connaissances humaines, which contains the bulk of his speculation on the origin of language, the literature began to multiply.
In 1751 Diderot published his *Lettre sur les sourds et muets,* in
which he discussed the foundation of language and the relationship of speech and gesture. The *Encyclopédie* contained several
articles on the subject: Jaucourt's "Langage," Cahuzac's "Geste"
and "Chant," d'Alembert's "Caractère," and Turgot's "Etymologie."
In 1754 came Rousseau's *Discours sur l'origine de l'inégalité parmi
les hommes.* Rousseau, avowedly influenced by Condillac[14] although differing from him, considered the problem of the relationship between the beginnings of knowledge and the beginnings of
language as part of his attempt to show the obstacles placed by
nature in the way of civilization.

By 1760 interest in the subject was clearly becoming intense,
and the list of books written about the genesis of language, either
exclusively or as part of the study of primitive culture, grew longer
with each decade, until nineteenth-century positivism made suspect
all speculation on questions beyond the reach of observation.[15]
During its period of respectability, however, the subject elicited
such works as these: Maupertuis, *Réflexions philosophiques sur
l'origine des langues et la signification des mots;*[16] Antoine-Yves
Goguet, *De L'Origine des lois, des arts, et des sciences et leurs
progrès chez les anciens peuples* (1758); Nicholas Sylvestre Bergier,

14. Rousseau, *Discours sur l'origine de l'inégalité,* in *Œuvres complètes,*
1, 245.

15. This attitude was made official in 1866, when the statutes of the
newly founded Société de Linguistique de Paris forbade all communication
on the subject of the origin of language. See Jespersen, *Language,* p. 96. In
the twentieth century, however, there has been a reaction against this
restriction, of which Jespersen is a prominent example.

16. There is a problem about the date of Maupertuis' book. It was
published in 1756 with a note that twelve copies had been published and
privately circulated some years before. Condillac received one of the copies
as a gift from the author in 1750 (Letter to Maupertuis, *Œuvres phil., 2,*
535). This date gives it certain priority over Rousseau and possible priority
over Diderot, but it does not threaten Condillac's standing. See Kuehner,
Theories, p. 24, n. 16.

Les Eléments primitifs des langues (1764); Charles de Brosses, *Traité de la formation mécanique des langues et des principes physiques de l'étymologie* (1765);[17] Nicholas Boulanger, *L'Antiquité dévoilée* (1766); Claude François de Radonvilliers, *De La Manière d'apprendre les langues* (1768); Herder, *Abhandlung über den Ursprung der Sprache* (1770); Court de Gébelin, *Le Monde primitif, analysé et comparé avec le monde moderne, considéré dans son génie allégorique, et dans les allégories auxquelles conduisit ce génie* (9 vols., 1773–84); l'Abbé Copineau, *Essai synthétique sur l'origine et la formation des langues* (1774). Voltaire also discussed the origin of language, without committing himself to any particular theory, in the articles "Alphabet" and "Langues" in his *Dictionnaire philosophique* of 1764.

The genetic analysis of the human mind, so well typified by Condillac in the 1740s, became by the 1760s a sort of quasi-anthropology. It was an inevitable development. The eighteenth-century conviction that the key to anything—reason, human nature, society, religion—lies in its origins, was bound to arouse interest in man's primitive history, an interest reinforced by travelers' tales of savage peoples, noble or ignoble, in the Americas and the several Indies. Still, even in the 1760s, interest in primitive culture was rarely for its own sake, nor was it pursued in the light of a genuinely evolutionary understanding of history, such as emerged in the next century. Rather, the search for the primitive was undertaken, for the most part, in order to shed light on some aspect of man's present condition and often to suggest ways of improving it.

Condillac's concern with the origin of language, however, reflects an earlier stage. The section on language in the *Essai sur l'origine* was not anthropological. He did not consider the origin

17. This work incorporates the essentials of two *mémoires* which De Brosses read before the Académie des Inscriptions et Belles-Lettres in 1746, the year of Condillac's *Essai*. However, De Brosses' work was of a completely different sort, in method and intent, being based on the physiology of the vocal organs, and making use of extensive linguistic classification. See Kuehner, pp. 35–36.

or structure of early society; he was not interested in the realities of primitive culture. He was, however, engaged in a search for the primitive. But this did not mean to him what it meant to Rousseau, for example. Condillac was not seeking the underlying nature of man. He did not wish to assess the value of civilization. He was not a social critic. He had a problem—or, rather, three problems—to solve in his psychology of knowledge, and he sought the answers to those problems in the origin, nature, function, and development of language. First, he had to show how man, beginning as the passive object of changing sensations, could take control of his mental processes and become master of his understanding. Condillac claimed that man accomplished this by the invention of language. When he had words to stand for things, he could manipulate chains of associated ideas at his pleasure, and this capacity opened the door to fully developed reason. However, this answer raised another question. How did man invent language? Does language not suggest an innate rationality or at least some kind of mental attribute preceding experience? It was in an attempt to answer this question, which challenged his whole philosophy, that Condillac really became involved with the genesis of language. He had to show that language, too, could be explained as the product of experience. Finally, since he tended to define error as a function of careless or vague language, and since he also always asserted that nature teaches us valid ideas and good language, it became necessary for him to explain how error had arisen in the first place. This, also, led him into his investigation of the formation of language.

Condillac again took up the origin of language in the *Grammaire*, the first volume of the *Cours d'études* for the Prince of Parma (in which he shows, incidentally, that he was keeping up with current primitive studies by citing Goguet, De Brosses, and Rousseau).[18] In the *Grammaire* he had another purpose in considering the origin of language: a quest for a model of the way in which language ought to be constructed. In the *Essai* his search for the primitive had

18. "Motif des études," *Œuvres phil.*, *1*, 419; *Grammaire*, in *Œuvres phil.*, *1*, 432, n. 1, and 433, n. 1.

been explanatory, the use of genetic analysis as the key to under-standing a set of phenomena. In the *Grammaire* the normative use of the primitive prevails. The primitive, the original, the natural—this was the ideal, and it implied not barbarism or crudeness but rationality, symmetry, truth. Condillac's concept of the primitive was not based on empirical investigation. It had little to do with a concrete primitive, with the way real individual men actually conducted their lives and learned to think and communicate. It was a primitive akin to the statue-man, abstracted from experience, reduced to a formula, freed from extraneous details that would tend to obscure its precise outlines. Or, to revert to an image used earlier, it was the potentially symmetrical gem hidden beneath the "unnatural" rough and uncut diamond of actuality.

This concept of the primitive as simple, rational, and universal accounts, in part, for the way Condillac went about establishing the origin of language. It is not that he did not try to be empirical. He used concrete examples from time to time, but usually in that most unprimitive language, French. Still, if human nature is at all times and everywhere the same, and if the natural products of human reason and experience must be uniform, one language will in fact do as well as another to illustrate the principles of lan-guage formation. Besides, Condillac had no more idea than any of his contemporaries of the real antiquity of man. He accepted the biblical tradition that Hebrew was man's original language. Indeed, no one in the eighteenth century, however unscriptural his outlook, was prepared to challenge the assumption that Hebrew was at least one of the original languages. By the chronology then used, Greek was a very early language, second only to Hebrew in antiquity, and followed in turn by Latin. This led to two assump-tions about the formation of language: first, that its development from primitive cries of joy and warning to a large vocabulary and a complex grammar was extremely rapid, and second, that the structure of modern languages is really very little different from that of the most primitive languages. Therefore, since it could be assumed that the structure of modern language corresponds to and reveals the way in which language was originally formed, it is not at all surprising that Condillac should expect to find the genesis of language by analyzing French and Latin (he does not seem to have known Greek or Hebrew).

Condillac's method, however, depended much less on the empirical data he thought to find in French and Latin than it did on a priori reasoning from the fundamental principles of his philosophy. He began with a supposition reminiscent of the statue-man and of his "observation" of animals. He postulated two children after the deluge, separated from society before they had learned to speak, and he reconstructed, on the basis of his sensationalist psychology, the manner in which they would have formed a language.[19] From that point it was only a matter of showing how, on his principles, the present and historically known states of language and the arts could have been attained. This method Condillac admitted to be conjectural. We cannot, he said, really know how it happened, but it must have come about in a manner similar to the one he described.[20]

Language originated, according to Condillac, in man's natural, instinctive, and physical capacity for expression. In its most primitive beginnings language was individual, not social; expressive, not communicative. For the first language consisted of those natural and spontaneous cries and movements of the body with which man, like animals, responds to certain situations and expresses certain feelings—fear, joy, pain, hunger, contentment. They are not intended, at the beginning, to communicate these feelings. Indeed, these cries and gestures are so instinctive to the race that they can scarcely be described as intended at all. They are the individual's undeliberated self-expression, but they are not peculiar to the individual. The uniformity of physical conformation of the members of the same species means that each individual will instinctively express the same feeling or respond to the same situa-

---

19. This fiction, incidentally, avoids the theological problems involved in talking about the first origins of language.

20. *Essai,* in *Œuvres phil., 1,* 103.

tion with the same cry or action. Natural language, then, is a
universal and instinctive expression of feeling through cries and
gestures.[21]

In order to become a language in the usual sense of the word,
this instinctive expression must become communicative and deliberate. It must convey ideas from one person to another and it
must be intentionally used for that purpose. It is necessary, therefore, to explain how man became conscious of the utilitarian possibilities of his expressive actions and how he developed them
beyond the limited store provide by nature. The key to man's
transition from spontaneous, noncommunicative language to deliberate, communicative language lies in three characteristics of the
species: universality, sympathy, and the association of ideas. The
first step was the instinctive sympathetic response of one man to
the expressions of emotion of another just like himself:

> For example, the one who was suffering because he was
> deprived of an object his needs made necessary to him
> would not confine himself to uttering cries. He would make
> efforts to obtain it, moving his head, his arms, and all parts
> of his body. The other, moved by this spectacle, would fix his
> eyes on the same object, and feeling in his soul emotions which
> he could not yet explain, he would suffer on seeing his un-
> happy companion suffer. From that moment he would feel
> himself inclined to help him, and he would obey this feeling
> as far as he could. Thus by instinct alone men asked for help
> and gave it to one another.[22]

21. Ibid., pp. 60–61.
22. Ibid., p. 61. Condillac contradicted this explanation in the
Grammaire, perhaps because he felt uneasy attributing so much to instinct:
"This language [of action] is natural to all individuals of the same species;
nevertheless, all need to learn it. It is natural to them, because if a man who
has not the use of words shows with a gesture the object he needs, and
expresses by other motions the desire that this object gives birth to in him,
it is, as we have just noticed, a result of his constitution. But if this man had
not observed what his body does in such a case, he would not have learned
to recognize the desire in the movements of another. He would not therefore

By accident and instinct, then, expression had become unintentionally communicative. Gradually, through the familiar mechanism of association, natural cries and gestures became linked with the objects or situations that gave rise to them—the need for certain things, fear of particular places, animals, kinds of food, and so on: "For example, one of them, on seeing a place where he had been frightened, would imitate the cries and movements that were signs of fear in order to warn the other not to expose himself to the same danger."[23]

Now these growing habitual associations both extended the range of natural communication and opened the way to consciousness of it. Man, reflecting upon his feelings and actions, became aware, albeit vaguely and inarticulately, of the association of signs with things and began the deliberate invention of arbitrary or conventional signs by analogy with the natural signs he had acquired by instinct. The final step had been taken in transforming unconscious natural expression into real language.

The nature of primitive language as it limped and stuttered its slow progress was concrete and crude. Man could not form abstractions. Since his experience was with individual material objects, his vocabulary was limited to names of objects, invented in the order of experience and need. The first words were names like "tree," "water," "fire." As man came to extend the range of thought and meaning to include abstractions or descriptions of mental phenomena, he did not know how to extend his vocabulary except by analogy with the material things he knew. Hence the first abstract words were figurative, depending upon an extended or quasi-poetic meaning given to concrete words. Modern languages

---

be capable of intentionally doing the like in order to make himself understood. This language is not, therefore, so natural that it is known without being learned." (*Œuvres phil., 1,* 428–29.) According to this explanation, then, the transition from expression to communication was conscious, deliberate, and the result of learning, rather than accidental, instinctive, and the cause of learning.

23. *Essai,* in *Œuvres phil., 1,* 61.

still reveal this phenomenon: "Having always perceived motion and rest in matter, having noticed the tendency or inclination of bodies, having seen that the air is agitated, overcast, or made light, that plants develop, grow strong and then weaken, men talk of the 'motion,' 'rest,' 'inclination,' and 'tendency' of the soul, they say that the mind is 'agitated,' 'overcast,' 'enlightened,' 'develops,' 'grows strong' and 'grows weak.' "[24]

Primitive language was poetic because of its inventors' limited vocabulary and brief experience with language. Primitive man would have been unable to hear the small differences in accent or subtle variations of pitch which characterize modern speech. His speech, therefore, was akin to music, although lacking a sustained melody. He spoke with marked rhythmic stresses and pronounced differences in pitch in order to make himself understood.[25] The poetic and musical quality of primitive speech was reinforced by the continued influence of the original language of cries and gestures. Natural language had been emphatic, crude, concrete, and its early spoken offshoot inevitably preserved its characteristic imitativeness, imagery, and rough-hewn expressiveness. Moreover, in a society without writing, memory was vital in the preservation of solidarity and continuity, in handing down law and religion from generation to generation. Poetry and music, gesture and dance not only lent dignity to solemn occasions in the community but provided natural mnemonic devices to ensure that the legends, laws, myths, and lore of the society not be forgotten.[26]

24. Ibid., p. 87.

25. Condillac regarded modern Chinese, with its use of tones to give different meanings to the same syllable, as a continuation of this primitive characteristic (ibid., p. 64). He does not tell us his source of information about the Chinese language, but travel literature was abundant enough in the eighteenth century to account for it. The Jesuits, in particular, had acquainted Europeans with the existence of a highly developed civilization and culture in China.

26. Although his discussion of the character of primitive language is based primarily upon the characer of Latin and on what he had heard of the character of Greek and Hebrew, Condillac did include a few illustrative references to the languages of contemporary primitive peoples. Although

It was not long, however, before man invented a written language to convey to absent persons the thoughts that he had already learned to communicate by articulate sounds. The invention of writing, unlike the invention of speech, was in no sense accidental or instinctive. It was a deliberate creative act of man's intelligence. But man still had to work within a framework of experience governed by the influence of the language of action, and his first written signs were attempts to reproduce "the same images which they had already expressed by actions and words, and which had from the very beginning made language figurative and metaphorical."[27] Inevitably, then, the first attempt at writing was the drawing of a simple picture. Although Condillac discussed—or, rather, borrowed Warburton's discussion of—the evolution of picture-writing into hieroglyphics, he was extremely vague on the still more significant development of the alphabet. He talked as if hieroglyphics naturally evolved into the running phonetic script we are familiar with today. But although the transition from the natural representation of picture-writing to the conventional symbolism of hieroglyphics was important and certainly required a creative intelligence, it is based on quite a different principle from that of the still more important phonetic script. The jump from conventional signs representing whole words to conventional signs representing sounds must have been an enormous step in the history of communication and indeed in the progress of civilization. Apparently, however, neither Condillac nor Warburton gave it much thought.

---

travelers' tales flooded the market in the eighteenth century, Condillac cited only one of them: C. M. de la Condamine, *Relation abrégée d'un voyage fait dans l'intérieur de l'Amérique méridionale* (Paris, 1745). From this he learned that South American Indians have too cumbersome a system of numbers to count past twenty, and that their language fortunately lacks such abstractions as "substance," "essence," and "being." (*Essai,* in *Œuvres phil., 1,* 41, 87.) He also referred to the social uses of dance and music among Negroes, Caribs, and Iroquois, without citing the source of his information (ibid., p. 80).

27. Ibid., p. 95.

Condillac's theory of the origin and development of language was in so many ways a new departure (Mandeville's discussion being too brief and Warburton's too specialized to count as more than hints of what was to come) that it might be profitable to examine it in relation to the theories of his contemporaries.

The break with rationalism not only permitted but demanded the formation of theories of the origin and growth of language. Condillac and his fellows did not believe that language originated as an expression of reason, since man does not possess reason except as he acquires it, or at least realizes it, through experience. So while the traditional rationalists had a ready-made explanation for the impulse to language, the sensationalist had to find an alternative in man's experience. Condillac's philosophy did not permit him to take the evolution of language for granted as given in the nature of man. The imperatives of sensationalism and genetic analysis required him to explain just how, as a result of experience working on man's natural needs and capacities, language could have evolved as a rational tool. This meant that Condillac and the sensationalists, unlike the rationalists, were interested in the nature and history of primitive language.

The methodological character of Condillac's search for the primitive was, as we have pointed out, a rationalist's ideal—an abstract model. The substantive content of his primitive, however, was anything but rational, as the nature of the impulse to language illustrates. As we have just seen, in Condillac's theory man's earliest language of cry and gesture did not originate in a desire to communicate an idea, or even a feeling, to his fellows. He was instinctively, spontaneously, and quite unself-consciously expressing his own momentary moods and passions. Since there was no intent to communicate, the presence or absence of another person was a matter of indifference. Alone or in company, when primitive man was in pain, he cried out; when he was afraid, he cowered; when he desired something, he reached for it; when he felt joy, he laughed. The form his expressions of emotion took reflected no rational appropriateness but the physiological necessities of his own body.

It would seem, then, that the passions, not reason, are basic to man, that the emotions of the soul and the needs of the body, not the logic of the mind, are the given elements of humanity which ultimately dictate behavior. Reason, along with deliberate communication, must be learned.

It would be difficult to imagine two thinkers more different in temperament and philosophy than Condillac and Rousseau, and yet Rousseau's intellectual debt to Condillac was great. From Condillac he learned that reason is not innate and that language originates in feeling, not in thinking.[28] These were critical ideas, part of the philosophical foundations of Rousseau's decisive break with the rationalist assumptions of the Enlightenment. The idea of the emotive origin of language took on a radical significance for Rousseau, impressed as he was by the uniqueness and irreducible diversity of things, which it could not have had for Condillac, still persuaded of their uniformity. Condillac believed that he was giving full value to the concreteness of experience when he argued that man's first words must have been the names of sensible objects—words meaning "tree," "river," "animal."[29] But Rousseau maintained that "tree" is already an abstraction at least once removed from experience. Man's first words, he argued, must have meant "this tree," "that tree," "this river," "that river." Moreover, there would have been no etymological connection between the words signifying "this" tree and "that" tree, because primitive man would not have known how to recognize and classify them according to their similarities. He would name them as unique experiences.

Rousseau, in his theory of the origin and development of speech, could not bridge the gap between the fundamentally atomistic character of experience and the highly abstract character of conventional

<hr>

28. See Jean Morel, "Recherches sur les sources du Discours de l'inégalité," *Annales J. J. Rousseau,* 5 (1909), 143–59.

29. Cf. *La Logique,* in *Œuvres phil.,* 2, 379, where Condillac pointed out that children always overgeneralize when they learn words. Every plant is a "tree" to them.

language. He ended with an unresolved dilemma. If language was necessarily anterior to thought, so much the more was thought necessarily anterior to language. If the world presents itself to man's senses in discrete and unclassifiable units, and if man's reason is not innate and prior to experience, then there is nothing in the nature of things experienced to bring forth the abstracting and classifying processes which underlie rational thought. Yet we have rational thought and we have language. The point of Rousseau's paradox was to draw the lines between nature and civilization, to show that reason and language are the products of civilization and not of nature, indeed that nature puts such obstacles in the way of the development of these attributes of civilized man that it cannot be imagined how he overcame them. However the trick was accomplished, it was clear to Rousseau that it was done contrary to nature.[30]

Condillac's insights into the origin and nature of primitive language, which impressed Rousseau even while he criticized them, and which are still current in twentieth-century speculation,[31] were all antirational in character. The impulse to speech and gesture was expressive, not communicative, emotive, not logical. As a result, primitive language was rhythmic and highly metaphorical, chanted poetry rather than spoken prose. Morever, when language became utilitarian, it did so under the pressure of need, not as a free act of

30. Rousseau, *Discours sur l'origine de l'inégalité,* in *Œuvres complètes, 1,* 245ff.

31. A description of primitive language as far richer in tonal variety and more complex in phonic structure than modern language, as well as the statements that primitive language was unanalytic, concrete, and highly poetic in nature, are all to be found in Jespersen, *Language,* pp. 418–31. Twentieth-century theories about the form the first speech took have been classified into four types (ibid., pp. 413–16): the theory that speech began as imitation of animal cries (usually referred to as the "bow-wow" theory), that it was an instinctive expression of feeling (the "pooh-pooh" theory), that it reflected a kind of inherent mystic harmony between sound and sense (the "ding-dong" theory), and that it grew out of tribal work or action in which muscular effort evoked a rhythmic chant (the "yo-he-ho" theory). Condillac's theory belongs to the "pooh-pooh" school.

autonomous reason.[32] Survival value determined the direction of early language development. Practical reason, shaped by the experience of pain, the knowledge of deprivation, hunger, danger, and death, governed the order of word formation. The mechanism behind the growth of language was not logic but the involuntary, almost accidental association of ideas. Indeed, there seems little room, in this picture, for the pure light of reason.

If we give Condillac's theory another turn and look at it from a slightly different angle, we shall find reason once again. For even though Condillac denied the innate or pure rationality of man, he left that of nature intact.[33] Nature, full of laws and purposes, makes use of man's passions to teach him reason. The haphazard irrational struggle to seek pleasure and avoid pain, which Condillac described as the dynamic force behind man's mental development, takes on a systematic, purposive, and rational character when seen in the light of cosmic planning. Man is moved to cry out by needs and passions which lie below the level of rationality, but the universality of those passions, the single human nature shared by all men, gives his blind inarticulate cries meaning to other men. Moreover, this common human nature, provoking each man to recognize himself in all other men, is the spring of identification and sympathy, the spontaneous emotional response that is the condition for making rational communication out of mere instinctive expression. Finally, the association of ideas, mechanical, habitual, and often arbitrary, provides the logical structure for emergent speech. Now the law by

32. Rousseau has his own version of the emotive impulse behind language. According to him, speech began and first developed as the expression of pleasure, passion, sentiment, and love, rather than of pain and need. Rousseau, *Essai sur l'origine des langues,* in *Œuvres complètes,* 2, 422ff.

33. It should be noted that Locke also appealed to a rational Nature —i.e. God—working behind the scenes to ensure the ultimate reliability of our acquired knowledge: "The infinite wise Contriver of us, and all things about us, hath fitted our senses, faculties, and organs, to the conveniences of life, and the business we have to do here." *Essay concerning Human Understanding* (II.23.12), *1,* 402.

which the association of ideas operates is a mechanical and contingent law. It carries no guarantee of rationality. If x and y occur together, x and y will be associated in the mind of the observer, but nothing in this law provides that x and y will have an intrinsic relationship that makes their association objectively rational. It might be supposed, then, that a language developed on the principle of the association of ideas would also not be objectively rational but would be haphazard and arbitrary. However, Condillac's faith in the natural order came to the rescue. His universe of cause and effect, regularity and symmetry—still the rationalist's Great Watch—is sufficient guarantee that those things which man associates together in his mind are also associated in the nature of things. The humble and suspicious origins of man's reason—the animal, the passionate, and the mechanical in him—do not negate his reason, for all the cosmos has conspired to make it good.

It is not, then, surprising to find that Condillac's analysis of grammar and the evolution of language beyond the primitive was simply another version of the conventional rationalist theory. Man's acquisition of language precisely paralleled his acquisition of reason. Both reflect his experience and his reflection upon his experience, but his developing reason holds a certain priority over his developing language. Language, in Condillac's view, developed and took on grammatical structure as an analytic method—that is, as a form—*the* form, according to Condillac, of reason. Language, in other words, once out of swaddling clothes, is nothing other than the vocal expression of reason, just as it had been from its very inception for the traditional rationalist. Experience provides the content of language, the names of objects and actions, and the circumstances in which growth occurs; but reason—that is, analysis, analogy, and the association of ideas—provides the form.

The form of language means, of course, its grammar. Condillac, in his capacity of tutor at Parma, used his theory of language in studying French grammar. Grammatical science was in its infancy in the eighteenth century. There was much confusion about its aims, its techniques and method, and its philosophical presuppositions. The principles of comparative grammar had not yet been formulated. In keeping, however, with eighteenth-century interest in language in general, there was a great deal of lively, although often incidental, discussion of grammar, in which nearly all the philosophes engaged at some time or other. The background of this discussion was the famed *Grammaire de Port-Royal,* whose principles served as the point of departure for virtually all philosophic discussion of grammar in the eighteenth century.[34]

The *Port-Royal Grammar* supplanted two alternative approaches to the subject. Medieval grammar had been prescriptive in nature, laying out rules of correct usage which ought to be followed in composition. It was governed by two major assumptions: first, that Latin is the model language whose structure should be copied by all languages, and second, that the study of grammar, the first subject in the *Trivium,* is not an end in itself, because grammar shares with logic the role of a tool in the service of rhetoric, which in turn serves theology as the technique of disputation.[35] There was also a postmedieval grammatical method that had arisen from man's growing awareness, in the sixteenth and seventeenth centuries, of the varieties of human life, thought, and behavior. The tendency toward cultural relativism that cosmopolitan experience fostered affected approaches to the study of language and gave rise to a new school of grammarians. Vaugelas' *Remarques sur la langue française,* which appeared in 1647, was the representative work in France. Vaugelas made the important and new assumption that languages are an expression of convention, not of nature, and that therefore there is no "right" order which a language ought to follow. A language must be taken as it is and studied empirically. The grammarian should not prescribe laws; his business is with facts—to ob-

34. See Guy Harnois, *Les Théories du langage en France de 1660 à 1821* (Paris, 1929), pp. 13–18; Léon Vernier, *Etude sur Voltaire grammairien et la grammaire au XVIIIe siècle* (Paris, 1888), pp. 65–66; Edouard Maynial, "Les Grammairiens philosophes du XVIIIe siècle," *Revue Politique et Littéraire,* 40 (1903), 318; Kuehner, *Theories,* p. 15.

35. Harnois, *Les Théories du langage,* p. 17.

serve, to describe, to verify, and to report them. "They are greatly deceived," Vaugelas observed, "and sin against the first principles of language who want to reason about ours, and who condemn many generally accepted usages because they are contrary to reason. For reason is not a factor here; there is only usage and analogy."[36]

Against both these approaches to language stands the *Grammar* of Port-Royal, first published in 1660. The Port-Royal grammarians, Lancelot and Arnauld, shared to a certain extent the pedagogical intent of the medieval grammarians, but for them the teaching of correct usage did not imply either the belief that the study of grammar is a means to an end, the mere acquisition of a technical skill, or the limitation of the grammarian's function to the collecting of rules which are given in the tradition. The *Port-Royal Grammar's* primary purpose was neither to prescribe rules nor to report facts but to explain the structure of language, to account for French grammar on rational principles. The assumption behind this aim was the purest Cartesianism—that language is a reflection of an innate human reason. The laws of grammar express, point for point, the laws of thought. The most important consequence of this assumption for grammatical study was a doctrine which the philosophes accepted without question—that there is a general and universal grammar common to all languages, and that the peculiarities of each individual language are merely incidental and unimportant variations that do not obscure their basic and wholly rational underlying structure.

Condillac, as a grammarian, was well within the Port-Royal tradition, to which he paid deserved tribute in his *Grammaire.* Like the Port-Royal grammarians, he believed that the structure of grammar corresponded to the structure of human reason. However, having a different notion of the nature of reason, Condillac did not simply repeat the *Port-Royal Grammar,* which assumed an innate reason expressing itself immediately in a fully developed grammar, whose parts parallel the elements of logic. Condillac assumed an acquired reason. The development of reason was accompanied, step

36. Quoted ibid., p. 20.

by step, by the growth of language, whose structure reflects the order
of the acquisition of ideas. For Port-Royal the laws of thought must
first be grasped in order to learn grammar, while for Condillac
grammar should be used as a means to the understanding and mas-
tery of the laws of thought. Grammar is "the first part of the art of
thinking," because a language is nothing but an "analytic
method."[37]

To understand what Condillac meant by defining language as an
analytic method we must return to his theory of the origin and development of language, as he does himself in the *Grammaire*. The
language of action expresses ideas just as we have them—in clusters,
several at a time. That is to say, the ideas which the language of
words would render as a logical sequence—e.g. "I see a wolf; wolves
are dangerous; wolves cannot climb trees; we must climb that tree
immediately"—are in fact experienced not as a sequence but simultaneously. Moreover, when expressed with spontaneous gestures and
natural cries, they are expressed simultaneously, or very nearly so. It
is only when he has the use of an artificial and symbolic language
that man can analyze such a cluster of ideas into its constituent
parts.[38] Thus the progress of analysis and the progress of language
were interdependent developments in human thought, and grammar
reflects not the given and static categories of reason but the steps in
the evolution of the analytic method.

Approaching the study of grammar from this point of view, Condillac devoted nearly half his book to what he called the "analysis of
discourse"—the examination of the symbols that languages give us
for analyzing thought, or, in more conventional language, the "general grammar" that will reveal the universal elements and rules common to all languages. He undertook to subject language to a genetic
analysis which would lay bare its fundamental structure. His starting
point was the language of action. By showing how the language of
action could itself be transformed into an analytic method once the
symbolic principle was introduced to replace its primitive natural
expressiveness, Condillac demonstrated the use of the three keys of

37. *Grammaire*, in *Œuvres phil.*, *1*, 427.
38. Ibid., p. 430.

language formation: analysis, analogy, and the association of ideas. In this connection he was much interested in the sign language of the deaf and dumb, which of course is as artificial and analytic as any spoken language.[39]

The process of converting spontaneous expression into an analytic language appears simple enough where the names of sensible objects are concerned, but the process men followed to analyze their own thoughts in order to name their inner experiences seems more difficult to reconstruct. Condillac found the key to the problem in the figurative character of the names of the operations of the understanding: they were named by analogy with the operations of the senses. Here is his reconstruction of the development of the verb "to be," which, it should be noted, he defined as meaning "to have sensations."

> As I have supposed that the word "attention" was given to the action of the organs when we are attentive by sight, hearing, or touch, so I suppose that the words "to be" were chosen to express the condition in which each organ is found when, without action on its part, it receives the impressions that objects make on it. On this supposition, it is evident that "to be" joined to "eye" will mean to see; and joined to "ear" it will mean "to hear." This word will then become a name common to all impressions, and, at the same time that it expresses what seems to happen in the organs, it will also express what happens in fact in the mind. When an abstraction is made from the organs, "to be," spoken alone, becomes synonymous with what we call "to have sensations," "to feel," "to exist." Now that is precisely what the verb "to be" means. Reflect on yourself, Monseigneur, and you will see that it is thus that you came to grasp the meaning of this verb.[40]

Condillac then went on to perform the same sort of analysis of the formation of combinations of words, such as the inflected form "I am," and to show how sentences are made up.

39. Ibid., p. 429, n. 1.
40. Ibid., pp. 446–47.

Having prepared the way by considering how the elements of all language came to be, Condillac turned to French grammar itself—the parts of speech, the conjugation of verbs, the use of dependent clauses, and so on. In this he was not at all original, and his work calls for no extended discussion. Acknowledging his eclecticism, he cited several of the standard works of grammar and linguistics as the basis of his own. Besides the *Port-Royal Grammar,* he referred to Du Marsais' *Des Tropes* (1730) and *Principes de grammaire* (1769), Duclos' commentary on the *Port-Royal Grammar* (1754), De Brosses' *Traité de la formation mécanique des langues* (1765), and Beauzée's *Grammaire générale* (1767).[41] Condillac's only personal contribution was to eliminate technical jargon in an attempt to explain grammatical usage in simple and everyday language.

A corollary to the eighteenth-century faith in a universal grammar was the equally rationalist notion of a "perfect" language. Such a notion implied that once the state of perfection had been achieved, language should and could remain fixed and unchanging, for change could only mean corruption and decline. This idea was quite in keeping with the failure of the philosophes to recognize both the haphazardness in the history of language and the inevitability of continued change in a living language. Seeing language as the natural expression of universal reason, whether immediately formed or historically developed, they felt that a perfect conjunction of language and reason was possible, and that man, dominated by his reason, would then have no further need or impulse to change his language. In spite of the fact that some of the philosophes—Condillac among them—often asserted that language was more the product of convention than of nature, in their hearts they were convinced of the contrary. Since nature, in their image of it, implied a state of perfection, the conclusion was perhaps inevitable.

41. *Grammaire,* in *Œuvres phil., 1,* 427; 432, n. 1; 469, n. 1. At the time Condillac composed the *Grammaire* for the Prince, only Duclos' commentary and Du Marsais' *Des Tropes* were available. He must have consulted the other works and perhaps expanded his own, when he was preparing the *Cours d'études* for publication after leaving Parma.

For Voltaire the state of perfection in language had already been reached in the classical French of the *Grand Siècle*. Indeed, it has been pointed out that all of Voltaire's observations on the subject of language and grammar were dictated by his concern to preserve · seventeenth-century French unchanged. For conformation to reason and *le bon sens,* for clarity, purity, and resonance in all genres, the French of the century of Louis XIV, according to Voltaire, could not be surpassed and would remain forever fixed.[42] D'Alembert likewise felt that French had been perfected in the preceding century as a literary instrument, but he advocated the revival of Latin as the international language of science and philosophy.[43] Diderot had a similar bias in favor of French, but not necessarily the French of the past century. Although he felt that the vital components of a *langue perfectionnée*—namely, the analytic tools of a fully developed grammar and the aesthetic qualities of syllabic and periodic harmony—had already entered the language, its real perfection depended upon the achievement of universal knowledge that was still to come. When man had perfected his knowledge, there was no question but that he would communicate it in French: "French was made to instruct, enlighten, and convince; Greek, Latin, Italian, and English to persuade, move, and deceive. Speak Greek, Latin, or Italian to the people, but speak French to the wise."[44] When knowledge has become perfect and cosmopolitan, universal grammarians and lexicographers will be needed to systematize French, to stop change and decay so that no knowledge will be lost. To that end Diderot suggested a rigid system of analytic definitions given in dead languages, preferably using quotations, so that corruption would not enter by the back door, through changes in the meaning of the words that make up the definition. Moreover, he recommended orthographic reform in the direction of phonetic spelling, a uniform, fixed, and logically based grammar, and a

42. Vernier, *Etude sur Voltaire grammairien*, pp. 9, 53, 62.

43. "Discours préliminaire," *Encyclopédie, 1,* lvi.

44. Quoted in H. J. Hunt, "Logic and Linguistics: Diderot as 'grammairien-philosophe,'" *Modern Language Review, 33* (1938), 226.

reactionary aesthetics that would prescribe a fixed and general vocabulary for all poetry.[45]

Although Diderot placed the development of a perfect and universal French in the future, he did not really call for much change in the language. Both he and Voltaire were quite well satisfied with the French they knew. Condillac, however, was not. Condillac approached language primarily as a logician, which meant that the literary values that counted heavily with Voltaire and Diderot carried little weight with him. He was not impressed by the grace and sophistication of classical French, nor was he convinced of its clarity and precision.

As far as Condillac was concerned, all modern languages were only degraded remainders of the dead languages that had preceded them.[46] Far from exhibiting improvement or progress after crude beginnings, they have lost the primitive virtues taught by nature. Condillac summed up these virtues in the word "analogy." Primitive language was made up of words formed not arbitrarily but by the strictest analogy with the ideas they stand for. Every word invented by primitive man had some kind of intrinsic correspondence to the idea it represented. Most frequently it was an imitative correspondence, as in naming an animal with an imitation of its characteristic cry, or an expressive correspondence, such as the naming of a human emotion with a word which seemed to express it by its tone or accent. At a more sophisticated level, words were formed by logical correspondence—that is, the extension of the meaning of an already existing word to a new but parallel idea. For example, if the language already contained a word meaning "to look," the phrase "to look with the ears" could be invented to mean "to listen," because both operations are characterized by an attentive disposition of the appropriate sense-organ. Another example might be the extension of a word with a concrete sensory meaning to a metaphorical usage that seems analogous, such as "a heavy heart."[47]

45. Ibid., pp. 230–32.
46. *La Langue des calculs*, in *Œuvres phil.*, 2, 427.
47. *Grammaire*, in *Œuvres phil.*, 1, 446.

On this basis primitive language allowed nearly perfect communication. Every word stood for either a simple idea known to all, because it was a direct and common sensation or perception, or a complex idea whose constituent simple ideas were clearly indicated by the word itself. Thus a high degree of accuracy was possible, for everyone knew what he was talking about in the most literal sense. Had languages continued to grow naturally, every language would contain within itself the whole history of culture, clearly recognizable.[48] Etymology would be equivalent to an entire course of science, philosophy, and the arts. There would be no disjunction between words and knowledge. Every scientific or philosophical term would be totally self-explanatory.

Unfortunately, however, languages did not develop according to nature. Man became careless as culture advanced beyond mere necessity and subsistence. Nature's great aids in enforcing her commandments, the sanctions of pleasure and pain, no longer operated with such direct effectiveness, because men had the leisure to concern themselves with things irrelevant to their survival or even to their physical comfort. In these new areas of human concern pain would not be the immediate consequence of error, and so errors grew and multiplied, piling one upon the other, until not even pain could point the way back to truth and accuracy. Men became, and remain, content to say almost what they mean and to understand almost what others are trying to tell them.[49] Language has degenerated into jargon, in which spurious metaphysical questions, which would never have arisen if language had retained its purity, are disputed. Language, in short, has become completely detached from both logic and reality.

There is, however, one significant exception to this bleak picture. Algebra, which Condillac regarded as nothing more nor less than a language, is still pure, exact, and analytic—the very model of what a language ought to be.[50] This claim can be best understood in the

48. *La Langue des calculs*, in *Œuvres phil.*, 2, 427.
49. Ibid., p. 419.
50. Ibid., p. 420.

light of three other assertions which Condillac often made about language—namely, that the art of reasoning is a well-made language, that a language is nothing but an analytic method, and that grammar is the first part of the art of thinking. In other words, language is identified with analytic logic, and there is no more perfect example of analytic logic than algebra. The solution of an algebraic equation is to be found in a series of analytic propositions in which the unknowns are extracted from the givens. For Condillac this is the only legitimate form of reasoning. From this point of view the parallel between the vocabulary of algebra—i.e. numbers—and the vocabulary of his ideal language becomes clear. Any number implies all possible relationships contained within it, and these relationships are extracted by analysis. Thus twelve equals six plus six, equals seven plus five, equals two times six, equals three times four, equals ten plus two, and so on. This series of identical or analytic propositions is simply the process of making explicit the ideas already implicit in the number twelve. Now if every word stood for an idea whose parts were as clearly grasped as are the parts of the number twelve, then all propositions would be identical or analytic propositions, and would be as absolutely reliable as algebraic equations.

Condillac illustrated his meaning by reminding the reader of his explanation of the understanding. He claimed that this was an analytic demonstration in the strictest logical sense, because, since all the faculties of the understanding are fundamentally identical with the faculty of sensation, his demonstration did no more than make explicit that which was already implicit in the idea of sensation. Ignoring the blatant *petitio principii* involved, Condillac even went so far as to cast it in the form of a simultaneous equation.

> Now to ask what is the origin and generation of the faculties of the human understanding is to ask what is the origin and generation of the faculties by which man, capable of sensations, conceives things by forming ideas about them. It is immediately seen that attention, comparison, judgment, reflection, imagination, and reasoning are, with the sensations, the known elements of the problem to be solved, and that the origin and

generation are the unknown elements. These are the data in which what is known is mixed with what is unknown.

But how can we separate the origin and generation, which are the unknown elements, from the others? Nothing is simpler. By origin we mean the known factor which is the principle or the beginning of all the others; and by generation we mean the manner in which all the known factors come from a first known factor. This first element, which is known to me as a faculty, is not yet known to me as the first. It is therefore properly the unknown element which is mixed with all the known elements, and which we must separate. Now the most casual observation shows me that the faculty of sensation is mixed with all the others. Sensation is therefore the unknown quantity that we have to separate in order to discover how it becomes successively attention, comparison, judgment, etc. This is what we have done, and we have seen that as the equations $x - 1 = y + 1$ and $x + 1 = 2y - 2$ pass through different transformations to become $y = 5$ and $x = 7$, sensation likewise passes through different transformations to become the understanding.[51]

The relevant implication of this exercise is that reasoning equals calculation, and words, like numbers, are, or at least should be, signs of exact ideas to be manipulated in various relationships. To show how this can be done, Condillac began the *Langue des calculs*.

The purpose of this unfinished work was to examine the "grammar" of algebra so that it might be appropriated by all language. Or, to put it more precisely, Condillac set out to formulate for the first time the grammar of algebra. He was, as he pointed out, approaching algebra as a metaphysician rather than as a mathematician, for the mathematicians do not realize that algebra is a language and therefore it has as yet no grammar. Only metaphysics can provide it with one.[52]

51. *La Logique*, in *Œuvres phil.*, 2, 410–11.
52. *La Langue des calculs*, in *Œuvres phil.*, 2, 429.

Condillac based his analysis of the grammar of algebra on what he presumed to be the origin of all mathematical calculation—namely, counting with fingers. By showing how the fundamental arithmetical operations—addition, subtraction, multiplication, and division—can be done with fingers, he tried to get at the principle of analogy on which the language of calculation is based. Numbers, he argued, are the signs of ideas that man expressed with fingers in the prelinguistic stage of his development. If the names of numbers are to be truly useful, they should be invented by analogy with finger-counting. For the most part, the names of numbers do express this analogy: our number system is based on a unit of ten because we have ten fingers. Unfortunately, however, the system is made imperfect by the existence of anomalies like "eleven" and "twelve," which Condillac would rename "ten plus one" and "ten plus two." This is an abuse or corruption which has crept only into our decayed modern languages. More primitive languages, like Latin, still preserve the ancient analogy. Nevertheless, in general, even in modern languages numbers are models of the principle of analogy, which should be used as the basis for all language.[53]

Condillac asserted that if modern languages could be remodeled according to the principles of algebra, they would lose the character of arbitrariness and capriciousness which presently disfigures them. This would be an improvement in taste as well as in communication, for he felt that what are considered to be beauties of style are only beauties by convention and should be supplanted with a more rational and natural set of criteria. In order to achieve this goal, he suggested that men should take lessons from ignorant and primitive people, who, because they are still disciples of nature, have not yet made an art of false reasoning and capricious language.[54] Their words are as perfectly formed as numbers. They are genuinely signs or tokens of experience.

53. Ibid., pp. 426–27.
54. Ibid., pp. 419–20, 427.

Perhaps the most surprising of Condillac's recommendations is his rejection of the idea, so dear to the hearts of his contemporaries, of a single universal language of science. The result of such a universal language, he felt, would be that while everyone could understand it equally, no one could understand it very well.[55] For once, we see Condillac's rationalism tempered by a real concern for concrete experience. Arguing that even numbers evolve out of experience and are named by analogy with it, he asserted that all language must equally evolve from experience, and the analogy must be preserved for the sake of understanding. Since each people has a unique history and formulates its language as a reflection of its history, words from an alien culture cannot be adequate signs of ideas and cannot serve the fundamental purpose of communication. Condillac excoriated modern languages for their habit of borrowing words from one another—words which can have no analogy with the experience of the borrower. He drew a picture of the French pillaging from other languages like barbarians. "Our languages seem to be only what remains after ravages and devastations. They resemble our empires: everything turns out badly if it was badly begun."[56]

Condillac did not share the dream of a single perfect language because his criteria of perfection were both rational and empirical, both universal and particular. All languages ought to approximate the language of algebra, and insofar as they succeed, they will resemble one another in the perfection of their clarity. But each language must also reflect the unique experience of the people that has evolved it, and insofar as it meets this criterion, it will be different from all other languages in the perfection of its force and integrity. Instead of one perfect language, then, there would be many in Condillac's ideal world—the difficulties of international communication being compensated for by the perfect understanding within each community.

55. Ibid., p. 463.
56. Ibid., p. 427.

7. Empirical Aesthetics and the Disintegration of the Classical Ideal

> Poetic style is . . . a style of convention; this is so in every kind of poem. . . . To try to discover the essence of poetic style would be vain. It has none. Too arbitrary for that, it depends on associations of ideas that vary as much as the spirit of great poets; and there are as many kinds as there are men of genius capable of putting their stamp on the language they speak.

> If these associations vary with the spirit of the poets, so much the more do they vary with the spirit of nations, which, having different customs, manners, and characters, could not associate all their ideas in the same way. So of two equally perfect languages, each has its beauties, each has expressions for which the other has no equivalent . . . . Whether [these] beauties belong exclusively to one language, or can pass from one language to another, they are equally natural, for nothing is more natural than associations of ideas that have become habitual.[1]

In asserting the uniqueness and intrinsic value of each culture, Condillac was expressing a new stage in the development of French taste. The aesthetics of classicism had recognized neither historical change nor cultural diversity. "For the classicist there are only beautiful works or ugly works, which have neither age nor nationality, and which must all resemble one another by the principle of their beauty or their ugliness. A tragedy may be by Sophocles or Racine, a discourse by Demosthenes or Bossuet: what makes the discourse or the tragedy worthy of eternal admiration is an iden-

---

1. *De L'Art d'écrire*, in *Œuvres phil. de Condillac*, *1*, 605–06.

tical essence, an equal conformity to the unique type of perfection."[2] The classical ideal of created beauty rested upon a set of assumptions about the nature of things and the nature of man which were common to many branches of seventeenth-century thought. Beauty, like truth, is one—the same for every time and every place and every manner of man, because all men possess the sovereign power of reason, universal and uniform, and it is to reason that beauty speaks and by reason that beauty is created. At the same time, the classicists felt that their absolute ideal of beauty had only been attained in a few times and a few places. The cultures of antiquity, of Renaissance Italy, and of their own France were their three models of aesthetic perfection.

In the eighteenth century these doctrines, although still prevalent, were being eroded by the discovery of other cultures, other arts, other literatures. By and large, the eighteenth century was still convinced that the Age of Louis XIV had been an era of artistic creativity with few peers and no superiors, and that French culture was in general of a higher order than that of the rest of Europe—not to speak of the rest of the world. But English and German culture—or, for that matter, Chinese or Hottentot culture—were no longer universally dismissed as unworthy of a Frenchman's attention. The discovery and appreciation of alien cultures compelled the admission that valid art and literature could be created outside the canons of French taste; that genuine beauty could not be circumscribed by the three unities, by *le bon sens,* or by the careful classification of genres. This admission in turn forced a reevaluation of the assumptions and methods of aesthetic theory. Classicism did not disappear as a result; it continued to live right through the eighteenth century. But side by side with classicism—sometimes in the thought of a single individual—appeared ideas that were fundamentally at odds with it. In sum, French artistic doctrines and aesthetic systems in the eighteenth century almost universally reflect a tension between the dogmas inherited from the classicism

2. Emile Krantz, *Essai sur l'esthétique de Descartes* (Paris, 1882), p. 16.

of Boileau and the intellectual forces tending to undermine them.[3]

Condillac was caught in this tension, just as he was caught in the tension between Cartesian rationalism and Lockean empiricism, and between the objectivity of the new science and the subjectivity imposed by the new philosophy. Indeed, there is a parallel among these various intellectual tensions. I have discussed above[4] the shift in philosophy from metaphysics to epistemology, and within the latter, the shift from a search for an objective, externally oriented epistemology to an acceptance of a subjective epistemology that is little more than a branch of psychology. In other words, concern had shifted from the objects of knowledge to the nature of knowledge and, finally, to the mechanics of thought and perception. In the field of aesthetics one can observe an analogous movement from discussions of the nature of beauty and the extent to which external objects conform to an absolute standard of beauty to discussions of the perception of beauty or aesthetic judgment and the artistic process. In both cases there is manifest a loss of confidence in man's ability to know and understand that which is outside him, and a consequent retraction of vision to what is inside him—the subjective, the individual, the relative. For much of the eighteenth century this change occurred within the framework of the classical ideal, just as epistemological skepticism developed within the framework of scientific certainty and as the doctrines of empiricism so often appeared in rationalist clothing. Condillac, never one to tread gracefully between two poles of thought, put together his aesthetic doctrines out of the literary preferences of a disintegrating classical ideal and the new orientation of psychological and cultural relativism.

The internal connections between classical aesthetics and Cartesian philosophy have been widely explored and debated.[5] Some

3. See Gustave Lanson, "Les Idées littéraires de Condillac," *Etudes d'histoire littéraire* (Paris, 1929), p. 212; and John Richardson Miller, *Boileau en France au dix-huitième siècle* (Baltimore, 1942), p. 147.

4. See above, p. 22.

5. See Krantz, *Essai sur l'esthétique de Descartes;* Lanson, "L'Influence de la philosophie cartésienne sur la littérature française," *Etudes d'histoire*

writers, such as Emile Krantz, have been struck by the parallels between classical and Cartesian modes of thought to the point of finding in the philosophy of Descartes (who did not write about art or literature) the key to French classical aesthetics. Others, led by Lanson, have argued, on the contrary, that Cartesianism, with its rejection of the authority of antiquity, its exclusive concern with pure ideas abstracted from all human content, and its principled insensitivity to poetry and passion, delivered a mortal blow to the classical tradition, robbing it of the elements of sensibility and imagination which are the life of any art.

Although we cannot here enter into the debate, it does seem clear that the Cartesian philosophy has an ambiguous relationship to classicism, confirming some classical doctrines while annulling others, so that the classicism of such professed Cartesians as Perrault, Fontenelle, or Terrasson has a distinctly different flavor from that of the lawgiver of French classicism, Boileau. Specifically, Cartesianism confirmed the classical belief in the essential uniformity and timelessness of great art, in the universality of good taste, and in the existence of a set of aesthetic rules which are the codification of reason itself, and to which any artistic creation must conform if it is to be acceptable to good taste. On the other hand, Cartesianism negated the classicist's reverence for antiquity and minimized the role of the passions and the imagination in art, preferring a pure and uncontaminated reason to hold unique jurisdiction over all human creativity and judgment. In short, a Cartesian aesthetics would tend to transform poetry into philosophy, and art into science; witness Fontenelle's observation that even eloquence would profit from the application of the geometric spirit.

Perhaps a clue to the essential difference between the classical and the Cartesian approach to art and beauty can be found in Krantz' statement (which refers to both approaches as if they were

---

littéraire, pp. 58–96; Wladyslaw Folkierski, *Entre Le Classicisme et le romantisme* (Paris, 1925), p. 212; Cassirer, *Philosophy of the Enlightenment*, chap. 7, sects. I–III; Miller, *Boileau en France*, Pt. I.

one): "It must not be forgotten that the seventeenth century began by deprecating, almost denying, history, and that the first article of the Cartesian manifesto is a proud rupture with the past."[6] The difficulty here—and the clue—is that the history deprecated by classicism is not precisely the same as that denied by the Cartesian manifesto. The classicist denied history as a process in which there could be a legitimate change of values; that is, he denied that different historical epochs could claim their differing artistic experiences to be equally valid or—insofar as they deviated from the universal norm—to be valid in any degree at all. Historical variation could simply be plotted as a greater or less degree of deviation from the one true standard of cultural value. And, for the classicist, this one true standard had been most perfectly embodied in the historical past: in the culture of classical Greece and Rome. The aesthetic rules of Aristotle, which codified the Greek artistic experience, were taken as authoritative because they reflected universal reason, understood by the classicist as *le bon sens*—the common, rational, educated response of the cultivated man of all ages. The past, then—or a part of the past—was uniquely venerated by the classicist because it presented him with both the models, which any writer or artist must imitate if his work is to have value, and the rules that guide the process of imitation. Creation, then, can be nothing more than intelligent, sensitive, scrupulous imitation of a perfect object that already exists.

Now it is precisely this use of the past which the Cartesian was rejecting when *he* denied history. The classicist bowed to the authority of antiquity because it embodied reason; the Cartesian rebelled against the authority of antiquity in the name of reason, understood by the Cartesian not as *le bon sens* (which may, after all, be only a collection of habits and prejudices) but as philosophic or geometric reasoning. The critical, questioning, doubting reason of the philosopher demands that, just as truth can only be discovered by starting afresh and accepting no guide and no authority

6. Krantz, *Essai sur l'esthétique de Descartes,* p. 16.

but one's own reason, so beauty can only be created by conforming immediately to reason, and not through imitation of what has gone before. Thus the disciples of Descartes are to be found on the side of the Moderns in their quarrel with the Ancients. And thus they tended to judge literary works by their conformity to the new rules of clarity and distinctness, rather than to the old rules of unity of time, place, and action. The fact that the Cartesians often ended by making the same judgments on the new basis as the classicists had on the old only points up the continuity of taste and the lack of creative innovation in the late seventeenth and early eighteenth centuries. The Moderns were scarcely avant-garde in their preferences, but they do reveal a marked inner shift in the philosophical foundations of aesthetic judgment.

In the first quarter of the eighteenth century another shift begins to manifest itself in the appearance of an empirical aesthetics. The publication in 1719 of *Réflexions critiques sur la poésie et sur la peinture* by the Abbé Dubos is the first real sign of this development. Dubos and his successors, of whom Condillac is one, put forward still another view of the relationship of history and reason, and of the uses of history and reason in the formation of aesthetic judgments. The empiricists rejected both the classical and the Cartesian versions of a universal reason embodied in rules establishing a single aesthetic ideal. Instead, they saw reason as a method of inquiry into the evidence, a systematic investigation of facts, which in turn led them to a new assessment of history, not as a source of authority, but as a source of evidence. The empiricist critic neither reverenced nor rejected history; he regarded it simply as a collection of phenomena to be studied. Man's entire cultural experience, then—his works of art and literature, his manifestations of creativity and genius, his changing tastes and aesthetic responses —may all be legitimately taken into account in the development of an aesthetic theory. With Dubos, and still more with Condillac, aesthetic inquiry ceases to be a branch of metaphysics and becomes a part of anthropology and of psychology.

This new concentration upon the data of human experience,

upon what the history of culture has actually been, led to two significant new ideas: that sentiment has played a more important role than reason in man's aesthetic experience, and that every age, every culture can claim validity for its own art. The two ideas are by no means unrelated. The first can be taken to imply—and later would be taken to imply—the subjectivism and individualism of art, and the second becomes the basis for recognizing the autonomy of cultures. Both point to the adoption of an aesthetic relativism springing from the private emotional experience of each individual and from the unique cultural experience of each society which stands at the opposite pole from the rationalistic absolutism of classical aesthetics.

Nevertheless, this evolution in aesthetic doctrine was still not accompanied by a revolution in taste, and certainly not by an explosion in artistic creativity and originality. French taste had definitely enlarged by mid-century. It could accept and enjoy a far wider range of artistic and literary works than could an earlier generation, but it still centered on the works of seventeenth-century France and, above all, on those of classical antiquity. The fact is, the men of the Enlightenment had all been nourished on the classical tradition, which was still the very heart of education in their time. It was part of their blood and bones. Furthermore, they did not have the grounds for turning against this part of their own heritage that they had for turning against the Christianity in which they also grew up. On the contrary, the pagan classics provided a familiar and easily accessible alternative tradition to that of Christianity.[7] The philosophes, then, while breaking with the absolutist philosophical doctrines on which seventeenth-century classicism had rested, continued to cherish and to imitate the works which that classicism had valued.

7. See Peter Gay, *The Enlightenment: An Interpretation* (New York, 1966), for a perceptive, thorough, and illuminating discussion of the relationship of the philosophes to both Christian and classical history. This is one of the few general works on the Enlightenment to appear in recent years which is full of new material and new insights and yet does not strain after novelty, much less fall into the perversity which has characterized so much recent interpretation of the period.

Gustave Lanson places Condillac squarely in the middle of this development. He asserts that Condillac made a vigorous attempt to construct a theory that would take into account the real state of contemporary French taste, and that would justify an appreciation of the foreign works in which Frenchmen had come to take pleasure without at the same time demanding the sacrifice of the classical tradition. This, says Lanson, was the principal step between the absolutism of Boileau and Perrault, on the one hand, and, on the other, the insistence of the *idéologues* on the right of each people to express itself in its literature.[8]

Cartesians and empiricists agreed that the method of aesthetic inquiry is no different from the method of scientific inquiry: a rational investigation of the forms of art in search of the universal law or principle that will explain it. Newton's universal law of attraction found its aesthetic parallel in, for example, the imitation of *la belle nature* of Charles Batteux's *Les Beaux-Arts réduits à un même principe* (1746). Condillac, of course, also considered the forms of art to be amenable to scientific analysis, but unlike both classicist and Cartesian, unlike either Ancient or Modern, he did not take the artistic products of his own time, or those of the great creative epochs of Western civilization, as the primary elements to be analyzed and classified. Instead, he looked for the primitive origins of art; or, to put it more precisely, in seeking the origins of language, he also found the origins of art. It is on the basis of his understanding of the origins of art that Condillac formed his theories of the nature of the artistic impulse and the criteria of artistic perfection. Like his theory of the origin of language, his genetic analysis of the forms of art is a characteristically abstract and imaginary reconstruction of man's primitive cultural development. Defending his method, Condillac conceded that

> some perhaps will take this whole history for fiction, but they must at least grant its probability. I have difficulty believing that the method I have followed has often led me astray, for my aim has been to advance nothing except on the supposition

8. "Les Idées littéraires de Condillac," *Etudes d'histoire littéraire,* p. 212.

that every language was formed on the model of the one that immediately preceded it. I have seen in the language of action the germ of all languages and all arts that can serve to express our thoughts. I have observed the circumstances suitable for developing this germ, and not only have I seen these arts form, but I have even traced their progress and explained their different characters. In a word, I have, it seems to me, plainly demonstrated that things which to us appear so singular were most natural in their time and that nothing has come about except what might have been expected to come about.[9]

There are no cultural accidents in Condillac's universe. Given the nature of things and the nature of man, language and the arts had to be what they have in fact become. If man's cultural experience is so determined in accordance with a rationally comprehensible scheme, does this then imply the absolute uniformity of the classical aesthetic ideal? Does it suggest that the forms of art can be codified into rules and genres of universal applicability? It would seem not, for the thrust of Condillac's analysis is toward the differentiation of artistic experience and even toward the relativity of aesthetic judgment.

Condillac's search for an understanding of art in its origins led him to attack one of the most cherished activities of classical aesthetics—the classification of genres. Observing that the forms of art were first invented by men who had no models to copy, Condillac asserted that the categories into which these forms were subsequently placed are artificial and arbitrary, that they cannot and should not serve as limits to creation. To the man who wrote the first comedy, for example, the essence of a play of this kind consisted only in the notion that he himself had made of it. It was not given in the nature of things. Later writers of comedies have added to this first notion and, in so doing, changed the essence of comedy —something we also have the right to do. Instead, however, "we consult the models that we have today and we form our ideas

9. *Essai*, in *Œuvres phil., 1,* 103–04.

according to those that please us most. Consequently we only admit
certain plays into the class of comedies and exclude all others."[10]
The result is a dispute about names, not ideas—a dispute which is
profoundly irrelevant both to the creation and the appreciation
of works of art.

Before one concludes, however, that for Condillac the possibilities
of artistic creation are infinite, one should take into consideration
his remarks on the fine arts in the *Traité des systèmes:*

> The fine arts . . . seem to precede observation and they must
> have developed to some extent in order to be reducible to a
> system. The fact is that they are less our work than nature's.
> Nature initiates them when she shapes us, and nature has al-
> ready perfected them when we think of explaining them. All
> the arts are really only the development of our faculties. Our
> faculties are determined by our needs, and our needs are the
> consequence of our organization. Nature, therefore, by organiz-
> ing us has begun everything.[11]

This is reminiscent of Condillac's argument that nature uses man's
random and irrational desires to teach him reason.[12] Whenever
Condillac looked at human experience from within man, he came
up with a fragmented, even atomistic, interpretation which de-
stroys reason and leads to aesthetic and moral chaos. In order to
rescue himself from this chaos, he looked at the same experience
from the point of view of nature, whose order and rationality
and purpose are assumed. Thus, even though the first man to write
a comedy felt himself to be creating a new thing and autonomously
endowing it with its essential character, he was in fact simply
obeying his nature and Nature herself.

There is a sense, then, in which the classical genres *are* given in
the nature of things, after all. For since a rational and ordered
nature has a hand in man's creation of art, as in all his activities,

10. Ibid., p. 91.
11. *Traité des systèmes,* in *Œuvres phil.,* I, 215.
12. See above, pp. 162–63.

it is to be expected that the art he creates will follow rational and ordered patterns which may be retrospectively analyzed, codified, and classified. Rules and genres, like philosophical abstractions and scientific hypotheses, simply sum up the results of a careful observation of the phenomena. In other words, they are descriptive, not prescriptive, laws. They may be adequate tools for investigating the creations of the past; they may even contribute to the activity of creation by helping the artist or writer to organize and discipline his art. But they cannot, and should not, dictate the forms which this activity may take simply on the basis of the forms it has taken. Nature must be allowed to do her work freely—behind our backs, so to speak. The artist must pursue his inclinations spontaneously, in accord with the spirit of his language, his culture, and his private genius. When we treat the rules and genres as if they were the very law of nature, instead of being merely convenient expressions for a part of nature's works, we paralyze the activity of nature. This is when a culture becomes rigid and artificial. Indeed, the conversion of genres into stereotypes precisely parallels the conversion of a hypothesis into a metaphysical principle, or a custom into a prejudice. They all mark the point at which man turns his back on nature—whose continuing guidance alone guarantees the processes of creation, discovery, and change upon which progress depends—and submits instead to the misguidance of history translated into dogma.

The constructive role of nature in the formation of culture, and the destructive role of history, are underlined in Condillac's substitution of expression and utility, as the motivating forces in art, for the classicist's (and the Cartesian's) imitation. Imitation requires the conscious yielding of the present moment to the superior claims of historical example. (In practice, the Cartesian imitation of *la belle nature* comes to the same thing as the classicist imitation of the perfect models which are a legacy of the past, because *la belle nature* turns out to be best exemplified, and therefore most easily imitated, in already existing models.) Expression and utility, on the other hand—which reduce to man's physical mechanism and its needs—are nature's immediate instruments for leading man through all the changes of time, place, and circumstance to the achievements which make him unique in the cosmos: the use of reason, the development of science, the discovery of God and God's moral imperatives, the formation of society, and the creation of art.

T. M. Moustoxidi places Condillac among the originators of the aesthetics of expression, a movement culminating in the twentieth century in philosophers like Croce and Dewey. Moustoxidi rests his case on the assertion that "a single fundamental idea" governs Condillac's explanation of the origin of art: "the arts and writing have the same origin as language and are the supreme manifestation of man's need to express himself."[13] It seems to me that this interpretation of Condillac's theory—and with it his relation to Croce and Dewey—must be qualified. To begin with, Condillac did not really endow man with a basic need to express himself. The natural cries and gestures constituting the primitive expression which is the germ of language are, as we have seen, automatic reactions to certain stimuli—a variety of expression which Croce himself sharply distinguished from aesthetic expression,[14] and which Dewey denied the very name of expression.[15] In any case, for Condillac it was not a distinctive human impulse but a physiological mechanism he shares with the entire animal world. The role of this physical expression in the origin of language and art is no more than to provide the raw material from which they can be developed as man makes the mental association between the stimulus and the response and discovers that he can control the sounds and gestures he makes. At this point in the development of both language and art the object ceases to be expression and becomes communication, which is a function of utility.

13. T. M. Moustoxidi, *Histoire de l'esthétique française, 1700–1900* (Paris, 1920), p. 51.

14. Benedetto Croce, *Aesthetic as Science of Expression and General Linguistic,* trans. Douglas Ainslie (rev. ed. New York, 1922), p. 95.

15. John Dewey, *Art as Experience* (New York, 1934), pp. 60–61.

I have already discussed the transformation of spontaneous animal expression into the conscious use of symbols for the purpose of communication—that is, to convey essential information to another person so that he may act upon it. Now in this primitive language there was a potentially artistic element which was a result not of the richness but of the poverty of language. The sounds of primitive speech approached what we call music, with marked stresses and wide variations in pitch, because primitive man lacked the sensitivity to perceive the subtler modulations of modern speech-patterns. The vocabulary was poetic, depending heavily upon concrete images, because primitive man knew only concrete things and had too limited a vocabulary to communicate except by perceptible images. In the same way, the visual arts began as a means of preserving communication when phonetic script was far beyond the cultural grasp of man. And, of course, a large part of the most primitive forms of communication consisted of gesture or dance, more vivid and immediate than the resources of primitive language. These potentially artistic elements existed because they were the best man could do in his attempts to communicate. In time he would surpass them when he perfected prose, phonetic script, and abstract logic.[16]

The utilitarian potentialities of music, poetry, and dance determined not only their origin but the early stages of their development. Rhyme, melody, and rhythm, for example, were aids to memory before the advent of written language. The dance added solemnity and significance to communications of import to the community.[17] A second kind of utility here enters into man's cultural history. The human understanding had formed in response to a utility whose goal is simply survival, or at most the avoidance of pain. But language, at whatever degree of development, is a social phenomenon, and its real progress could only occur in the context of society. Thus communication originated to warn of danger or to identify a food supply—the extension of the impulse

16. *Essai,* in *Œuvres phil., 1,* 81.
17. Ibid., p. 80.

to self-preservation to include others.[18] But as generations passed and man became more sophisticated and his social organization both more complex and more stable, there evolved a kind of social utility whose goal was not merely the preservation of the individual, whether self or other, but the preservation of the society, with all of its particular institutions and ways of cohesion. This kind of social utility was a critical factor in the further development of the artistic elements associated with communication:

> The object of the first poetry is clear. When societies were first established men could not yet afford to concern themselves with pure embellishment, and the needs which had obliged them to come together limited their vision to those things that were useful or necessary to them. Poetry and music, therefore, were only cultivated to make known religion and laws, and to preserve the memory of great men and the services they had rendered to society. . . . This was the only means available since writing was not yet known. Moreover, all the monuments of antiquity prove that these arts, at their birth, were intended for the instruction of the people. The Gauls and the Germans used them to preserve their history and their laws, and among the Egyptians and the Hebrews the arts were in some sense a part of religion. This is the reason that the ancients wanted education to have as its principal object the study of music, a word I take in the full extended meaning they gave to it.[19]

Art, then, had its origin and first development in response to the pressures of individual survival and social utility, its character shaped by other than aesthetic values.

Utilitarian ends sharply limited the possibilities of artistic expression. Music and poetry, for example, could not become independent of one another so long as both were conceived as auxiliaries to social cohesion. And, of course, the mere fact that

18. Ibid., p. 61.
19. Ibid., p. 81.

the worth of an artistic project was judged by nonaesthetic criteria
—by how well it served its social and communicative function—
tended to stultify the development of artistic values. In fact, perhaps
it would be accurate to say that until music, poetry, painting, and
dance were appreciated for their own sake and judged apart from a
utilitarian function, they were not art, properly speaking, at all
but merely particular modes of communication which could serve
as the raw material of art whenever man got around to discovering it.

The discovery of art evidently occurred when men became aware
of a pleasure in the sound of music or the rhythm of poetry quite
independent of its social and didactic content. At the same time, the
invention of writing and the greater sophistication of language les-
sened the need for music and poetry as aids to memory and instruction. Therefore, for the first time, music and poetry could and
did develop solely for the pleasure they convey. Condillac seems
to have taken two views of the nature of this pleasure. In the first
place, there is the purely sensual pleasure of harmony or rhythm,
which apparently is a function of man's given sensual equipment.
Condillac argued that man discovered harmony by accident and
that it was an immediate, which is to say unlearned, source of
pleasure. "Since prosody was extremely varied when language
originated, every inflection of the voice was natural. Chance, therefore, could not fail to lead men occasionally to passages that pleased
the ear. These were noticed, and repetition made them habitual.
Such was the first idea of harmony."[20]

Besides a natural and immediate response to certain artistic
forms, Condillac attributed aesthetic pleasure to the expression of
emotion contained in a work of art. When men began to experience the pleasures of music, for example, they discovered that it
not only produced pleasure in the ear, but that it had an independent
effect on the soul as well. The sound alone, without words, could
arouse in them a variety of emotions, "from joy to sadness, or even

20. Ibid., p. 73.

fury."[21] The explanation of this experience is that there is a parallel between the sounds of music and the natural cries which are man's instinctive expression of emotion. At first, only men of the most delicate sensibilities perceived this parallel in music and responded to it. Other men, observing the experience of their fellows, were prompted by sympathy and curiosity to respond in a similar manner. The experience was talked about and repeated; everyone wanted to share in it. In such a conducive atmosphere many were soon equally affected by the music, sympathy and the association of ideas being the mechanisms by which the aesthetic experience was transmitted. What nature had taught to a few, convention conveyed to the rest.

The aesthetic impulse, then, like language and indeed like reason itself, is a by-product, not a part, of man's natural endowment, although, to be sure, and again like language and reason, it springs from man's natural capacities. Man, pursuing activities aimed first at bare survival and subsequently at comfort, found a gratuitous source of pleasure—gratuitous because it contributes nothing to his survival and is not even necessary to his comfort. Motivated by the pleasure, he continued to explore the possibilities of this new experience and to evolve the various forms of art that human culture knows.

In discussing the origins of art, Condillac emphasized the universal in man—the organization of his senses, his instinctive sympathy, his spontaneous expression of emotion in cries and gestures. But in dealing with the evolution of art beyond its primitive manifestations, Condillac focused upon a mechanism which, though universally possessed, is the source of differentiation and uniqueness—the association of ideas. For it seems that the substance and content of all the forms of art derive from the particular experiences of a people and the unique set of associations to which these particular experiences give rise. Moreover, each people has its own character and genius, which is most directly reflected in its lan-

21. Ibid., p. 74.

guage, which in turn dictates the character of its literature. In his *Art d'écrire* Condillac raised the question:

> What is art? . . . What is the beauty which is its effect? And how is taste, which judges beauty, acquired? . . . How can [these questions] be answered if we do not have precise ideas of the things called "art," "beauty," and "taste"? And how can we give precision to these ideas if they change from people to people, and from generation to generation? There is only one way of understanding so complicated a subject; it is to observe the circumstances that come together in various times and places to form what is called in each language poetic style.[22]

Condillac did not mean that beauty is whatever it has been thought to be or that all art is of equal merit. He was arguing for an empirical philosophy of art which would find its aesthetic standards in the history of art itself, rather than in the rational conception of *la belle nature.* Indeed, Condillac maintained that the professedly absolute ideal of *la belle nature* is itself culturally conditioned, varying from one country to another, reflecting only the prevailing fashion. *La belle nature,* then, does not transcend the history of art but is one of its products and is equally subject to empirical investigation.[23]

Condillac did not himself try to work out a systematic empirical aesthetics. His concern with aesthetics was, after all, incidental and almost entirely concentrated either on problems of literary criticism, notably in his manual of literary style for the Prince of Parma, or on art as an aspect of the history of culture. The latter is of

22. *De L'Art d'écrire,* in *Œuvres phil., 1,* 603.

23. *Essai,* in *Œuvres phil., 1,* 82. Semantic difficulties, which are always with us, are seldom more acute than in the words "history" and "nature." Condillac appeals from history as an unyielding authority to history as the record of man's changing experience, and therefore from nature as an absolute ideal made manifest in a few eternally authoritative models to nature as a guiding activity whose manifestations will change with circumstances.

special interest because of Condillac's espousal of a cyclical interpretation of history.

Condillac held that all cultures go through a cycle of infancy, progress, and decadence. The mechanism of the cyclical movement is to be found in a psychological cycle springing from the inherent opposition between imagination and analysis. In the infancy of a language, imagination and feeling are dominant. Language is simple and limited, and the analogies by which figurative expressions are invented are immediately obvious. The literature of this period is also simple, with few genres and little subtlety. In time the language begins to have fixed principles and a unique character. This is the period conducive to genius and to great literature: "When a genius has discovered the character of a language, he expresses it vividly and sustains it in all his writings. With this help, the rest of the men of talent, who could not previously penetrate it themselves, perceive it keenly and express it by his example, each in his own genre. The language is enriched little by little from the many new styles." A period of great productivity is launched as language and literature enrich one another. "Talents flourish. All the arts assume the character proper to them, and superior men appear in all genres."[24]

But no language is capable of infinite development or of giving birth to an unlimited number of fruitful genres. This fact paves the way for a period of decline, which, like the period of achievement, is inaugurated by the work of a genius. For when a language has original writers in each genre, then a man of genius must innovate to surpass them. "But because the styles analogous to the character of the language were grasped by those who preceded him, all he can do is to deviate from analogy." While he might be successful in carrying off his experiment, those who come after him and try to imitate him will perpetuate not his success but the defects intrinsic in the style he has created. "Then is born the reign of subtle and indirect thought, precious antitheses, brilliant paradoxes,

24. Ibid., p. 101.

frivolous twists, affected expressions, superfluous words, and to sum it all up, the jargon of wits spoiled by a bad metaphysic. The public applauds. Frivolous and ridiculous works, born only for the moment, multiply. Bad taste passes into the arts and sciences, and talent grows increasingly rare."[25]

The transition between the second and third stages is marked by a loss of balance between imagination and analysis. "Taste begins to decline as soon as it has made all the progress it can, and the era of decadence is a century growing ever more enlightened. Then there is more reasoning about beauty and less feeling for it."[26] There is an optimum relationship between analysis and imagination, but it is an intrinsically unstable relationship. It is the very tension between these two opposite faculties that holds them temporarily in balance at the peak of a culture's development, giving an illusion of harmony that must soon give way as the peak is passed.

Condillac's analysis of language and art is characterized by a series of oppositions. All languages share a common grammar that corresponds to the structure of universal reason, but every language has its unique character that must not be damaged by borrowing from another. Man invents the literary genres out of his own imagination, but there are a finite number of genres whose appropriate style is given in the character of the language. Art at its best must spring forth spontaneously, uninhibited by rules, and yet great art is produced only when the rules have been discovered and true genius is subject to them. The explanation for these oppositions lies, I think, in the ambiguity of the concept of nature in Condillac, the relationship he sets up between nature and conven-

25. Ibid., p. 103.

26. *De L'Art d'écrire*, in *Œuvres phil.*, *1*, 605. The notion of cycles in taste was not uncommon in the eighteenth century. It was held in one form or another by Dubos, Voltaire, Diderot, Marmontel, and Charpentier, among others. Perhaps d'Alembert's theory of cycles came closest to that of Condillac. See Henry Vyverberg, *Historical Pessimism in the French Enlightenment* (Cambridge, 1958), pp. 115–21, 192–94.

tion in human life and culture, and, in the last analysis, in the confrontation of his empiricist philosophy with his rationalist world-view.

"The natural consists . . . in doing something easily when, after much practice, one finally needs to practice no longer; it is art turned into habit. The poet and the dancer are both natural when they have attained that degree of perfection in which any effort to observe the rules is no longer noticeable."[27] Condillac's definition of taste reflects the same thought from another vantage point: "Taste is a manner of feeling so felicitous that one perceives the value of things without the aid of reflection, or rather without using any rule for judging it. It is the effect of an imagination which, having been exercised early on choice subjects, preserves their memory and naturally makes them models for comparison."[28] Condillac asserted that man is what he has acquired and that there-fore virtually nothing in human culture or in man's conduct as a social being can be called "natural" in the strictest sense of the word. Everything man is and has is the product of experience, of acquisition, of a departure from nature as symbolized in the statue-man—blank, mindless, passionless, expressionless. Consequently, when he talked about the "natural" in man's behavior, Condillac meant in part spontaneous and unforced or unreflecting behavior, but only in part, because he also meant something that is in con-formity with a certain order in the universe, something that is inherently right or proper or good or beautiful. Moreover, a man can only develop this kind of "natural" behavior or judgment after he has reflected on it and then internalized the fruits of his reflec-tion so that he need no longer be conscious of it. This can be ex-plained, I think, by Condillac's idea of nature as an objective force—rational and purposive. This is the nature that teaches man, by way of experience working on his primary nature and latent capacities, to be rational, to appreciate beauty, and to apprehend the good almost in spite of himself and certainly without his deliberate

27. *De L'Art d'écrire,* in *Œuvres phil.,* 1, 603.
28. *Essai,* in *Œuvres phil.,* 1, 34.

intention. In this sense art is an expression of nature rather than an imitation of it.

The relevant consequence of this twofold view of nature is that when Condillac looked at human culture from the outside, from the point of view of its relationship to the universe, he saw order and universality, because it reflects nature; and when he looked at human culture from the inside, from the point of view of man's experience of it, he saw diversity and uniqueness, because it reflects the fact that each man and each people must learn nature's single lesson in its own way through its own unique experience, endowing it with its own specific content. Therefore the general form and structure of language is uniform, because it is the product of a single nature working on a universal set of mental mechanisms, but each language has a unique character, because its vocabulary is built out of a particular cultural history. Since the general nature of language is fixed and uniform, the possible literary genres are given and finite, but within each language they must be invented as particular acts of human creativity and endowed with the style appropriate to each genre in that language. Given this finite structure imposed upon human expression, art must be characterized by a discoverable set of rules, but the human experiences of artistic creation and aesthetic judgment are characterized by the dominance of spontaneity and feeling over rational calculation.

In human terms, then, "nature" is convention which has developed in response to the dictates of "nature" in a larger sense. The result of this approach is an aesthetic theory that makes possible the coexistence of a bias toward French classicism as an artistic ideal with a recognition of the intrinsic value of the art of other nations and other times. While each nation must express its own experience of nature, it is possible that some experiences—like that of seventeenth-century France—more nearly reflect the true character of nature. In this way the psychological subjectivism and cultural relativism implicit in Condillac's empirical approach to the works of man are modified and redirected by his rational understanding of the works of nature. Condillac's essentially traditional aesthetic judgments do not rest easily on their new foundation, a foundation that in the long run provides the basis for the total destruction of those judgments. Classicism and empiricism are not compatible, and that Condillac was caught in the tension between them without being able to resolve it was one more example of the disparity in his thinking between new doctrines and old assumptions.

8. The Education of a Prince

Education:

The care taken to form the body and mind of a child.

At first he is swaddled and deprived of the use of all his members. Eventually his hands are freed, but his body is enclosed in a kind of box. . . . Afterward come the leading-strings with which the child is held up for fear he should learn to walk by himself. . . .

As for his mind, it is filled for seven or eight years with fairy tales, ridiculous superstitions, and fears of all kinds. For another eight years the child's memory is burdened with things he is kept from understanding. He learns his own language haphazardly, but he studies a primer and with the aid of a dictionary he can soon travesty in Latin sentences he does not understand. He has completed the course in the humanities.

At fifteen or sixteen the course in philosophy begins. . . . He learns by heart the old copy books dragged in the dust of the school. . . .

These studies completed, a young man enters the world . . . a dull blockhead, unless nature has been stronger than education.[1]

Condillac wrote this angry denunciation of contemporary education while he was himself engaged in forming the body and mind of a child. In the spring of 1758 he had traveled to the North Italian duchy of Parma to be tutor to the young Prince Ferdinand. Evidently Condillac was selected because he was known for just the right combination of fashionableness and moderation in his

---

1. *Dictionnaire des synonymes,* in *Œuvres phil. de Condillac, 3,* 232.

views. The Duchess Louise-Elizabeth's comments on her choice in
a letter to her husband are revealing:

> As to his religion, I have made inquiries of several people,
> and all reports were just what we could have wished. In spite
> of this book [the *Traité des sensations*], which they say is
> somewhat metaphysical, I think that we shall have nothing to
> reproach ourselves with on this choice, either in this world
> or the next. But I must warn you that the Jesuits were
> dumbfounded to lose even more ground with us.[2] They could
> not complain at first, the choice being so generally praised, but
> finally they are beginning to murmur about the book. Our
> son must be a good Catholic, but not a doctor of the Church.
> Controversial questions would be of no use to him.[3]

The tutor to a son of the Spanish Bourbons could not have a reputation for heresy, but on the other hand, Parma was undergoing its
own Enlightenment, largely under French influence, and it was
desirable to fill the post with someone who represented the new
ideas.[4] Condillac seemed the perfect choice. He was to share his
duties with a former military officer, M. de Keralio,[5] who held the
post of *gouverneur*, while Condillac was the Prince's *précepteur*.

Parma under the Bourbons has been called "the Athens of Italy."[6]

---

2. Presumably a reference to the antiecclesiastical policy which Parma
followed under Dutillot. See Bédarida, *Parme et la France*, pp. 359ff.

3. Quoted ibid., p. 412.

4. See Gabriel Maugain, *Etude sur l'évolution intellectuelle de l'Italie
de 1657 à 1750 environ* (Paris, 1909), for a detailed discussion of the
French-inspired Italian Enlightenment, in which Parma shared.

5. Louis Félix Guynement, Chevalier de Keralio (1731–93). After
leaving Parma, Keralio became professor of tactics at the *Ecole militaire* in
Paris. In 1776 he was appointed inspector of all French Ecoles Militaires,
and on the side acted as spy and propagandist for Benjamin Franklin. (See
Claude-Anne Lopez, *Mon Cher Papa* [New Haven, 1967], pp. 192–93.)
He was the author of a number of books on tactics and military history. In
letters to the Duc de Nivernais, Condillac habitually referred to Keralio as
"the Ogre" (*Œuvres phil., 2, 545*).

6. Bédarida, *Parme et la France*, p. 1.

That the duchy was in advance of the general state of Italian culture
was largely due to the efforts of Guillaume-Léon Dutillot, who
dominated Parma from various high offices of state between 1749
and 1771. Dutillot was a genuine *uomo universale,* whose advocacy
of enlightened despotism was doubtless nourished by confidence
in his own ability to do all things well. Not only was he skilled as a
diplomat, politician, economist, and administrator, with a Cartesian
passion for order and regularity, but he also had a deep and more
than amateurish interest in the arts, letters, and sciences. He was a
bibliophile who put together a magnificent private collection while
reorganizing Parma's public library; he encouraged the growth
of the University of Parma; and he had a particular interest in the
reform of the theater. Above all, he attracted to Parma a significant number of distinguished men of letters, most of them
French. Dutillot's interests were shared and encouraged by Don
Philippe, the father of Condillac's pupil, but the real energy and
initiative behind Parma's intellectual revival were Dutillot's own.[7]

The nine years Condillac spent in Parma provided him with a
splendid opportunity to test his theories. Since all his work was
fundamentally directed to the theoretical question of how man
learns, and to the practical question of how he can avoid error and
acquire truth, a program of education was the natural fulfillment
of his speculation. In spite of the fact that his efforts were not
rewarded by their outcome—Don Ferdinand seems to have been
of mediocre ability[8]—Condillac felt that practice amply confirmed
his theories of knowledge and psychology.

The *Cours d'études* of eighteen volumes which Condillac put together for the young Prince takes its place in a substantial body of
seventeenth- and eighteenth-century writing on education. It is

7. Ibid., pp. 71ff.

8. See Gabriel Compayré, *Histoire critique des doctrines de l'éducation
en France depuis le seizième siècle* (2 vols. Paris, 1911), 2, 150. See also
Diderot's reference to Condillac as "as good a teacher as his student is bad."
"Plan d'une université pour le gouvernement de Russie," *Œuvres complètes,*
3, 494.

scarcely surprising that the Age of Enlightenment should have been marked by a general reappraisal of the aims and techniques of education. The very name and concept of enlightenment assumes the transformation of man and society through education—through the diffusion of new ideas and the teaching of new methods of thought. Moreover, the existing schools and universities of France were under the exclusive jurisdiction of the Catholic clergy until 1762. This meant that they were quite naturally dedicated to the preservation of the traditional classical and Christian culture, rather than to its replacement by the secular and scientific culture desired by the philosophes. Therefore, although the schools were by no means as narrowly reactionary as they were painted by their enemies, they did represent, to a greater or lesser degree, a conservative temper which damned them in the eyes of the philosophes.

The impulse to educational reform, partly a product of the spirit of criticism, was reinforced by the more positive factors of new philosophical and psychological doctrines. The close connection between epistemology and educational theory is obvious. A revolution in ideas about the nature of knowledge and the process of acquiring it clearly calls for a corresponding revolution in education. Moreover, the widespread acceptance of Locke's philosophy in eighteenth-century France had special implications for education even beyond those of the ferment of new ideas generally. An environmentalist orientation toward the nature of man puts a significant burden on education. If man's mind begins as a *tabula rasa,* anything can be written upon it. Those who are responsible for his rearing and education can make of a man, intellectually and morally, whatever they wish, provided they have the technical capacity. It is of the utmost social importance, then, to know what one's educational aims are and to know how they can be fulfilled. For all these reasons we find in the Enlightenment an intense interest, expressed both in speculation and in practice, in the problems of education.

French education was dominated by the Jesuits in the seventeenth and most of the eighteenth century—that is, until their expulsion in 1762. The Jesuit system of education, embodied in the *Ratio studiorum* of 1599,[9] was essentially the medieval one adjusted to accommodate the new ideas of Renaissance humanism. The basis of Jesuit teaching was Greek and Latin; its aim was eloquence. For students who went beyond the normal eight- or nine-year program —and those who did so usually intended to enter the order—this education in rhetoric and the humanities was completed by three years of philosophy, which meant Aristotle. Although the heart of Jesuit education was literary and scholastic, the *Ratio studiorum* did contain a provision for the teaching of mathematics and science as peripheral studies.[10] This modest provision became the basis for a remarkable flourishing of mathematics in the French Jesuit schools.[11] Although the Jesuits were far from up-to-date in their physics and astronomy (the Copernican system was not taught until after 1700, and then not in all colleges), they presented an impressive curriculum in arithmetic, geometry, and such practical applications of mathematics as navigation, optics, and architecture. It cannot be without significance that the Jesuits educated so many of the anti-Jesuit intellectuals of France: Descartes, Montesquieu, Fontenelle, Voltaire, Diderot, Buffon, Condorcet, and possibly Condillac.[12] Perhaps the mathematical teaching of the Jesuits helped to form a point of view which made their literary and philosophical studies, as well as their teaching methods, appear narrow and reactionary.

By the middle of the seventeenth century, Jesuit domination was threatened by two rival groups of religious educators, the Oratorians and the Jansenists, both somewhat more receptive to new ideas and creative of new methods than the older order. While the Jesuit schools were at open war with Descartes, the Oratorians and the

9. Unrevised until 1832.

10. François de Dainville, *La Naissance de l'humanisme moderne: Les Jésuites et l'éducation de la société française* (Paris, 1940), p. 60.

11. See André Schimberg, *L'Education morale dans les collèges de la Compagnie de Jésus en France sous l'ancien régime* (Paris, 1913), pp. 513–23.

12. See above, p. 7.

Jansenists introduced the Cartesian spirit and philosophy into education. The Oratorians developed new goals, new methods, and new subject matter in their teaching. Besides mathematics, they taught experimental physics, history and geography, and the philosophy of Descartes.[13] French instead of Latin was used in the classroom in all subjects through the fourth year, and in history throughout.[14] The aim of education in the schools of the Oratory was to create precision of judgment, and this in turn was seen to have value only as a means to regulate the will. It was an intensely Christian education, but one which reflected the new light of philosophy and learning. The Cartesian outlook is especially evident in the observations, made in 1683, of Père Lamy, the great educational theorist of the Oratory, on the best means of forming the judgment. "There is no study more appropriate for exercising the judgment than geometry and the other parts of mathematics. . . . Geometry furnishes models of clarity and order, and . . . it accustoms the mind unconsciously to reason well."[15] The Jesuits, by contrast, were interested in mathematics only for its practical applications; their model of reasoning was still the Aristotelian syllogism.

The Oratorians were much influenced by the Jansenists who, although their schools were founded later, seem to have been more actively creative and articulate in educational theory.[16] The Jansenist aim was also to produce a critical and reflective judgment, and their method was a direct application of Descartes' *Discourse*

13. See Paul Lallemand, *Histoire de l'éducation dans l'ancien Oratoire de France* (Paris, 1889), pp. 241–63.

14. Compayré, *Histoire critique, 1,* 216.

15. Quoted ibid., p. 227.

16. The first Oratorian college was founded at Dieppe in 1614. The Jansenist schools of Port-Royal began in 1638 and were finally dispersed in 1660, having suffered so many interruptions in the interval that they really operated as an organized institution for only fourteen years. (H. C. Barnard, *The Port-Royalists on Education* [Cambridge, 1918], p. 25.) Their influence is all the more remarkable for the brevity of their operations and is in part due to the writings of the Port-Royalist educators Arnauld, Lancelot, and Nicole, most of whom were not published until after the schools had ceased to exist.

on Method.[17] Reason must yield only to the pure and clear evidence of truth, not to authority. Therefore all teaching must appeal to the judgment and not to the memory. The principle of instruction must be to lead the student from the known to the unknown. This meant, for example, that the student should first learn French thoroughly and then use it as the key to classical and foreign languages, in contrast to the traditional practice followed by the Jesuits of teaching the rules of Latin by rote from grammars written in Latin. The schools of Port-Royal proposed to teach by usage and not by rules, to take children as they are and work through their natural interests and aptitudes, teaching them only what they can understand and never what they can merely memorize.[18]

The major common effect of the new philosophy on educational attitudes was probably to introduce the idea that learning must be an individual process because it requires that each individual subject what he learns to the test of his own judgment. From this common viewpoint epistemological variations led to variations in aim and technique. For Descartes the test was reason and the purpose of education was to form the mind. For Bacon, the other major seventeenth-century source of educational ideas, the test was experience, and the purpose of education was to accumulate useful knowledge. In the eighteenth century, under the inspiration of Locke, a fusion of the two aims took place.

Locke was the real fountainhead of eighteenth-century theories of education. Not only did his *Essay concerning Human Understanding* set out the epistemological and psychological framework in which most of the philosophes worked, but his own *Thoughts concerning Education,* published in 1693 and translated into French two years later, had a more direct influence, especially on Rousseau. Locke's educational aim was Baconian—the acquisition of useful

17. The Cartesian influence in Jansenist education came from Antoine Arnauld, who did not share Pascal's antipathy to Descartes, and who perhaps "does not altogether represent the primitive spirit of the movement." Barnard, *The Port-Royalists,* p. 43.

18. Compayré, *Histoire critique, 1,* 227.

knowledge. This meant that he would eliminate Greek altogether from instruction, and reserve Latin for the "gentleman."[19] He was far more concerned that the student learn to speak and write effectively in his native language and in a living foreign language than that he should bog down in a dead language fit only for professional scholars. In addition, he would replace rhetoric and logic with training in letter-writing and extemporaneous discourse.[20]

Locke's conception of education as the accumulation of useful ideas and good mental habits stems from his psychology. He regarded the faculties of the mind as given; they can be fed material to work on in the form of ideas. Thus the mind can become more efficient with use, but its activity does not change or develop. Education, in Locke's view, can be only quantitative, the accumulation of sound ideas to be available in the memory. In the Cartesian tradition education was a qualitative process dedicated to the development and perfection of reason, but for Locke reason is the process of reasoning, a relatively simple and mechanical operation of the faculties to which memory is the key, rather than a special quality resident in the mind. This view is much more apparent in the post-Lockean associationists, but even in Locke himself the tendency is clear. The process of reasoning is a sequence of associated ideas, in which agreement or disagreement, coherence or incoherence, are looked for. If this is the case, then clearly the raw material not only of knowledge but of reasoning itself consists in acquired ideas. The more ideas a person has, the more far-ranging his reason will be. Moreover, the basic skill with which his reason operates is the same at all levels. As far as his limited quantity of ideas allows, a child can reason, can run through a sequence of ideas, as well as a man. All this had its effect on Locke's ideas of teaching technique. He rejected, for example, the approach to language of the Port-Royalists, who taught grammar as the inner logic of a language and held that a child could grasp this inner

19. *Some Thoughts concerning Education*, ed. R. H. Quick (Cambridge, 1902), pp. 138–39, 170–71 (sects. 164–65, 195).

20. Ibid., pp. 151, 162–64 (sects. 172–73, 188–89).

logic because it corresponds to the innate structure of reason. For Locke there is no such innate structure. We can only learn discrete ideas received through the senses. Therefore memory, rather than reason in the Cartesian sense, is the key to learning. Of course, Locke did not therefore return to the old system of learning the rules of grammar by rote, which would have seemed obscurantist to him. He advocated learning language by usage and repetition without reference to grammar.[21] Locke's theory of education, then, would select subject matter on practical grounds and develop its techniques according to the basic philosophy that knowledge is derived exclusively from experience. These ideas, somewhat modified, reappeared in Condillac.

Besides the developments in general educational theory in the seventeenth century, developments in the more specialized field of princely education must be taken into account. Here, too, new conceptions and attitudes appeared. The fatuousness and frivolity of La Mothe le Vayer's instruction of the young Louis XIV gave way to the seriousness and dignity of Bossuet's attempts to prepare the Dauphin for his destiny as heir to the throne, and this in turn was succeeded by Fénelon's humanity, tact, and flexibility as preceptor to the Duke of Burgundy. In part, of course, these differences must be attributed to differences of talent and temperament among the three tutors themselves, but there is also at work here a genuine and perceptible process of revision away from traditional attitudes toward the prince as a being apart. In the place of these attitudes we can see the growing and salutary conviction that the prince is no different from other men in his makeup, and that insofar as he has unique educational needs, they arise from the demands of his office and not from the sanctity of his person.

The education of Louis XIV was first entrusted, in 1644, to Hardouin de Péréfixe, later the Archbishop of Paris. Not much is known of his teaching except for a little manual he wrote for his pupil's moral education—the *Institutio principis,* a rather con-

21. Ibid., p. 138 (sect. 162).

ventional list, in Latin, of the virtues proper to royalty. In 1652 Péréfixe was succeeded by La Mothe le Vayer, about whose methods and principles a good deal more is known. In 1640, in the hope of being appointed tutor, he had composed a small treatise, *De L'Instruction de Monseigneur le Dauphin,* and in the 1650s, after his appointment, he put together a set of textbooks for Louis. From these it appears that La Mothe le Vayer combined a traditional and unimaginative attitude toward the methods and matter of education with a bland complacency before the position of kingship. He seemed to feel that a king needs to know not more but less than an ordinary man, with the result that he rejected many studies as beneath the royal dignity, thus watering down even the traditional program of education. Grammar, for example, he considered too base a study for a prince. Arithmetic is for merchants; Latin is not suitable; history is not even worthy of being considered. A little astronomy is permitted—just enough for Louis to have a clearer idea of the position of his kingdom in the world. Music is acceptable, provided that the king never forgets his station while singing. The subject matter of the textbooks appears substantial enough—geography, rhetoric, morals, economics, politics, logic, and physics—but La Mothe le Vayer presented them in the form of superficial and simpleminded summaries of the doctrines of Aristotle. The most important royal education of all, according to Louis XIV's tutor, is physical training, and especially hunting. Indeed, La Mothe le Vayer wondered why the noble sport of hunting was not included among the seven liberal arts.[22]

In reaction against the kind of absurdity represented in Louis XIV's education, and with an eye to the forthcoming education of the Dauphin, Nicole of Port-Royal published a book called *De L'Education d'un prince* in 1670, in which he set forth a program of princely education in the light of the reforms of Port-Royal. The book is said to reflect particularly the thought and spirit of Pascal.[23] Nicole was not at all awed by the majesty of princes. On

22. Compayré, *Histoire critique,* 1, 294–98.
23. Ibid., p. 279.

the contrary, his first concern was to point out both the moral responsibilities and the moral hazards of the princely estate. A young prince needs—in a tutor—a master, counselor, and friend. Instead, he finds only a courtier. Accustomed to flattery and indulgence from an early age, he never learns that he belongs to the state and not to himself.[24] Moreover, since he never learns the discipline and austerity of a moral life, he is subject in later years to the problem of boredom which is chronic to those whose passions have always been violently stimulated and who in time inevitably exhaust their desire for any sensual object. Finally, never having been encouraged to love books, princes grow up ignorant, intellectually lazy, and ill-equipped to perform the service to which they are called.[25]

Nicole need not have worried about the spirit in which the Dauphin's education would be undertaken. Entrusted as it was to Bossuet, it had to be pursued with energy, high-mindedness, and even austerity. Bossuet's earnest efforts, like Condillac's with the Prince of Parma, were rewarded with only indifferent success, which some have blamed on the Dauphin's limited abilities and others on the unsuitability of Bossuet's personality for the needs of a child.[26] Certainly there is a disproportion, even an incongruity, between the lofty intelligence and moral grandeur of the tutor and the modest talents and languid temperament of the pupil which cannot have made for congeniality. Be that as it may, Bossuet's understanding of his duties represented a clear advance over that of La Mothe le Vayer. All the knowledge the seventeenth century had at its command was put before the young Prince. Specialists were called in to teach him mathematics, physics, and anatomy, using actual demonstrations and experiments. Bossuet himself took charge of literary and philosophic studies, introducing a number of innovations in method. He composed for the Prince a Latin grammar in French prose. He had him read the classical authors straight

24. Pierre Nicole, *De L'Education d'un prince* (Lyons, 1670), p. 2.
25. Ibid., pp. 28–33.
26. Compayré, *Histoire critique, I,* 312.

through to understand their thought, instead of confining him to fragments. He made history a central study, with special emphasis on the history of France. Although Descartes was not included in the program, Bossuet taught the Cartesian principles that philosophy begins with oneself and rises to God, and that the purpose of the study of rhetoric is to speak with logic and clarity. It was, in short, an education in the new manner of the great reforms of Port-Royal and the Oratory.[27]

In 1689 Fénelon was appointed tutor to the Dauphin's son, the Duke of Burgundy. In this capacity he made use of some of Bossuet's writings—notably the Latin grammar and the essay *De La Connaissance de Dieu*—but he also introduced some techniques of his own reflecting the new psychology of experience. Fénelon's fundamental pedagogical principle seems to have been that one learns by doing. He avoided teaching the Duke rules of grammar and instead gave him models, encouraging him to imitate them and to learn the rules by his own observation after correct usage has become habitual. Like Rousseau, Fénelon believed in the usefulness of contrived experience, so he devised situations by which the prince could learn for himself such things as the evils of an ungoverned temper, without ever realizing that he was being taught. Moral training proceeded by planned scenes and by fables that Fénelon composed, drawing his material from the Duke's own life and character. In recognition of the maxim that learning depends upon attention, and attention depends upon interest, Fénelon sought always to fit his instruction to the prince's own experience and to so vary the subject matter that the prince would never become bored.[28]

It can be seen, then, that the later part of the seventeenth century bequeathed to the eighteenth a rich heritage in educational experience and speculation. In education, as in science and philosophy, the first half of the eighteenth century was distinguished more for

27. Ibid., pp. 305–11.
28. See Gabriel Compayré, *Fénelon et l'éducation attrayante* (Paris, 1910), pp. 51–79.

the diffusion and practical application of the ideas of the preceding century than for original thought of its own. More and more schools, serving ever wider circles of society, were being established, most of them dedicated to ideals of educational reform. Aside from the rise of a secular spirit in education, widespread for the first time in the eighteenth century, not much was added to pedagogical theory before mid-century. In 1762 the Jesuits were expelled from France. The same year saw the publication of *Emile,* a fitting symbol as well as a major cause of a new era in educational thinking. The new element, hinted at before but never so systematically or explicitly worked out, was the appeal to nature as the true basis of a sound education.

In 1762 Condillac had been four years at Parma, bringing up the Prince according to his own idea of a "natural" education, with the explicit aim of "teaching him to think."[29] For Condillac, teaching the Prince to think meant teaching him good mental habits. He proposed to do this by making the Prince conscious from the outset of his methods of learning and thinking. What these good habits are, and the ways in which the Prince was encouraged to learn and to apply them, involves many of Condillac's doctrines about men, reason, nature, and science. For Condillac's educational program is closely related to his sensationalist psychology, to the centrality of the association of ideas in his concept of human reason, to his idea of nature as the ultimate authority for all we know and do, and to his belief in the unity of knowledge.

The first principle of Condillac's psychology of learning is that we have acquired all our ideas through our senses. Its second principle is that we only retain ideas that grasp our attention. Attention, in turn, is a function of desire, which is an operation of the will arising out of the experience of pleasure and pain. In practice, these principles meant that the Prince would learn by observation and that he must be motivated to learn. In order to be motivated to

---

29. "Discours préliminaire," *Cours d'études,* in *Œuvres phil., 1,* 399.

learn, the child must be able to understand what he is taught, and not forced to repeat words he does not comprehend; and he must be interested in what he observes, must see its relevance to his own experience and needs. His desire to learn can be helped along by the pleasures of a self-love gratified by success, but this alone cannot overcome the disgust engendered by being forced to learn what he sees no need to learn.[30] Condillac suggested, therefore, that as a beginning the tutor must enter the child's world, see things as he does, play with him, and excite his curiosity through his own natural activities.[31]

As a doctrinaire sensationalist, Condillac rejected the notion—cherished among men since at least the Greeks—of an age of reason. The idea that a child cannot profit from serious education until he reaches the age of reason, said Condillac, originated in man's habit of teaching by general principles instead of by observations. Forgetting that general principles (if true) are merely abridged expressions comprehending a mass of observed data, teachers have begun at the wrong end, attempting to get children to understand such principles although they have not made the observations which constitute them. Finding that their charges do not follow the instruction, they conclude that they do not yet have the power of reason. To this, Condillac replied that "at no age can one comprehend the general principles of a science without making the observations that lead to these principles. The age of reason, therefore, is the age at which one has observed; and so reason will come early if we engage children in making observations."[32]

Condillac's view of reason in children was similar to Locke's. The process of reasoning, resting upon the association and comparison of ideas acquired through observation, is the same for all subjects and all ages. Although in the statement quoted above,

30. Ibid., pp. 398–99.
31. "Motif des leçons préliminaires," *Cours d'études,* in *Œuvres phil.,* 1, 408.
32. "Discours préliminaire," *Cours d'études,* in *Œuvres phil.,* 1, 397.

Condillac implied that reason must be taught by teaching observation, a few pages later he claimed that it appeared of itself in children even before they are instructed:

> When Newton, observing the bodies on the surface of our globe, said, "they weigh toward the center of the earth, therefore the moon weighs toward the same center, therefore the satellites weigh toward the center of their principal planet, therefore all planets weigh toward the center of the sun," what more is involved in these reasonings than in this: one says *"punira,"* therefore one will say *"récompensera"?*
>
> The Newton who expounded the system of the world did not reason otherwise than the Newton who learned to touch, to see, to speak; he did not reason otherwise than the Newton who developed his own sensations. Both observed; both compared; both judged; both drew consequences. Age has only changed the object of study, but the reasoning of the mind is always the same operation.[33]

From the beginning of their conscious experience, then, children reason by reflecting upon their experience and comparing the ideas that their experience gives them. There is, however, a second type of thinking, different from thinking by reflection but growing out

33. "Motif des leçons," *Cours d'études,* in *Œuvres phil., 1,* 407. Perhaps the question of the development of reason can be clarified by making a distinction between reason as a process and its application. In Condillac's eyes the process of reason is a simple operation consisting of analysis, analogy, and the association of ideas, which anyone, a child or a savage as well as an educated adult, not only has the capacity to perform but actually does perform—often unconsciously—with respect to the most basic activities of life. Development occurs in two ways: in the application of reason to an ever-widening range of material, and in making the process conscious so that it may be deliberately and effectively applied to every question. Thus Condillac's theory that the development of language reflects the development of reason (see·above, pp. 162–63) means only that the growing scope of reason must find expression in a growing vocabulary and a more complex formal structure.

of it, which is subject to special hazards. This is thinking by habit. Habitual judgments were once learned by reflection, but they have become so familiar to the mind that they occur in too rapid a sequence of associated ideas for the mind to notice the process. Thinking of this kind is appropriate, according to Condillac, to such things as judgments of taste. The special danger involved is that if the series of ideas that make up the judgment is badly formed, either with respect to the ideas in themselves or with respect to their relation to one another, then the judgment will be false, and since it *is* habitual and therefore unconscious, it is generally beyond the reach of criticism and correction. Therefore it is of paramount importance in educating children to teach them good habits and, above all, to make them conscious of the way these habits are formed, so that they may from time to time reflect anew on the grounds of their formation.[34]

As Condillac had explained in detail in the *Essai sur l'origine des connaissances humaines* and the *Traité des sensations,* both types of thinking depend upon the association of ideas, which is the very mechanics of reason. Reflection, whether looked at as the process of comparing and judging, the process of reasoning by analogy, or the method of analysis,[35] requires the setting forth of a sequence of ideas related to one another in a logical or causal chain. Thus, even when individual ideas have been well made, faulty reflection may still occur when they are wrongly associated—i.e. when the merely contiguous experience of them, which may be nothing more than an accident of space or time, is mistaken for a genuine relationship.[36] It is the business of careful and attentive observation to guard against the dangers of erroneous association.

While effective use of association of ideas demands a good

---

34. "Discours préliminaire," *Cours d'études,* in *Œuvres phil., 1,* 400.

35. I am not suggesting that these are three different methods; in Condillac's usage they are, at bottom, the same process, but he speaks of the process now with one terminology and now with another, depending upon which aspect he wishes to illuminate.

36. "Discours préliminaire," *Cours d'études,* in *Œuvres phil., 1,* 400.

memory, training the memory is not the true goal of education. There is no point in teaching a child to remember words to which he connects no ideas, but if he has observed things carefully and formed clear ideas by reflecting on his observations, he will remember them without special effort. Association will be the means of recovering temporarily forgotten ideas: "He who has reflected much has retained much. If something escapes him, he can find it again, because reflections which have become familiar to him are linked to one another and can always lead him where they have led him before. On the contrary, he who only knows by heart knows nothing, practically speaking, and what he has forgotten he will not recover, or at least he cannot be certain of recovering it."[37] Memory is taken out of its rightful place if it is made an end in itself. Properly understood, memory, like all other mental processes beyond the level of simple sensation, is a function of the association of ideas. To train the faculty of association—that is, to stock the mind with well-formed ideas whose genuine interconnections are properly grasped—is the object of the teacher: this is what it means to teach a child to think.

Nature was Condillac's authority and guide in devising an educational method. The Prince will be taught the way nature first taught man, before he went astray over phantasms of his own making. This, of course, is nothing new for Condillac. It is a theme which he repeated from the moment he first stated his ideas about knowledge. But now for the first time he had a chance to demonstrate in practice what his "natural" method of education involved.

Condillac's idea of "the way nature teaches us" was drawn from the "experience" of the statue-man, combined with reflections on the primitive state of mankind. More precisely, it represents the superimposition of Condillac's own abstraction of man's nature, personified in the statue-man, upon his reading of contemporary primitive studies. He believed that the actual historical process in which nature instructed man was less accurate and effective

37. Ibid., p. 399.

than it ought to have been, because man did not know what was going on and so could not actively cooperate. Ignorant of the principles by which nature was teaching him, he learned accidentally and haphazardly. If he would become conscious of these principles, however, he could direct his own learning in the way nature would have it by eliminating the nonnatural aberrations accumulated by civilization, as well as the accidents of undirected experience.[38]

The idea of a natural education at once brings to mind the apostle of naturalism, Jean-Jacques Rousseau. The whole story of the relationship between the ideas of Condillac and those of Rousseau has not yet been told, and I cannot do it here. It is a complicated relationship that needs and deserves a careful and thorough investigation. At first glance, Condillac's highly intellectualized and abstract "nature," his notion that man must mold and manipulate it even while yielding to its lessons, his emphasis on the early training of reason, all suggest a very different "nature" from the emotional, spontaneous, and diversified "nature" of Rousseau. And yet a reading of *Emile* shows that not only was Rousseau's version of natural education fully as artificial and contrived as Condillac's, but that the epistemological and psychological principles upon which it rests were derived directly from Condillac. One could cite page after page in which Rousseau restated Condillac's doctrines, almost in Condillac's words: the need to train the senses to perform their function (a discussion couched in terms of a newly created man or statue); sense experiences as the raw material of an infant's thought before memory and imagination develop; the greater importance of preventing the child from forming inaccurate or confused ideas than of teaching him a large quantity of material; desire as the key to attention, which is indispensable to learning; the folly of teaching a child any idea before he is able to understand it; the dangers of error inherent in the way the mind forms complex ideas out of simple sensations;[39] the method of teaching the child to

---

38. Ibid., p. 398.
39. *Emile*, in *Œuvres complètes*, 3, 61–62, 67–68, 297–98, 313–14, 367–69.

correct the experience of his senses by the example of observing a stick partly submerged in water;[40] and so on and on.

Nevertheless, Rousseau was not Condillac. He had, to be sure, adopted Condillac's epistemology and all of its pedagogical consequences. However, in Rousseau's eyes epistemology was only a tool; for Condillac it was the whole of philosophy. Rousseau appreciated the technical advantages a sound epistemology gives to education: the mechanics of teaching depend upon an understanding of the mechanics of learning. But it was not the mechanics of learning that preoccupied Rousseau; it was the purpose of learning, which was to create a moral being, not an intellectual one. For Condillac, on the other hand, the mechanics of learning *was* its purpose. Indeed, they supplied Condillac not only with the techniques of teaching but with the substance and the end as well. His aim was to teach his student to understand the mechanics of learning so that he might himself take over the process of learning when he left his tutor's care. For Rousseau there was "only one science for children to learn—the duties of man,"[41] and only one means of teaching it—the cultivation of good moral habits through a "well-regulated liberty."[42] For Condillac there was also "only one science: the history of nature,"[43] and it is taught by the cultivation of good mental habits through a well-regulated observation. Condillac was wholly concerned with the realm of the intellect. His

40. Ibid., pp. 374–75. In this passage, incidentally, Rousseau asserted, with Condillac, that any process of comparing ideas is a process of reasoning, that children therefore reason as soon as they have any ideas in their minds, and that, by implication, they can and should be taught to reason well. This contradicts the more frequently cited passage (ibid., p. 119) in which Rousseau rejected Locke's maxim that children should be reasoned with, on the grounds that reason is man's "last and choicest growth" and beyond the capacity of children. It seems to me that the passage in support of teaching reason to children is consistent with the whole of *Emile,* and that the passage against it, usually cited out of context, in reality has only a specific and limited application to the teaching of deductive principles, which Condillac also condemned.

41. Ibid., p. 40.
42. Ibid., p. 124.
43. *De L'Art de raisonner,* in *Œuvres phil., 1,* 619.

program of education, like his life, lacks a moral or emotional dimension. Rousseau, on the other hand, was almost totally concerned with man as a moral being, and for him the training of the mind to form ideas, about nature or anything else, is a useful but subordinate technique. Reason, for Rousseau, was meaningless without a moral context. Morality, for Condillac, was just another system of well-made ideas.

The word "only," it is true, functions differently in Condillac's statement that the only science is the history of nature than it does in Rousseau's assertion that the only science for children to learn is the duties of man, as the qualifying phrase in the latter statement suggests. Rousseau was talking about priorities of knowledge, Condillac about the unity of knowledge. Rousseau was maintaining that children must first be taught the duties of man, because it is that which will make them men instead of animals. Without it, all other knowledge is corrupting; with it, all other knowledge is dispensable (although not necessarily undesirable). Condillac, on the other hand, was saying that no knowledge exists other than the history of nature, or, to put it more positively, that all knowledge is comprehended in the history of nature. Since this was a first principle of his system of education, it follows that there is then only one method of inquiry, and it was by teaching that method that he expected to open all doors of knowledge to the Prince. Because of our limited capacities we must cut up the history of nature into several branches, but we ought not to lose sight of the fact that we are always talking about the same small body of ideas looked at in different ways.[44] Most importantly, we divide the history of nature into two parts: physics, which is the science of sensible truths (truths perceived by the senses), and metaphysics, the science of abstract truths. Each is necessary to the other:

> Whatever the subject of our studies, abstract reasonings are necessary to grasp the connections of sensible ideas, and

44. "Motif des études," *Cours d'études,* in *Œuvres phil.,* I, 421.

> sensible ideas are necessary in order to make abstract ideas and
> to define them. Thus we see that from the first division the
> sciences return to one another. Also they lend aid to one
> another, and it is in vain that philosophers try to put barriers
> between them. It is very reasonable that minds limited as ours
> are should consider them separately, but it would be ridiculous
> to conclude that it is of their nature to be separate. We must
> always remember that there is really only one science, and
> if we know truths which seem to be detached from one another,
> it is because we are ignorant of the bond that joins them into
> a whole.[45]

The final expression of the unity of knowledge is that, for Condillac,
just as there is only one science, there is also only one true proposition: "the same is the same." All valid logical propositions are
reducible to a statement of identity.

The meaning of Condillac's naturalistic method was most apparent in the first months of his program, when his teaching was,
to say the least, unconventional. He inaugurated the education of his
seven-year-old charge with nothing less than a course in psychology
and anthropology, before going on to the more conventional program of French and classical literary studies which occupied the
boy until his eleventh year. For, as we have indicated earlier, Condillac's notion of a natural education was to teach the way nature
first taught us, but with a crucial difference: the student is to be
made conscious of the processes involved, so that the haphazard
character of the really natural education may be replaced by a
systematic direction which will preserve the purity of nature's
intent better than nature could do herself. Thus we find that the
very first month of the program was devoted to the principles of
Condillac's psychology of knowledge. Condillac insisted that the
boy had no difficulty in learning these principles because he taught
him through his own observations:

> To carry out my plan I had to be friends with my student
> and put myself entirely in his place. I had to be a child rather

45. *De L'Art de raisonner,* in *Œuvres phil., 1,* 619.

than a tutor. Therefore I let him play and I played with him, but I made him notice everything he did and how he had learned to do it, and these small observations on his games became for him a new game. He soon came to recognize that he had not always been capable of movements which, until then, he had believed to be natural. He saw how habits are contracted, how to acquire good ones and to correct bad ones.[46]

Then, with his curiosity excited, the philosophical child went on to realize that he had not always had the same ideas and that all his ideas originated in the senses. He learned, still by self-scrutiny (aided by Condillac's simplified summary of the theories of the *Traité des sensations*), to recognize the different operations of the soul, the different kinds of ideas and how they can be classified, generalized, and analyzed. His preliminary education was capped by a discussion of the difference between the soul and the body, and the cosmological argument for the existence of God.[47] (It is interesting that Condillac chose to introduce his philosophy of religion at precisely this point. Is it perhaps intended to guard against the boy's pursuing his newly acquired sensationalist doctrines to materialist conclusions?)

Armed with Condillac's psychological doctrines, the Prince was now prepared for the second stage in his experience of natural learning: a repetition of the experience of primitive man, but without its haphazardness. For Condillac wanted the child to recapitulate the education of the race, to pursue the order of learning, as well as the method of learning, of primitive man. Man began, according to Condillac, by learning the things necessary to his survival and comfort, then went on to form judgments of taste, and finally began to reason on matters of speculation. Thus the Prince was to begin with the earliest knowledge of a society just leaving the state of ignorance: the formation of laws and customs, handicrafts, astron-

46. "Motif des leçons préliminaires," *Cours d'études*, in *Œuvres phil.*, 1, 408.

47. "Précis des leçons préliminaires," *Cours d'études*, in *Œuvres phil.*, 1, 409–18.

omy, rudimentary agriculture, and commerce.[48] His text—aside, that is, from his own activities and observations—was a simplified version of Goguet's *De L'Origine des lois*. His interest in the subject was aroused by urging him to compare his own childhood with the childhood of the world.[49] One regrets that Condillac does not give more details of this stage of the Prince's education, because it could have been an original, creative, and fascinating project. The one concrete instance he provides was not his idea at all, but Keralio's: this was the Prince's education in agriculture, which was conducted in a garden adjoining the boy's apartment: "The prince dug his field, sowed the wheat, watched it grow and ripen, and gathered it in. More interested in his garden once the flowers had been removed from it, he wanted to plant other grains, and he wanted to see different kinds of trees grow. He was then almost at the same point at which man was when he had provided for his most pressing needs."[50] It is startling, however, to find that, simultaneously with the reading of Goguet's history of primitive man, the boy (still only seven) was put to reading Boileau, Molière, Corneille, and Racine, which would seem to contradict and defeat the purpose of recapitulating the experience of the race. Indeed, the whole idea seems to have been buried beneath the weight of the literary program that followed it so closely, and one is left to wonder just how far Condillac had thought through his own ideas.

Apparently Condillac's real interest in primitive man as a pedagogical model was to inspire a method, rather than to yield a source of substantive teaching. The history of man's development provided a basic order—necessities, taste, speculation—and, above all, the procedure of going from the known to the unknown, one of Condillac's most often repeated formulas.[51] By this he meant, primarily, leading the Prince from his own observations to the

48. "Discours préliminaire," *Cours d'études*, in *Œuvres phil.*, *1*, 400–02.
49. "Motif des études," *Cours d'études*, in *Œuvres phil.*, *1*, 419.
50. "Discours préliminaire," *Cours d'études*, in *Œuvres phil.*, *1*, 401.
51. To be found also, of course, in Descartes and in the Port-Royal Manuals, but with quite a different meaning.

formation of abstractions or general ideas or judgments, rather than teaching him general principles from which knowledge is to be deduced.

In practice, Condillac quickly passed the stage of teaching necessities—perhaps on the grounds that the Prince of Parma would not be much affected by problems of survival and comfort—and moved immediately to the cultivation of the boy's taste. Going from the known to the unknown in this realm meant giving the Prince models of good taste and letting him observe for himself, for "his observations led him naturally to the discovery of the rules of the art of speaking."[52]

The Oratorians and the Jansenists not only had led the field in making French the normal vehicle of instruction, but were also responsible for the idea that a language is best learned by extensive reading of good models, rather than by the rote learning of grammar. By 1700 French language and literature were well established in most non-Jesuit schools and colleges in France. On the other hand, Condillac certainly added something new when he taught the Prince to analyze critically the structure of a play: "We read some comedies of Molière, some tragedies of Corneille, some of Racine, and we made for ourselves the idea of a drama. The prince understood how an action is exposed, unfolds, and reaches its denouement. He saw how the denouements are prepared, how they are led up to without being given away. He observed the art with which character is sustained. He distinguished the episodical characters and he judged their contribution or lack of it."[53] The plays of the great dramatists, the poetry, satires, and epistles of Boileau, and the letters of Mme. de Sévigné were the models of good French that Condillac used. These were supplemented, but only after much reading, by Condillac's own *Grammaire* and *De L'Art d'écrire*, and *Des Tropes* of Du Marsais. In Condillac's eyes literary studies were simply a branch of the art of reasoning and led naturally into a study of logic and from there into science. All knowledge is one,

52. "Discours préliminaire," *Cours d'études,* in *Œuvres phil.,* 1, 402.
53. "Motif des études," *Cours d'études,* in *Œuvres phil.,* 1, 419.

and all thinking is, at bottom, the creation of analytic systems
based on the logic of identity:

> What is the *Grammaire?* It is a system of words representing
> the system of ideas in the mind when we want to communicate
> them in the order and with the relationships that we perceive.
> The *Art d'écrire* is nothing but the same system, carried to
> that point of perfection of which it is capable. While studying
> these things one after another, we really just keep getting
> back to the same fund of ideas. Consequently, what we study
> continually recalls what we have studied, and nothing is
> forgotten.
>
> The art of reasoning, or the art of conducting one's mind
> in the search for truth, is not a new art for someone who al-
> ready knows the operations of his soul, and whose taste is
> beginning to form. But it was a question of exercising the
> prince's reasoning on new objects, and this was the occasion
> of giving him new knowledge.[54]

The new knowledge was the Newtonian system of the world, approached through its greatest popularizers, Mme. du Châtelet,
Maupertuis, and, of course, Voltaire. Condillac's *Art de raisonner*
itself—after describing the three kinds of evidence: feeling, fact,
and reason—was an elementary textbook of Newtonian physics.
In Condillac's scheme of education, science and his own philosophy
took the place of the Aristotelian philosophy of the scholastics and
the Jesuits and the Cartesian philosophy of the Oratorians and the
Jansenists. For Condillac taught no philosophy but his own, no
logic apart from that of mathematical physics, and no cosmology
but the Newtonian. The Prince concluded his first two years of
study by reading the selections from the Marquise du Châtelet's
edition of Newton, Cotes' preface to the second edition of the
Principia itself, Voltaire's letter on Newton and the second part
of his *Eléments de la philosophie de Newton,* and excerpts from
the books of Maupertuis. In subsequent years the Prince's mathe-

54. Ibid., p. 421.

matical, scientific, and technical education was continued by Keralio, who taught him arithmetic, algebra, geometry, hydrostatics, hydraulics, astronomy, geography, and military architecture. His whole education was capped by the performance of a course in experimental physics by two anti-Cartesian monks of the Order of St. Francesco di Paula, Père le Sueur and Père Jacquier, imported from Rome for the purpose, and by the study of differential calculus.

In between Condillac's own teaching of elementary popular science and the more advanced scientific training given by his colleagues, came Latin, more French literature, and a great deal of history. Latin instruction proceeded by the approved Jansenist method of waiting until he had a thorough grasp of his own language before beginning the second, and of not teaching him words that represent ideas he does not understand. Following at first the method of interlinear translations and good French paraphrases developed by Du Marsais, Condillac and Keralio guided the Prince through the conventional list of Latin authors: Horace, Vergil, Ovid, Livy, Cicero, Caesar, and Tacitus. Since, wrote Condillac, he knew his own language well and learned Latin by comparing it with what he knew, the Prince learned Latin easily and developed no distaste for it.[55] In these years—that is to say, at the ages of nine and ten—the Prince's knowledge of French literature was further extended by reading all of Voltaire's plays, as well as the *Henriade* and the *Essai sur la poésie épique,* additional plays of Corneille and Molière, and all the plays of Regnard, and rereading all the plays of Racine.

More interesting than the literary program is the six-year course in history which occupied the major part of the Prince's attention from his eleventh year to the end of his education. Again, Condillac was not an innovator in introducing history to his course of study. The Oratorians had done so too, and Bossuet's great *Discours sur l'histoire universelle* was written for the Dauphin. Condillac also wrote his own text—the twelve-volume *Histoire ancienne* and

55. Ibid., p. 422.

Histoire moderne—which gives us an opportunity, in passing, to
see how he understood history and for what purpose he thought
it should be taught.

To begin with, history is a source of lessons, especially for someone with a ruler's responsibilities. Condillac's history is full of
didactic admonitions: "The study of history, Monseigneur, will
make you aware of the injustice of most wars." "The unhappiness of
so many centuries, Monseigneur, must teach you how important
it is to judge things by what they are in themselves. It is above all
the duty of a sovereign to unravel the truth in the middle of the confusion created by the passions of men and the interests of parties."
"You see, Monseigneur, that this system [stoicism] leads only to
enthusiasm."[56] For Condillac believed that it was the Prince's
business to dominate the historical process, which he could only
do by understanding it. The process itself he saw in two forms: the
progress of the human mind and an ever-recurring cultural cycle of
barbarism, enlightenment, and barbarism again. Each stage of enlightenment achieves more than the preceding stages, so that man's
reason does make progress over the ages, limited and halting
though it may be. But in terms of any given nation, society, or culture—which is the concern of princes—it is the cycle, rather than
the progress, which is most apparent. Each culture must go through
the stages of the barbarism of innocence, enlightenment, and the
barbarism of luxury and decadence. But by understanding the
causes and relations of these cycles, a ruler may encourage or retard
them, as seems desirable. The cyclical mechanism may be found
in the interaction of three factors: revolutions of the mind, revolutions of customs and morals, and revolutions of government.

> Now by the morals of a nation is understood its habits,
> customs, and usages, considered in relation to the good and
> evil arising from them.
>
> You see therefore that manners and morals are subject to
> all the revolutions of the human mind. They are not the same

56. *Histoire ancienne*, in *Œuvres phil.*, 2, 98, 147, and 79.

among peoples who have always been barbarians, among those who are enlightened, and among those who have fallen back into barbarism. . . .

But as revolutions of the human mind produce parallel revolutions in manners and morals, revolutions in manners and morals produce parallel revolutions in government. Thus government depends upon morals, as morals depend upon the manner of envisaging human actions.

These three things being produced in this order react on each other in the contrary order. I mean that the government influences morals, and morals influence the manner of thinking.[57]

An effective ruler who understands these forces can control them to some extent and therefore control the history of his nation and the happiness of his people. The extent to which a prince does this determines whether he is worthy to rule.[58]

His whole instruction of the Prince in history—from the Creation to his own time—was presented in the light of his cyclical theory and his didactic purpose. In the tradition of Voltaire, Condillac understood history to include not only war and politics but the customs of society and the life of the mind. Indeed, if anything, he gave more space than Voltaire to cultural and intellectual developments. The final long chapter of his history is an account of the revolution in letters and science since the fifteenth century.

Thus ended the education of a prince *en philosophe* and *en géomètre*. The Duchess Louise-Elizabeth had indeed nothing to reproach herself with. This was scarcely a dangerous education. There were few novelties in it, and as always, Condillac carefully, if unenthusiastically, observed the proprieties of Catholic orthodoxy. Nevertheless, it was a program conceived in a new spirit, certainly contrary to that of the Jesuits, who would have liked to educate

57. "Introduction à l'étude d'histoire," *Œuvres phil.*, 2, 9. The ideas expressed here were undoubtedly drawn from Dubos and Condillac's brother Mably.

58. Ibid., p. 10.

the Prince of Parma. As a case study in the application of Condillac's philosophy, it is incomplete. One cannot quite see the connection between the order of nature as witnessed by Goguet's *Origine des lois* and the French classic drama. Still, the program *is* Condillac, with all his strengths and weaknesses, his areas of originality, and his baffling moments of obtuseness. The Prince was his real-life statue-man, and if he did not live up to expectations, it was not altogether Condillac's fault. Humanly speaking, Condillac comes through the pages of the *Cours d'études* as a patient, tactful, and considerate, if not exactly inspiring, teacher. Given these virtues and the Prince's inherent mediocrity, his system probably worked as well as any other.

9. Nature, Need, and Value: Economics as an Analytic System

> The object of a science is, properly speaking, a problem which, like all problems to be solved, contains known and unknown factors. In the science of economics the known factors are the means that we know to be effective in producing abundance in some areas, the unknown factors are the means remaining to be discovered for producing abundance in all ...
>
> Among the means of producing abundance, I see first the cultivation of land. But, if agriculture seems necessarily to begin before commerce, it is certain that it can be perfected only insofar as commerce is established and extended. Thus a perfected agriculture, that is to say, one which produces the greatest abundance, presupposes commerce. Commerce presupposes exchange, or, what is at bottom the same thing, purchases and sales. Purchases and sales presuppose that things have a price, and price presupposes that they have a value.
>
> These are the known factors. However confused they still are, I at least see clearly in what order they rest upon one another; and this order ... shows me that the value of things is the first idea to be developed and defined.[1]

It went against the grain of Condillac's solitary temperament to become identified with a sect or movement, or to allow himself to be drawn into the turbulence of public controversy. Nevertheless, in the years following his return to France he devoted his attention to a subject of acute public concern and violent partisan debate: the principles of political economy. In the France of the *taille* and the

---

1. *Le Commerce et le gouvernement* (hereafter cited as *Commerce*), in *Œuvres phil. de Condillac*, 2, 247–48.

tax-farmer, of the monopoly and the *douane,* of bad harvests and bread riots, this was no abstract or academic matter of interest only to armchair theorists or salon dilettantes. The prosperity of the great merchants, the livelihood of the *petite bourgeoisie,* and the very survival of the lower classes depended upon the wisdom and soundness of the economic policies pursued by the government, and it was precisely these policies which were at issue in the conflict of divergent interests, mutually hostile cliques, and opposing schools of thought. In the center of the conflict stood the physiocrats, who, as advocates of a sweeping reform of the nation's economic structure, offered the greatest threat to those who feared the consequences of change, and the greatest promise to those who hoped that economic reform would be the salvation of France. It is perhaps too much to say that Condillac "fought side by side with his physiocratic friends for economic freedom"[2] during his second period of residence in Paris—one who lived so much in retirement could scarcely have been in the thick of the fight—but he did form personal and intellectual connections with them which bore fruit in 1776 with the appearance of the quasi-physiocratic work *Le Commerce et le gouvernement considérés relativement l'un à l'autre.*

The birthplace of physiocracy[3] was the Court of Versailles itself, where François Quesnay—physician-in-ordinary to the King, by grace of Mme. de Pompadour—presided over gatherings of friends

2. Paul Meyer, *Etienne Bonnot de Condillac: Ein Wegbereiter der ökonomischen Theorie und des liberalen Gedankens* (Zurich, 1944), p. 13.

3. The name was not bestowed upon the movement until 1767, when *La Physiocratie* of Dupont de Nemours appeared. Until then, and often thereafter, Quesnay's followers were known simply as the "Economistes." The substantial body of literature concerning the physiocrats is dominated by the four comprehensive works of Georges Weulersse, upon which I have relied heavily: *Le Mouvement physiocratique en France de 1756 à 1770* (2 vols. Paris, 1910); *Les Physiocrates* (Paris, 1931); *La Physiocratie sous les ministères de Turgot et de Necker (1774–1781)* (Paris, 1950); and *La Physiocratie à la fin du règne de Louis XV (1770–1774)* (Paris, 1959). Weulersse, incidentally, believes that Quesnay, "great lover of Greek and of made-up words," must have invented the term "physiocracy," even though it was Dupont who gave it currency *(Les Physiocrates,* p. 21).

and followers in his suite, known as the *Entresol*. Here Quesnay zealously propagated the economic principles he had first begun to develop for the *Encyclopédie*,[4] and which he had given final, though brief, form in the *Tableau économique* of 1758. His growing circle of disciples included the elder Mirabeau, whose *Philosophie rurale* (1763), written in collaboration with Quesnay, became the "Pentateuch of the . . . sect";[5] Pierre-Samuel Dupont de Nemours, who, as secretary to the intendant of Soissons, helped to infiltrate the administrative class; the brilliant King's advocate at Orléans, G. F. Le Trosne; P. Mercier de la Rivière, a former colonial official now retired from public affairs; and the Abbé Nicolas Baudeau, founder of a journal modeled after Addison's *Spectator*, the *Ephémérides du Citoyen*. Quesnay could also count as allies the former disciples of economist Vincent de Gournay (d. 1759), notably Morellet and Turgot.

The importance of a new school of economic thought was underlined and encouraged by the economic condition of France in the mid-eighteenth century. The burden of taxation for the Seven Years' War—coming at a time when France had not yet recovered from the strain of supporting the foreign and domestic glory of the Sun King—fell with especial severity on those least able to bear it, the peasants and the artisans. Their distress was aggravated by a periodic scarcity of grain that drove the price of bread—and they ate little else—violently upward. Indeed, the critical condition of French agriculture, plagued by bad harvests and hampered by trade restrictions and poor farming techniques, was the source of gravest concern to the reformers. French industry, stifled in its growth by regulations inherited from the corporate economy of the Middle Ages and expanded by the power-oriented policies of mercantilism, could not catch the tide of industrial revolution at the flood, but lagged in the stagnant backwaters, passed up by the surge of progress.[6]

4. In the articles "Fermiers" and "Grains."
5. Weulersse, *Les Physiocrates*, p. 9.
6. See Henri Sée, *La France économique et sociale au XVIIIᵉ siècle*

The physiocratic program called for far-reaching changes in the economic policies of the state, based on an analysis that may be fairly described as the first attempt to comprehend the economic order as an objective system. The physiocrats assumed that economic activity is a part of the order of nature and that it will, if allowed to operate freely, follow the laws of nature to the maximum advantage of society. Governing the operation of these laws of nature as applied to economic life are the two concrete principles of self-interest and the sole productivity of agriculture. Self-interest dictates the economic choices of each individual, and in a competitive market these choices will fix wages and prices at their "natural" level. The level of prosperity of any society is determined by the state of its agriculture (which, for the physiocrats, meant all extractive industries, mining as well as farming), which alone yields a product in excess of the cost of production, and which, therefore, is the sole source of wealth. From these principles the physiocrats derived their reform program: the diversion of capital from industry to agriculture in order to encourage farming on a larger and more efficient scale, thus increasing production; the freeing of all branches of commerce, and especially the grain trade, from duties and restrictions; and the replacement of the burdensome and complex system of taxation by a single tax to be imposed upon the net income from land.

In the 1760s the pressure of the nation's economic problems and the persistence of Quesnay's evangelizing activities bore fruit in government policy, both locally and nationally. The formation of *sociétés d'agriculture* throughout France served to promote the new doctrines in the provinces and to encourage improved agricultural techniques. Many of these societies worked in close collaboration with sympathetic local officials, such as the intendants of Limoges (this was Turgot), Soissons, and Caen, and the Parlements of

---

(Paris, 1925), for a brief but lucid discussion of the general economic condition of France, and his *L'Evolution commerciale et industrielle de la France sous l'ancien régime* (Paris, 1925) for a more extensive discussion of the problems confronting industry.

Toulouse, Rennes, Grenoble, Aix, and Rouen. As a result of this activity, in certain localities commercial restrictions were relaxed and such onerous burdens as the *corvée* were dropped. At the national level the new emphasis on agriculture was signaled by the creation of a special committee responsible for French agricultural policy. Beginning in 1764, the royal government issued a series of edicts and declarations which established the liberty of the grain trade, slightly simplified the tax structure, and limited the stultifying privileges of certain monopolies and corporations. As might be imagined, this change in the direction of French economic policy raised up powerful enemies, especially among the commercial and industrial classes. The inevitable opposition received a powerful assist when the years following 1764 saw a series of bad harvests, making bread scarce and driving up prices. The lower classes, most immediately affected by this stroke of bad fortune, held the new economic policies of the government responsible, and public opinion turned powerfully against the physiocrats. The Encyclopedists, who had blown hot and cold on the subject anyway, now lined up clearly in opposition. In January 1767, when Condillac returned to Paris, the physiocrats were in retreat, protesting in vain that bad harvests and not free trade were the cause of the population's distress.[7]

Condillac arrived in Paris with his interest in political economy already awakened. Guillaume Dutillot, the Prime Minister of Parma, had encouraged the economic development of the duchy during the years of Condillac's residence with a policy combining features of mercantilism, physiocracy, and the ideas of Gournay. For his private library he snapped up the writings of Gournay, Quesnay, Mirabeau, Dupont, and the rest almost as soon as they appeared. Moreover, in imitation of the activities of the *économistes* of France, he saw to it that Parma had her own *société d'agriculture*.[8] Situated at the Court as he was, Condillac could hardly have escaped being aware of these developments. His interest in them is

7. Weulersse, *Les Physiocrates,* pp. 18ff.
8. Meyer, *Condillac,* p. 8 and nn. 1 and 2.

indirectly confirmed by his known contacts with the Italian political
economists, Beccaria and Gherardo, and by the emphasis placed
upon economic matters in the two *Histoires* of the *Cours d'études*.[9]
Thus, upon finding that political economy and the doctrines of the
physiocrats were the talk of Paris, Condillac needed only free time
to take up these issues seriously—and free time he had in abundance
once the problems connected with the publication of the *Cours
d'études* were out of the way.

It is not too much to suppose that the final stimulus provoking
Condillac to write *Le Commerce et le gouvernement* was the appointment of his old friend Turgot to the office of Controller
General.[10] Certainly *Le Commerce et le gouvernement* turned out
to be, among other things, a lively defense of the policies of the
Turgot ministry at a time when it was under heavy attack and near-
ing its fall. Moreover, Condillac's independence of the doctrinaire
approach of the physiocrats echoed that of Turgot, who also held
himself aloof from the sect, even while sharing many of its ideas.
To an outsider like Grimm, Condillac's book appeared to be one
more presentation of physiocratic doctrine—one which, owing
to its author's eminence, the physiocrats should welcome.[11] But to
the members of the sect themselves *Le Commerce et le gouvernement* was an exercise in heresy. It was bitterly denounced by both
Le Trosne and Baudeau as a betrayal of the "Master."[12] In fact,
the book was enormously eclectic, full of hints of the physiocrats, of
Gournay and Turgot, Richard Cantillon, Locke, Galiani, Graslin,
Morellet, and Condillac's brother Mably. And yet the book has an
originality to it, an originality which is pure Condillac and which
perhaps reveals itself first and most strikingly in its method.

9. Ibid., pp. 9–10.

10. Turgot may even have been responsible for Condillac's final success
in getting the *Cours d'études* published in Paris in 1775. See above, p. 13.

11. Grimm, *Correspondance littéraire, 11,* 54.

12. See Auguste Lebeau, *Condillac économiste* (Paris, 1903), pp. 37–39.
Lebeau quotes in full Baudeau's "Observations économistes à M. l'abbé de
Condillac" from *Les Nouvelles Ephémérides,* April 1776 (see Lebeau,
App. II, pp. 432–45).

Le Commerce et le gouvernement is of special interest as an example of Condillac's distinctive method, of its character and its defects, because it is Condillac's only systematic theoretical venture outside the realm of those philosophical inquiries which served as the basis of his method, even while they represented applications of it. That is to say, there is a kind of methodological reflexiveness, as it were, a constant self-referential factor, in Condillac's studies of psychology, epistemology, language, and education, because he is in those studies simultaneously working out, applying, demonstrating, and confirming his methodological principles. In his study of economics, on the other hand, Condillac was using his method—by now surely in its most mature and evolved state—to discover and expound the principles of a subject which did not itself have anything to do with the principles of method. Here for the first time is a genuinely external application of the method of analysis, making it possible to see it in action.

It will be recalled that Condillac defined language as "nothing but an analytic method." This phrase is the key to his approach to economics, for he states that his object in *Le Commerce et le gouvernement* is to supply a conspicuous lack in economic literature —namely, to create a language appropriate to economic science.[13] In order to do this, Condillac undertook a genetic analysis of economic activity which was the exact equivalent of his genetic analysis of psychological activity in the *Traité des sensations.* In both cases he employed a fiction: an abstract model freed from the distracting and confusing complexities of real life, the development of whose functions he could trace from their origins to their full growth, attaching precise names to these functions as he came to them. In the *Traité des sensations* the abstract model was the statue-man, and the functions were sensation, attention, memory, comparison, and so on—each becoming for Condillac a psychological concept whose meaning was clearly limited by the analysis. In *Le Commerce et le gouvernement* the model is a small, newly

13. *Commerce*, in *Œuvres phil.*, 2, 242.

formed, and isolated community, dependent for its material survival on its own industry and techniques. Out of Condillac's "observation" of the developing economy of this *petite peuplade,* as it learns to provide for itself with increasing efficiency, come the precisely determined economic concepts of abundance and scarcity, value and price, wealth, exchange, monopoly, and the rest.

Condillac understood these economic concepts as he understood the psychological activities of the statue-man—as abstract functions. He defined them in terms of specific actions taken and judgments made by his model community as it looked after its material needs. Moreover, he regarded these actions and judgments in as limited and abstract a context as possible by taking them at what he supposed to be their original, most primitive state—the way they were, or must have been, the first time they occurred, before they had been modified by extraneous habits or distorted by the pressures of a more complex culture. Thus, for example, he arrives at a functional definition of "price" by describing what happens when two members of the community—one having grown more wheat than he can consume but having no wine, the other having a surplus of wine but lacking wheat—become aware of each other's situation: "When we make each other offers, we bargain. When we agree, the bargain is struck. Then we consider that a *septier* of wheat is worth to you what a cask of wine is worth to me. This valuation that we make of the wheat in relation to the wine, and of the wine in relation to the wheat, is what is called 'price.' Thus your cask of wine is for me the price of my septier of wheat, and my septier of wheat is for you the price of your cask of wine."[14] This may be compared to the definition of "desire" derived from the statue-man's primitive experience:

> We could only feel ill, or less well than we have been, by comparing our present condition with those through which we have passed. The more we make this comparison, the more we feel the restlessness that makes us judge that it is

14. Ibid., p. 249.

important to change the situation. We feel the need of something better. Soon memory recalls to us the object that we believe could contribute to our happiness, and in that moment
the action of all our faculties is diverted to this object. Now
this action of the faculties is what we call *desire*.[15]

Condillac's attempt to establish a precise vocabulary for economics led him sometimes into simplistic definitions which brought
upon him the ready scorn of Baron Grimm. Referring to Condillac's
assertion that the place to which one brings the commodities one
proposes to exchange is called "market" *(marché)* because bargains
(marchés) are proposed and concluded there,[16] Grimm exclaims:
"That is admirable! Ah! if only we had studied sooner to know all
that!"[17] While one cannot but smile in sympathy with Grimm's
reaction, it might be somewhat misplaced. For it is Condillac's
whole point that a language properly made *is* self-evident and
obvious, that every word of such a language clearly reveals the
ideas it stands for. Thus, what he is trying to do in his step by step
establishment of economic terms, in which he does not neglect even
the most commonplace word, is to pattern the development of his
economic science after man's actual experience. The term "market"
may belong to everyday usage and appear to need no definition—
least of all Condillac's definition—but it stands for a complex idea,
and for Condillac the only way to understand a complex idea is to
analyze it into its simple ideas. Moreover, the best way to do that is
to begin at the beginning with the simple ideas and follow their
development and combination as they occur in experience.

As in the *Traité des sensations*, Condillac claimed that he was
following an algebraic method, proceeding from knowns to unknowns,[18] but, again as in the *Traité des sensations*, this claim is
more a salute to his methodological ideal than it is a real description
of his own procedure. However, the form of *Le Commerce et le*

15. *Extrait raisonné du Traité des sensations*, in *Œuvres phil.*, 1, 327.
16. *Commerce*, in *Œuvres phil.*, 2, 251.
17. Grimm, *Correspondance littéraire*, 11, 55.
18. *Commerce*, in *Œuvres phil.*, 2, 247.

gouvernement is a partially successful attempt to build a system of economics according to the prescriptions laid down in the *Traité des systèmes*. Condillac adheres with some fidelity to the two requirements of a valid system: that it rest on a true principle, which is a fact verified by experience, and that every part of the system be connected in a causal relationship. The true principle on which his economic system rests is that value, which is the most fundamental economic category, depends upon and varies with need, which is the most fundamental psychological category. He provides his customary kind of empirical verification for this principle through his hypothetical observation of the behavior of the members of his fictional community. He builds up the details of his system by continuing to observe the community in action in order to discover and demonstrate the causal chain from the most basic economic activities, involving only a simple exchange of such necessities as wheat and wine, on up to the complex operations of banking, credit, and government regulation. The whole system—although he does not say this himself—seems intended to be reducible to the identical proposition, "need equals need."

If need is at the root of man's economic activity in Condillac's system, then we must inquire into his definition of need. Here it appears that a governing principle of Condillac's entire economic theory is that it is opinion, not fact, which determines everything. This is made clear from the very beginning, when he discusses the economic condition of his community in the most basic terms—i.e. whether it has an abundance or a scarcity of food:

> If a people could judge with precision the relationship between the quantity of wheat it has and the quantity it needs for its consumption, this known relationship would always make known, with equal precision, whether there is an abundance, a superabundance, or a scarcity.
>
> But it cannot judge this relationship precisely, for it has no means of being assured exactly either of the quantity of wheat it has or of the quantity it will consume . . . .

Nevertheless . . . it is always true to say that it believes
there is an abundance, when it thinks it has enough wheat to
eliminate all fear of want . . . and that it believes there is a
scarcity, when it thinks it does not have enough to dissipate
[all its fears]. It is therefore in the opinion of quantities,
rather than in the quantities themselves, that abundance, super-
abundance, or scarcity is to be found.[19]

Thus, at the most elementary level of economic organization, what
matters is not the actual relationship of the supply of a given
commodity to the community's need for it but the community's
opinion of that relationship. This principle remains valid as the
society grows more complex. Every man's economic actions arise
from his judgment: of his own needs, of the relative value of
commodities, of the likelihood of stability or change in the market,
of the advantage he may gain by selling or withholding his goods,
and so on. His judgment may indeed turn out to have been mistaken, but that is irrelevant, except as a corrective factor in the
judgments that will govern his future actions.

The sovereignty of opinion for Condillac displays itself most
strikingly and most consistently in his theory of value, which, in
turn, is the point about which the remainder of his economic doctrines revolve, as well as being the point that separates him most
markedly from the physiocrats. For Condillac value is not a quality
belonging to the object valued, but exists only in our judgment of it
and varies as our judgment varies. This notion precisely parallels his
theory of knowledge, in which the material characteristics of a body
likewise do not reside in the body (at least so far as we can form
any clear ideas about the matter), but exist in our perception of
them. Economic value, then, like the material world, is a subjective
phenomenon. The equivalence of the two doctrines can perhaps
best be seen in Condillac's own statements of them:

There is no doubt that there must be admitted in bodies
qualities that occasion the impressions they make in our

19. Ibid., p. 243.

senses. The difficulty that is claimed is to know whether these
qualities are similar to what we experience. No doubt what
causes us trouble is that, perceiving in ourselves the idea of
extension, and seeing no inconvenience in supposing something similar in the bodies, we imagine that there is also to be
found there something resembling perceptions of colors, odors,
etc. This is a precipitate judgment, based only on this comparison, and about which in fact we have no idea.[20]

People tend to regard value as an absolute quality, which is
inherent in things independently of the judgments we make,
and this confused notion is a source of bad reasoning. It must
be remembered that, although things have a value only because
they have qualities which make them fit for our use, they would
have no value at all for us if we did not judge that they in fact
have these qualities. Their value, therefore, is principally in the
judgment we make of their utility; and they have more or less
value only because we judge them more or less useful, or with
the same utility we judge them scarcer or more abundant.[21]

Condillac's theory of value reflects his theory of knowledge not
only in its subjectivity in a general sense but, specifically, in the
very source and nature of the judgments involved. We judge a thing
to have value because we can use it; that is, it answers our needs,
which in turn are established in the first instance by our physical
makeup. In the same way, the nature of our perceptual judgments
—the fact that they are made up of five distinct kinds of sensations, which nevertheless fit into a coherent whole that becomes
the material reality we project outside ourselves—is a function of
our physical organization. If we had other senses, we should perceive
the outside world quite differently.[22] If we had other needs, we
should value things differently; indeed, as we develop new needs, we

20. *Essai,* in *Œuvres phil., 1,* 9.
21. *Commerce,* in *Œuvres phil., 2,* 247.
22. *Essai,* in *Œuvres phil., 1,* 11.

do value things differently.[23] Thus, in both cases, attributes of things which are commonly supposed to have an objective and independent character are in fact entirely relative to us and to the way we are constituted.

Condillac's theory of value was a new departure in economic thought—a departure suggested by such contemporaries as the Abbé Galiani and Turgot, but not stated so clearly or maintained so consistently as by Condillac.[24] The emergence of a subjective theory of value in the eighteenth century is a fact of considerable significance both in terms of the history of economic thought and in terms of more general intellectual history. In the first case it is tied to the development of economics as an autonomous discipline, separated for the first time from religious, ethical, or even political considerations.

In the thought of the ancient world there had really been no economic philosophy as such, but only observations or rules about economic matters, expressed incidentally and piecemeal. The form of these rules and observations varied with the culture: for the Hebrews economic activity was subject to the same rigid and ritualistic codification as were all other aspects of human behavior; for the Greeks economic policy was thought to be subordinate to the pursuit of the good life, and any concern with it beyond what was necessary was regarded as a distortion of the moral ideal; the Romans tended to regard economic matters as juristic in nature, consisting of such legal relationships as the contract and the private ownership of property. In no case did these observations add up to an attempt to understand the workings of the economic order or to discover systematically rules that would raise man's economic level.

23. *Commerce,* in *Œuvres phil., 2,* 245.

24. Galiani, *Della Moneta* (Naples, 1750), of which large excerpts concerning value are translated in A. Dubois, "Les Théories psychologiques de la valeur au XVIIIᵉ siècle," *Revue d'Economie Politique* (Oct.–Nov. 1897); and Turgot, "Valeur et monnaies," *Œuvres de Turgot,* ed. Gustave Schelle (5 vols. Paris, 1913–23), *3,* 79–98. See Lebeau, *Condillac économiste,* pp. 311–19.

In the Middle Ages an economic philosophy developed, but it was thoroughly incorporated into the Christian world-view and subsumed under the heading of moral theology. In this context we find the clearest statement of an absolute and objective notion of value as a quality belonging to an object by virtue of the labor that went into its production, and the moral necessity of a "just" return for that labor. This general notion derived from suggestions in both Greek and Roman thought, but it formed the very heart of scholastic economics. In the sixteenth and seventeenth centuries the dominant approach to economics shifted from the moral philosophy of scholasticism to the political orientation of mercantilism. The mercantilists, regarding economic policy as an essentially amoral function of the power of the state, held an ambiguous view of value, in which they began to regard it as an extrinsic market phenomenon dependent upon exchange. In fact, the mercantilists looked at value in two ways—as an intrinsic quality depending upon man's needs and desires and the inherent fitness of things to gratify them,[25] and as an extrinsic quality, depending sometimes upon supply and demand, and sometimes upon the cost of production. In both cases value is something objectively determined by the operation of certain laws and relationships, but it has become a property that can change, instead of remaining, as in the medieval view, fixed and invariable.[26]

25. This view differs from that of Condillac by its omission of the subjective factor. The value belongs to the thing, even though it is determined by the relationship of the thing to need. For Condillac value belongs to the judgment made about that relationship. While for the mercantilists a thing may have value whether anyone thinks it has or not, for Condillac the opinion must exist in order for the value to exist, even though qualities of usefulness may in fact have to exist in the thing (like causes of sensation) in order to give rise to the opinion. Nevertheless, if the opinion is wrong (i.e. if the thing cannot in fact be used), the economic value remains. The object has value in the eyes of those seeking to acquire it and therefore has value (may be exchanged for something) for those seeking to sell it.

26. This necessarily sketchy and oversimplified account of previous economic thought is based on Lewis H. Haney, *History of Economic Thought* (3d ed. New York, 1936), chaps. 3–7.

The physiocrats distinguished between two kinds of value: value in use and value in exchange. On the whole, they paid little attention to the concept, but when they did, they concerned themselves primarily with value in exchange—a notion which they made very nearly synonymous with price. As such, they regarded value as a phenomenon determined entirely by the objective workings of the exchange mechanism, which functioned as part of the machinery of the natural economic order. In no sense did they see value, even value in use, as a subjective judgment or psychological phenomenon.[27] To make the concept of value a psychological concept was the achievement of those eighteenth-century thinkers—like Galiani, Turgot, and Condillac—who remained substantially independent of physiocratic dogma. Of these, only Condillac made it the heart of his economic philosophy, and it is the stress he placed on it, as well as the consistency with which he held to it, that both distinguishes him from his contemporaries and makes him a genuine forerunner of nineteenth-century economic thought, nearly all the schools of which agreed that value is a subjective and psychological concept, tied to utility and not to morals, and central to any sound economic analysis.[28]

The significance of a subjective theory of value for intellectual history in general is apparent in the relationship between Condillac's theory of value and his theory of knowledge. First of all, it marks the break, dating from the scientific revolution, between the world of "reality" and man's perception of the world, revealing the consequent philosophical withdrawal into man's mind as the only real world we know (whether considered in terms of fact or in terms of value), and whose contact with anything outside itself must remain an open question. At the same time, it marks the beginning of the fragmentation of the intellectual world into separate compartments, and specifically, the growing detachment from morals of the study not only of nature but of man himself. There are several stages to this process. Before the impact of Galilean science, the prevailing

27. See Weulersse, *Les Physiocrates,* pp. 216–18.
28. See Lebeau, *Condillac,* pp. 312–13.

world-view pictured a coherent cosmos in which economic values, perceptual judgments, moral concepts, religious acts, natural phenomena, and political relationships all fit together as parts of a given totality, whose ultimate meaning possessed a revealed and supernatural guarantee. In the seventeenth century this meaning was increasingly being sought within nature itself, which was still regarded as a coherent whole embracing both physical and moral phenomena. But in terms of practice and technique and the organization of knowledge, the different aspects of this whole were more and more separated from one another and studied as discrete units. The most highly regarded technique for studying any of these units came to be that which derived from astronomy and physics—namely, measurement—and wherever this quantitative technique was applied, the area studied became objectified or isolated from the world of human feelings and values. Economics participated in this process, and by the time of the physiocrats the concept of value, which for the medieval Christian philosopher was imbued with the notion of an absolute justice and belonged entirely to the fundamental moral structure of things, had become a mechanically determined quantity. Nevertheless, the physiocrats still regarded man as standing apart from the objective world of mechanized natural phenomena, by virtue of his autonomous reason, with which he could come to understand and control the external economic order. In the next stage, when value was made psychological, man's role in the economic order was implicitly objectified as he was reduced to a factor in that order. Instead of consciously controlling the economy by understanding it, man now unconsciously affected it through his opinions, including the misjudgments caused by his fears or his complacency.

Condillac stands squarely in the center of the fundamental ambiguity involved here. His exclusive concern with opinion points up the subjectivism and skepticism, bordering on solipsism, at the heart of his philosophy, and yet at the same time, as will soon be apparent, he restores an objective order of value through an appeal to nature, just as he had restored the order of reality which his epistemological subjectivism had so decisively called into question.

The contrast between Condillac's theory of value and that of the physiocrats is reflected in his discussion of the relationship between value and scarcity. There are those, he points out—and he means the physiocrats—who say that the value of an object is determined by its scarcity or abundance. But this notion puts the relationship backwards and makes the very ideas of scarcity and abundance meaningless by implying that there is some absolute quantitative measure involved. In fact, Condillac argues, a thing is scarce when we judge that we do not have as much of it as we need, and abundant when we judge that we have enough. Now these judgments do not establish value; rather, they presuppose it. That is, we must judge that we need a thing—i.e. that it has value to us—before we can possibly judge it to be scarce. Something we can do nothing with has no value no matter how little there is of it.[29]

On the other hand—and here a certain circularity begins to creep into the argument—Condillac cannot deny that the value of an object, although not created by its scarcity, is nevertheless affected by it. The fact is, Condillac concedes, we feel the need of something more acutely in time of scarcity than in time of abundance, therefore we attribute more value to it. Indeed, when there is a superabundance, so that there is more than we can use, the surplus may have no value at all, unless we can store it against future need. But future need cannot give as much value as present need, because we feel it so much less. Condillac's admission that scarcity and abundance cause value to vary thus does not really depart from his original contention that value is exclusively a function of need. "Since the value of things is founded on need, it is natural that a more keenly felt need gives to things a greater value, and that a less keenly felt need gives them less value. The value of things grows therefore in scarcity and diminishes in abundance." But, he goes on to say, "the

29. *Commerce*, in *Œuvres phil.*, 2, 246–47.

degree of value, utility being the same, would rest solely on scarcity or abundance, if this could always be known precisely; and then we would have the true value of each thing." Now this is somewhat confusing, because it suggests, in the first place, that there really is such a thing as "true value" if we only knew how to ascertain the precise relationship between supply and demand, and, in the second place, it appears to separate utility and need (by making utility an invariable, while need, presumably, is reflected in the variations of supply and demand), which he had previously made almost synonymous: "The value of things is therefore based on their utility, or, what comes to the same thing, on the need we have of them, or what still comes to the same thing, on the use we can make of them."[30]

This can perhaps be disentangled by the observation that Condillac is using the words "value" and "utility" in two ways, apparently without fully recognizing the fact, and that this ambiguity is, moreover, a derivative ambiguity resting upon one still more basic in his use of the word "need." Need, for Condillac, is sometimes an objective fact and at other times a subjective feeling. At first glance, he seems to be using value in two ways—as a certain quality (albeit a subjectively determined one) which has no real measure or variation but which we judge a thing simply to possess by virtue of the fact that we can use it; and, in a quantitative sense, as an attribute which, by its nature, does vary according to circumstances and can be measured.[31] But if we investigate the circumstances that cause value to vary, they turn out to be variations in utility, which upon still further analysis appear to rest upon the particular way in which he is thinking of need—the key to the whole problem. This is the way it works: man needs nourishment—this is an objective fact, and by virtue of this fact, anything which will nourish man has utility for him, and he therefore judges it to have value. In this sense both utility and value are simple qualities. At the

30. Ibid., p. 245.
31. See Lebeau, *Condillac,* pp. 323–25. Lebeau's analysis is that Condillac's use of *utility* is ambiguous, but I think the concept of need is still more basic.

same time, a commodity which in the abstract has this quality may not have it in a specific instance, if circumstances (such as super-abundance) end man's need for it. Thus wheat as such possesses utility and value for man, but a particular bushel of wheat, if it is in excess of the quantity men can consume before it rots, has no utility and no value, because it is in excess of man's need. In this case, too, in spite of the relative terms in which it is put, need is regarded as an absolute fact, upon which the simple qualities of utility and value depend.

Now consider what happens to value when it is derived from need, not as a fact but as a feeling. Condillac supposes a shortage of wheat in his community, a shortage of one tenth of the community's needs, and he remarks upon the reaction of the community to this situation:

> As they are complacent in abundance they fear in scarcity. Instead of one tenth which is lacking, they judge that they lack two, three, or more. They believe that they are on the point of having no wheat at all, and the lack of a tenth produces the same terror as if it were a third or a half.
>
> Once opinion has exaggerated the scarcity, it is natural that those who have wheat think of saving it for themselves; in fear of want they put in reserve more than they need. It happens therefore that the scarcity will really be total, or nearly so, for a part of the community. In this state of affairs, it is evident that the value of the wheat will grow in proportion as opinion exaggerates the scarcity.[32]

In these circumstances it is not the utility of the wheat, and not the actual need of the community for it, which grows or diminishes. Every bushel of wheat can be used, therefore every bushel has value in the simple sense. But every bushel is also the object of a greater quantity or proportion of desire—or *felt* need. No one person in fact needs more wheat than he needed in time of surplus, but since he

32. *Commerce,* in *Œuvres phil., 2,* 245–46.

feels his need more keenly out of fear that his need will not be met, he desires more intensely the quantity he does need, perhaps even to the point of forgetting how much he really needs and desiring an excess, and therefore he values wheat, both in general and in specific quantity, more highly. Thus value increases in response not to increased need-as-fact (utility) but to increased need-as-feeling (desire).

The increased value that a person places upon a bushel of wheat in time of scarcity means, among other things, that he will give more for it, which raises the question of the relationship of value and exchange. According to the physiocrats, one definition of value is that it consists in the relationship of exchange between one thing and another. Now presumably Condillac's quantitative concept of value would come close to this, but he explicitly repudiates it, on the same grounds as he repudiates the notion that value depends upon a degree of scarcity—i.e. that it reverses the order of ideas. Exchange does not create value; it presupposes it. For it is because things have value that people are willing to exchange them.[33] Even more precisely—and more clearly emphasizing the subjectivity and relativity of value—it is because people have *different* opinions of value that exchange can take place at all.[34] If what I buy from you did not have more value for me than what I give you for it, I would not make the exchange; and, of course, if you did not hold the opposite opinion, you would not make the exchange either. This is one of Condillac's most original and most hotly disputed notions: in an exchange each side gives less for more. The traditional notion was that in a fair exchange, equal value is given for equal value. But, according to Condillac, this idea rests on a false and absolute notion of value, or else value is confused with price. If value is properly understood as the esteem a person attaches to something because of the use he can make of it (or because of the need he feels for it), then it is clear that two people will attach different values to the same ob-

33. Ibid., p. 247.
34. Ibid., p. 273.

jects, and that in an exchange each party will give what he values less for what he values more.

The significance of Condillac's principle of value exchanged is even more apparent when one side of the exchange is in the form of money. For if Condillac's theory is valid, ten dollars may be at one and the same time of greater value than a certain quantity of wheat, and of less value. That is, to the buyer the ten dollars he pays for the wheat is worth less than the wheat, because he needs the wheat more. To the seller, on the other hand—who is selling his surplus over the quantity of wheat he can consume—the ten dollars is worth more, because he needs it to buy other things. This suggests that value only exists in individual minds, just as do color, distance, and shape in Condillac's epistemology. What we agree to call "red" may in fact be many different colors, as perceived in different minds. Likewise, what we agree to call "ten dollars" may be many different values, as compared to a commodity in different minds.

The physiocrats commonly used "value" and "price" to mean the same thing, and Condillac himself inadvertently slipped into this equivalent, thus confusing the issue somewhat. In his discussion of the relationship of value and price he returned to his qualitative notion of value: "As soon as we need a thing it has value; it has it by that alone, and before there is a question of making an exchange."[35] Price, however, is a concept belonging exclusively to the act of exchange, and is a means of measuring the exchange relationship between two things. Price, like scarcity and abundance, and like exchange itself, neither creates nor even measures value but presupposes it. According to Condillac, price measures value not in an abstract sense but in a specific comparison; that is, price is the measure of the value of one thing in terms of another. It is here that Condillac falls into the very confusion he criticizes the physiocrats for. In his theory price cannot even measure value in this comparative sense but instead expresses an agreed upon relationship which is quite apart from the relationship of value. The

35. Ibid., pp. 249–50.

equation: a certain amount of wheat equals ten dollars, expresses a price relationship, but in Condillac's theory this is not the value relationship. The latter must be expressed: a certain amount of wheat is worth more than ten dollars to one person, and the same amount of wheat is worth less than ten dollars to the other. Thus, while in any exchange there is only a single objective price, there are two subjective values. The price represents a kind of negotiation or bargain between the two values that does justice to both but is equivalent to neither.

Thus everything important in economics—including, as we shall see, productivity, labor, and money—rests on value, defined as a subjective opinion, which varies relative to the same object not only according to general circumstances but according to the person who has the opinion. The whole reduces ultimately to need, and the emergence of value out of need parallels the development of the human personality out of need as outlined in the *Traité des sensations*. It will be recalled that the statue-man's faculties were stimulated into activity by his experience of need—a physical condition expressed in terms of pain, which his will interpreted as desire and which impelled him to action to change his situation, assuage the desire, replace the pain with pleasure, and thus fulfill the need. As he repeated this process in many contexts and with respect to the several basic needs of the body, he was accumulating experiences, or sensations, which implanted themselves in his memory as clusters of associated ideas. These, in turn—as his experience grew and his store of remembered and associated ideas expanded— created new needs, because he developed an increased range and variety of sensations, both present and remembered, to compare and to prefer one over the other. This process is in reality nothing but the development, out of a universal human structure, of a unique individual, with a personality created from the particular com- bination of experiences that his needs and his environment have come together to produce.

The same process may be observed in the social and economic

activities of Condillac's *peuplade*. At first its members had only
those needs which their physical makeup dictated—most conspicuously, the need for food. A nomadic horde would satisfy those
needs as they arose, by hunting, fishing, and gathering wild fruit.
But there is a social process at work which begins to add new needs
or new forms of old needs. Once a society, however loosely constructed and rudimentary, has come into existence—as men, impelled by the helplessness of infants to form family units, and by
the discovery of the greater efficiency and security that cooperation
allows to form still larger units—there develops a need to preserve
the society. The nomadic horde becomes an agricultural community
which needs the greater security of a food supply produced by its
own efforts, and which also needs the more refined types of food
it has learned to create—cooked meat, baked bread, and so on.
Coincidental with these needs are the needs for a stable and
permanent shelter, for a wider variety of more durable tools and
pots, for a different type of clothing, for decoration, for more
sophisticated modes of social cooperation and economic organization, and so on. Such needs, although arising out of man's experience rather than preceding it, are no less pressing to him when he
has reached this stage of development, and they force him to seek
ever new and ever more complex ways of satisfying them, creating
ever new and ever more complex needs. Eventually (as will be apparent later), these needs wander further and further from the
course of nature, become really artificial needs, and lead to man's
corruption and society's decline. But at this particular point of
development, such needs still reflect a simple state of society, without luxuries or excessive rules and laws, and thus they constitute
progress. They also constitute history—the story of the unique
development and "personality," as it were, of the community. This
"personality," like that of the individual man, is composed of habits
the community has acquired in the course of its collective effort
to gratify its needs as they arose. Such habits include the values it
places on material things and the economic techniques it devises to

promote and expand the possession of things it endows with value, like the market place, the merchant's trade, minted money, banks, credit and exchange, and the rest: all are rooted in need.

Thus need is the fundamental spring of the mechanism of the social order for Condillac, and as such, it creates utility and therefore value. But there is another way of looking at the creation of value in society, and Condillac sets up another derivative sequence to account for it. Need, to be sure, creates value in the sense that it is our needs which determine what sort of things can have value for us. In another sense, however, *labor* creates value in that it is only through man's labor that the utility which things possess in the abstract becomes realized and that their potential value is actualized. Now this view is part of an attitude which separates Condillac from the physiocrats, because it is directly related to his notion of what constitutes, and what creates, wealth in society. At first he seems to line up with the physiocrats: "Wealth consists in an abundance of things having value, or, what comes to the same thing, in an abundance of useful things, because we need them, or finally, what is still the same thing, in an abundance of things that we use for nourishment, clothing, lodging, comforts, pleasures, amusements—in a word, for living. Now it is the land alone which produces all these things. It is therefore the unique source of all wealth."[36] But in fact Condillac's definition of wealth as an abundance of things having value opens up a whole new understanding of it. The physiocrats had regarded wealth as consisting in material stuff, and true productivity could only mean to bring into existence material stuff that had not existed before—specifically, by growing it or extracting it from the soil. Changing it did not count, because this did not increase the quantity and did not produce a surplus beyond the cost of the labor of change. But Condillac's introduction of value here, especially as he defined it, made it possible for him to deny the distinction (so dear to the physiocrats) between productive and sterile classes, and to explain that since both artisans and

36. Ibid., p. 255.

merchants added value to things, they created wealth, or, in other words, were genuinely productive. "It is the farmer who furnishes all the raw materials. But such raw material which . . . would be useless and without value becomes useful and acquires a value when the artisan has found the means of making it serve the uses of society."[37] Even the merchant who simply conveys things from one place to another adds value, by taking a surplus commodity from a locality where it has no value, because it *is* a surplus, to a place where it is needed and therefore does have value. Hence value is created where there had been no value, or less value, before.[38] Ultimately, then, utility, value, productivity, and wealth come from labor, and the wealth of any nation may best be measured not in terms of things possessed but in terms of work done, and this means the work of all: farmer, artisan, merchant, and even government, which, after all, provides the security and order without which economic activity—and therefore the production of wealth—would be impossible.[39] In this analysis Condillac, like Adam Smith,[40] reflects the pioneer thought of Richard Cantillon, who wrote: "The more Labour there is in a State the more naturally rich the state is esteemed," and supported his statement by working out the proportion of the population it is necessary to have employed to keep the rest in necessities, showing how labor beyond that proportion goes into those refinements and increases in commodities that make one state richer than another.[41]

Thus, far from being divided into productive and sterile classes, all citizens are mutually dependent for their economic well-being.

37. Ibid., p. 258.
38. Ibid., p. 263.
39. Ibid., pp. 314–15.
40. "Labour alone, therefore, never varying in its own value, is alone the ultimate and real standard by which the value of all commodities can at all times and places be estimated and compared. It is their real price; money is their nominal price only." *An Inquiry into the Nature and Cause of the Wealth of Nations* (I.5), ed. Edwin Canner (New York, 1937), p. 33.
41. *Essai sur la nature du commerce*, ed. Henry Higgs (London, 1931; 1st ed. 1755), pp. 87–91.

To dramatize this point, Condillac demonstrates that everything depends upon each class—the farmers, the proprietors, the artisans, and the merchants. It is, in fact, precisely the force of this mutual dependence which balances conflicting interests and divergent desires into a just order. Every man, if he could, would be a despot, but no one has the independence to be. So each gives up something in order to obtain the maximum benefit possible.[42]

Now this notion that labor determines the quantity of value and the wealth of the state led Adam Smith into an assertion about the relationship of population and prosperity which both Cantillon and Condillac rejected: "The most decisive mark of the prosperity of any country is the increase of the number of its inhabitants."[43] Cantillon had already suggested that the size of the population—which is, after all, different from the size of the active labor force—is not a measure of the wealth of the state, because it all depends upon how they live and how the quantity of goods is distributed among them. He cited the Chinese and the American Indians as two extreme examples of the density of population, neither of which, however, measures either extreme of wealth or poverty.[44] Condillac took up this idea, including the examples, and expanded it into a theory of optimum population which would be neither too small nor too large: "It is not then the greatest population considered in itself which ought to make us judge the prosperity of the state: it is the greatest population which, being considered in relation to the needs of all classes of citizens, is consistent with the abundance they all have the right to expect. Two kingdoms could be unequally populated, although their governments might be equally good or equally bad." China, for example, has an immense population, but the Chinese live only on rice and are nearly naked or dressed in cotton. "This great population thus proves nothing in favor of the government: it proves only that the land has

42. *Commerce*, in *Œuvres phil.*, 2, 300–01.
43. *Wealth of Nations*, p. 70.
44. *Essai sur la nature du commerce*, pp. 73–77.

great fertility, and is cultivated by hard-working men with few needs."[45]

Condillac is convinced, moreover, that there is a built-in mechanism in society regulating population—not, however, with the grim harshness of the otherwise similar mechanism described later by Malthus. But as long as the land can increase production in a community, the population will naturally increase—only to the saturation point, however, which will vary according to the tastes of the community. Thus it does not condemn humanity to a permanent level of bare subsistence; if a community has more needs, it will simply stop increasing, or even decline in numbers, sooner than another community with fewer needs.[46]

A large portion of *Le Commerce et le gouvernement* was devoted to a discussion of the economic activity engaged in by contemporary society. Here the effect of Condillac's method was significant. Following his characteristic functional and genetic approach, he sought to re-create the process by which the basic mechanism of the social order brought about the development of the specific economic machinery familiar to civilization. That is, he sought to describe the steps by which the pressure of need stimulated the response of creative labor, producing things of utility and hence of value, and through this experience creating ever new needs, demanding more creative labor, and so on, as well as to point out that this progressive process produced not only material things but techniques to facilitate the distribution of things. Thus Condillac presented a quasi-historical, or even quasi-anthropological, analysis of the invention of economic techniques quite similar in style to his discussion of the origins of language and art. And like his theories of language and art, his theories of economics were deeply affected by his method. His view of such fundamental aspects of economics as the division of labor, the market, money, the mechanism of exchange, and capital and interest was strongly conditioned by the fact that he understood each of them in terms of what he regarded as its probable origin.

45. *Commerce*, in *Œuvres phil.*, 2, 305.
46. Ibid., pp. 303–05.

This is most conspicuous in his analysis of the nature, function, and value of money. The mercantilists, of course, had regarded money—i.e. gold and silver—as the only real form of wealth, and this basic assumption was a governing factor in their advocacy of such economic policies as exporting as much (in goods) and importing as little as possible. Condillac, in common with the physiocrats, regarded this assumption as a delusion. But there they parted company, because, of course, the physiocrats simply substituted agricultural products for money as the only form of real wealth, while Condillac regarded any valued (i.e. useful or needed or desired) commodity, or even the labor going into such a commodity, as real wealth. Condillac viewed money as fundamentally just another commodity, but one with a special use and function in the economic machinery of any society beyond the most primitive. The invention of money was nothing more nor less than the invention of a standard measure by which the exchange of commodities in a more complex society could be facilitated. In principle, this measure could have taken any form. It took the form of metal, because metal, owing to certain specific attributes, was most convenient. Metal, however, became money only because it was already merchandise—that is, it already had a recognizable value dependent on its potential utility as tools, ornaments, and so on. The change from mere merchandise to money was a revolution, not because something altogether new had been created, but because a new technique had been found which was of revolutionary importance in the economic progress of society. Money, then, was metal whose value had been enhanced by the enhancement of its utility.[47]

Because the unique value of money rests on its use and not on its essence, Condillac argues that the nation's prosperity is to be measured not, as the mercantilists would have it, in the amount of money it possesses but, rather, by the extent to which its use facilitates commerce. In other words, it is the circulation of money in the society which is important, not the mere possession of it. Now the

47. Ibid., pp. 268–69.

amount of money in effective circulation may vary widely, depending on such factors as the size of the community, the size of individual enterprises within it, distances between places trading with one another, the use of credit as a substitute for the physical transfer of money from one place to another, and so on. Condillac sums this up by discussing the relationship between the reservoirs and the channels serving circulation. The reservoirs exist primarily in the towns, where money is spent and needed in relatively large quantities. Tenant farmers, proprietors, merchants, and artisans act as the means by which this money gets from the reservoirs into the channels. Condillac's analysis, as he acknowledges, follows that of Cantillon quite closely.[48]

The circulation of money, of course, involves the mechanism of banking and exchange, and here Condillac reflects a prejudice of his age in a violent denunciation of the banking profession—the only economic activity on which he passes a moral judgment. He charges the bankers with taking special advantage of their information regarding fluctuations of exchange from one time to another and one place to another, to manipulate interest rates (i.e. the price of money), and to obscure the workings of the exchange by veiling it in a jargon understood only by them. Thus a mechanism which is in reality quite simple and could be understood by anyone appears to be a mystery, and the bankers exploit the merchants who must depend on them for capital or credit or privileges of exchange.[49]

Nevertheless, Condillac has no animus against the business of money-lending as such. Since money is really just another commodity, there is no reason why it cannot be bought, sold, or rented like any other, and in Condillac's view this is what money-lending amounts to. He points out that the casuists who condemn lending money at interest do not condemn lending merchandise at interest, and that the legislators who forbid the former are even worse because they condemn it legally but tolerate it anyway. In both cases they do not really understand:

48. Ibid., pp. 274–77. See Cantillon, II.3–8.
49. *Commerce*, in *Œuvres phil.*, 2, 281–82.

The error into which the casuists and the legislators fall comes
solely from their confused ideas. In fact, they do not condemn
exchange, and they do condemn lending at interest. But why
would money have a price in one and not in the other? Are
lending and borrowing anything but an exchange? If, in the
exchange, one exchanges sums which are at a distance of place,
in lending or borrowing does not one exchange sums which are
at a distance of time? And, because these distances are not of
the same kind, must it be concluded that exchange in one case
is not exchange in the other? One does not see, then, that
lending at interest is to sell; that borrowing at interest is to
buy; that the money one lends is the merchandise that is sold;
that the money one must return is the price that is paid; and
that the interest is the income owing to the seller? Certainly,
if people had seen in lending at interest only merchandise,
selling, and income, it would not have been condemned; but
they have only seen the words "loan," "interest," "money," and
without taking into account what they mean, they have judged
that they ought not to go together.[50]

On the other hand, there are occasions when lending at interest is
bad, both morally and economically. Odious interest is that which is
excessive because it is unregulated by the mechanism of supply and
demand, taking advantage of the necessities of the borrower, rather
than making a mutually profitable transaction with a businessman
who sees an opportunity for genuine gain.[51] Interest of this kind,
which Condillac specifies as usury, is closely related to the problem
of monopoly, which likewise escapes the salutary regulation of
supply and demand, and exploits human necessity. Basically,
Condillac defines monopoly as "to sell alone." But in this sense it is a
neutral word describing an economic fact which may be good or bad
depending on the nature of the commodity sold. A monopoly in
superfluous commodities—his example is a painter who alone sells

50. Ibid., p. 285.
51. Ibid., pp. 286–87.

his own paintings—may be entirely legitimate and is certainly not harmful. In this case the price, even though it may be high, is not forced up at the expense of need, but depends on a free agreement between buyer and seller, since no one need buy a superfluous commodity at any price. A monopoly in necessities, on the other hand, is an unmitigated evil, and here Condillac's notion of what constitutes a monopoly is far more comprehensive. He argues that there is a monopoly in necessities whenever there are fewer merchants than there could be. This meant that all the commerce of eighteenth-century Europe was carried on by monopoly because the ubiquity of trade restrictions prevented the free expansion of competition in response to demand. In this situation prices are high—artificially high—and no one is free not to buy food, for example, if the price does not suit him. Only free trade could put an end to this undesirable situation.[52]

Condillac argues that the universal existence of monopolies is the result of a policy advocated by the mercantilists of each nation with the intent that each nation would increase its own advantage at the expense of the rest. Unfortunately, the real outcome of the policy gave no nation a genuine advantage but was injurious to all. The legitimate role of the state, according to Condillac, ought to be the protection of the free operation of the economic machinery rather than active interference in the machinery in a misguided attempt to protect itself and its citizens from the effects of free competition, both domestically and in relation to other countries. In a long section on the proper relationship of the government to commerce, Condillac catalogues "Injuries to Commerce."[53] They are nearly all acts of government: wars, customs and tolls, taxes on industry, privileged and exclusive companies, taxes on consumption, variations in money, borrowing by the government, regulation of the grain trade, and international jealousy. In all this, of course, he is in full agreement with the physiocrats, whose rejection of mercantilist economic policy he shared completely.

52. Ibid., pp. 294–95.
53. Ibid., pp. 330–55.

Now this raises the question of what Condillac regarded as legitimately owing to the state—that is, what kind of taxation, if any, is acceptable and just in his eyes. He and the physiocrats agreed that the government must have some income from its citizens in order to function. The physiocrats, starting from their basic notion that the only productive factor in the economy is land, argued for a single tax on the *produit net*—that is, the products from land over and above the cost of production. This, to them, was surplus and taxable, but nothing else should be taxed. Condillac has a similar, but not identical, idea—namely, that in the end taxation always falls back on the landowners, as the class that really puts up the money in society and therefore might as well be taxed directly. Salaried workers do not have the money to pay taxes and ought not to be required to. If any other classes are taxed, the landowners end up paying it anyway in the form of higher prices and wages. In a country that is not self-sufficient but depends on trade to live, the landowners will not be able to pay enough in public expenses, and the merchants will have to share the burden. But in this case the taxes are really paid by foreign landowners through what they pay to the merchants. In any event, Condillac here seems to feel that land is the ultimate source of wealth—but not of value.[54]

Philosophically, Condillac bases his case for a legitimate form of taxation on the classic eighteenth-century doctrine of the social contract:

> A civil society is founded on a contract, express or tacit, by which all the citizens agree, each for himself, to contribute to the common advantage.
>
> In general to contribute to this advantage, it is enough to be useful; and people will be useful whenever there is a state and they fulfill their duties to it.
>
> This manner of contributing is an obligation that all citizens, without exception, have contracted by coming together in the body of society.

54. Ibid., pp. 312–13.

A useless man is therefore not a citizen. A burden to society, he does nothing for it, and it owes him nothing.[55]

One of the forms the obligatory contribution to the common advantage takes is that of contributing, either by labor or by money, to the necessary public expenses. At the same time, Condillac, again in common with the physiocrats, upheld the notion of the sacredness of private property. But where the physiocrats regarded private property as virtually ordained of God and inviolable in the eternal scheme of things, Condillac based his theory on an "empirical" analysis of the historical origins of private property, which made it almost incidental, even accidental. Still, given the *fait accompli*, Condillac (unlike his brother Mably, who, also believing that private property was of human and historical origin, regarded it as an abuse and injustice to be abolished) believed that the right of private property ought to be respected. On the other hand, Condillac can speak of hirelings and day laborers as "coproprietors" of the produce of the land, whose share takes the form of the salary agreed upon.[56] His argument is that the ownership of land, which goes back to the actual divison made in the beginnings of society, is justifiably both hereditary and transferable. The result is that in time one man may come to own more than he can cultivate himself. Now while his right to the ownership of this much land is guaranteed by law and custom, he no longer owns all that the land produces, but owes some of it to those who work the land, who thus become coproprietors. The same divisions, Condillac goes on, exist in all great enterprises, which are made up of an owner, a manager, and workers. Thus, he concludes, all citizens by virtue of their work are coproprietors of the wealth of society, just as all citizens, by virtue of joining themselves to society, have an obligation to be useful to society.

In general, throughout his analysis, Condillac took a point of view that stressed the relative, the subjective, the historical, and the

55. Ibid., p. 311.
56. Ibid., p. 266.

empirical. He presented value as a relative measure springing solely from individual and subjective judgments. Both the workings of the economy and the existence of such perennial absolute abstractions as property rights and the social contract he justified or explained in empirical terms as resulting from a historical process, rather than as part of an absolute and given order of things. Yet Condillac ultimately returned to a rationalist, objective, and even absolute world-view in his appeal to nature as a moral norm for society. The key to this appeal is his distinction between "natural" and "artificial" needs. Natural needs are "a result of our makeup: we are made to need nourishment or not to be able to live without food." Artificial needs are "a consequence of our habits. Something which we could do without because our makeup does not create a need for it, becomes necessary to us by habit, and sometimes as necessary as if we were constituted to need it."[57]

Society occupies an ambiguous ground for Condillac in his distinction between the two kinds of needs, for its existence leads him to extend the concept of natural needs far beyond that of mere physical subsistence suggested in his definition, to include needs which one would suppose to be a result of habit rather than of makeup:

> The first needs our community develops are of the essence of the social order, which would cease if these needs themselves ceased. One is therefore justified in regarding them as natural. For if they are not so to a wandering savage, they become so to man in society, to whom they are absolutely necessary. This is why I shall call "natural" not only the needs that result from our makeup, but further those that result from the constitution of civil societies; and I shall understand by the word "artificial" those which are not essential to the social order, and without which consequently civil societies could subsist.[58]

57. Ibid., p. 244.
58. Ibid.

Thus society can be regarded as an extension of nature, the preservation of which is as "natural" as the physical preservation of the individual. On the other hand, it is only in society that the needs that Condillac calls "artificial"—and tends to condemn—can arise. Thus society is both a legitimate creation of the natural man and the source of his corruption and downfall.

Parallel to his distinction between natural and artificial needs, Condillac makes a distinction between natural and artificial value; indeed, one springs from the other. Things possessing a natural value, like wheat, have the same value for all, because all need them equally. Things possessing an artificial value, like diamonds, begin by having value only for a few. "But because the rich would obtain things of artificial value only insofar as they gave in exchange things of natural value, it is a consequence that artificial value, at least indirectly, becomes a real value for all. It is thus that things, useless to the greatest number, end by being of a general utility when they are judged equivalent to a thing necessary to all."[59] This, however, is the door that leads a society into luxury, and from luxury to corruption. For things of an artificial value, which can never become available to all and yet which come to be desired by all, constitute luxury; and when luxury (or excess) is introduced into a society, it begins to change its character, to go astray from the ways of nature, and to end by becoming totally corrupt.[60]

There are three stages in the development of society from its primitive beginnings to its corrupt end: crudeness, simplicity, softness. Unfortunately, the very arts necessary to bring it out of crudeness and into simplicity—Condillac's ideal—carry within them the tendency to overripen into softness and then to decay and rot. Progress in the arts is, up to a point, quite reconcilable with simplicity and indeed may be necessary to ensure the community's prosperity by expanding the available number of occupations. But progress tends to push on in the direction of ever greater refinement and the creation of ever more artificial needs and values eagerly sought after.

59. Ibid., p. 247.
60. Ibid., pp. 244, 309.

"It is then that the citizens, far from contributing by their labor to raise and consolidate the edifice of society, seem on the contrary to undermine its foundations. Luxury . . . will draw the artisans away from the most useful arts; it will entice the husbandman from the plow; it will raise the price of the things most necessary to life; and for a small number of citizens who will live in opulence, the multitude will sink into misery."[61]

There are three types of luxury, which are of ascending degrees of destructiveness, but which all tend to the corruption of morals: the luxury of magnificence, which is the least ruinous because the things involved are of a durable nature and preserve their value, like gold and silver vessels, statues, paintings, and so on; the luxury of comfort, which is more destructive because it is more contagious, is within the reach of a greater number of citizens, and tends to grow as the style of living becomes softer; finally, and worst of all, the luxury of frivolities, subject to the caprice of fashion, which induces a society to pursue objects whose value by definition is only fleeting. At this stage the economic and moral health of the society has totally collapsed.[62] Here again Condillac was severely critical of the mercantilist view, which advocated the deliberate encouragement of luxuries in the state, provided they were domestically produced, as a means of promoting employment and increasing the possession of rich goods, especially gold and silver. Even Cantillon looked with more sympathy on the production of luxuries than did Condillac, as better than nothing to create employment.

It should be noted that Condillac says at one point that luxury is a relative term, depending on the particular state society is in. That is to say, what would appear to be luxury or excess to a wandering and naked savage—such as leather shoes or a permanent shelter—is scarcely so to a man in society. And what might seem luxurious to a man in an early stage of society—ornamentation of clothes, a design on a pot—cannot be called excessive later on. But it remains clear that Condillac is not advocating a simple relativism of values here,

61. Ibid., p. 308.
62. Ibid., p. 310.

because he does have, ultimately, an absolute standard against which true luxury, or excess, can be judged and condemned. This absolute standard is found embodied in his depiction of an ideal community —namely, a community living in a state of simplicity, which of course means living according to the dictates of nature.

Condillac's community reveals the pastoral fantasies of a simple man. In the first place, agriculture is its mainstay, even after towns have grown up. Agriculture, being man's first art and the one from which all others derive, necessarily promotes a sober and laborious life, and does not allow the "softening" Condillac so deplores. In the second place, the society will have very few laws, there being no surer sign, in Condillac's eyes, of the corruption of morals than the multiplication of laws, which tend to be increasingly less observed by the self-seeking populace and must constantly be replaced by ever new, ever more complex laws, which are still less observed. In the simple society, on the other hand, order tends to maintain itself, since there are few material temptations and a great sense of community solidarity is felt by all the citizens. Such genuine differences as do arise between members of the community may easily be worked out in assemblies of the heads of families—the only real government the society needs. Finally, there will be complete economic freedom in the community. In particular, everyone will work at the labor of his choice. There will be no restrictions, either by families, by guilds, or by limited apprenticeships, on the occupation of each. There will, however, be the regulation of free competition, which will keep any given work from being overdone and will channel individual talents into a distribution of work most advantageous for the community as a whole. Thus the state will be rich from the work of all, and the society will be free, prosperous, and happy.[63]

This state of society is "natural" for Condillac, given the characteristics of the "nature" which is his standard of judgment. First, it is physically natural. That is, the society is still close to the soil,

63. Ibid., pp. 306–07.

and primarily concerned with the problem of physical subsistence, of fulfilling man's most basic physical need of nourishment. Second, it is organizationally natural. That is, the very simplicity of the social order reflects the simplicity of the natural order: there are few laws, and it tends in general to be self-regulating. Finally, it is morally natural. Moral virtue seems to be a built-in trait, spontaneous and unreflective.

It will be noted that the mechanism here which controls the relationship between man and nature is precisely the same—expanded to the social level—as that which Condillac developed in individual terms in the *Traité des sensations* and even more explicitly in the *Traité des animaux*. Nature shows man the right path by the needs she gives him. As long as he pursues this path, as long as he limits himself to fulfilling and responding to the needs nature has created, both physical and social, he is conforming to the moral order. When he departs from this path, when he creates needs for himself beyond those given him by nature, he becomes corrupt. Thus the link between man's subjective, essentially relativistic experience and an objective, absolute order is to be found precisely in what had seemed to be the very source of subjectivity and relativism: his needs.

10. The Enlightened Society

> In politics there is no perfect equilibrium, and the moment
> one believes it has been reached is precisely the moment when
> the balance is going to tip.[1]

The moral power of the Enlightenment sprang from the conviction
that ideas make a difference, that the difference they make is in this
world, not the next, and that what is at stake is neither the soul's
redemption nor the mind's serenity but the temporal happiness of
the whole man and the whole of mankind. The collective mission
of the philosophes was the destruction of the tangible and intangible
obstacles to happiness which, as they saw it, the evil intent of a few
had engendered and the inertia and ignorance of the many had
allowed to persist and to grow until they pressed upon society with
all the weight of centuries of acquiescence. In this mission—this
warfare—ideas were the ultimate weapon. Behind the play of
words and wit with which the philosophes snapped and slashed at
the Old Regime, stood the ideas of justice and toleration, of liberty
and law, of human dignity and human decency, of natural reason
and a rational nature, informing even their most light-hearted sal-
lies with a seriousness of purpose and a substantial vision against
which the moral frivolity and intellectual corruption of the de-
clining Old Regime must stand condemned.

Condillac's role in the struggle for an enlightened society was
less than heroic. Circumscribed by the caution of his temperament
and limited by his far from passionate nature, he employed his
arid vigor to tilt against relatively safe targets. Nevertheless, on occasion he, too, turned his thoughts to problems of political and social
order, particularly during and after his tenure at Parma, which

1. *Histoire ancienne,* in *Œuvres phil. de Condillac,* 2, 103.

had made him a close observer for ten years of political power in action and inaction. Moreover, his responsibility for the education of a future ruler quickened his interest in the techniques of ruler- ship and, inevitably, the nature of ruling, and the relationship, in fact and in justification, between ruler and ruled. Thus, in the *Histoires,* for the edification of his young charge, he speculated about the origins of society, the basis and nature of law, and the problem and place of sovereignty—in short, the philosophical issues that were typical of political and social speculation in the eighteenth century. With his interest in such subjects awakened, Condillac ended his term as tutor and returned to Paris, to find the city in the midst of controversy over the government's economic policy—a controversy which focused on his old friend Turgot. In this situation Condillac came as close to a polemical writing as he ever did in his life. *Le Commerce et le gouvernement* was, besides being a state- ment of the principles of political economy as he saw them, a spirited defense of the policies of the Turgot ministry and an assertion that they would have worked to save the economic life of France if only Turgot had been allowed to carry them out thor- oughly and systematically. Condillac dropped his guard somewhat in *Le Commerce et le gouvernement,* but even so, the book scarcely amounted to an assault on the Old Regime.[2]

Condillac saw himself essentially as an educator, and his area of competence as the theory of thinking. His mission to mankind was to clear away the metaphysical obscurities and the ill-founded prejudices that get in the way of intellectual lucidity, and to point out, by giving a theoretical explanation of the workings of the mind, the way to think and to accumulate knowledge without being sidetracked or misled. He rarely ventured, before his experience in Parma, into political, social, or moral problems, except as they touched on psychology or might serve as concrete examples of his

2. See above, Chap. 9, for the main discussion of *Le Commerce et le gouvernement.* In the present chapter, discussion of the book will be confined to those aspects of it which reflect Condillac's social and political, rather than economic, philosophy.

theory of thinking. Thus the major works of his early years refer
only occasionally and by indirection to the issues that seemed so
burning to Condillac's fellow philosophes. In the *Essai* he referred
in passing to the interaction of climate and government in the
creation of national character. In the *Traité des animaux* he discussed the concept of natural law and man's clear knowledge of his
duties as a citizen and a man, in order to show that man is more
than, and other than, an animal, in spite of the similarities of their
makeup. The most interesting and important of these incidental
forays into political and social philosophy occurs in the *Traité des
systèmes*, where he discussed, as one example among many, systems
in politics—their nature and necessity, good ones and bad ones,
and how the magistrate should use them to best effect. From these
scattered statements, direct and indirect, it is possible to discover
that Condillac, too, had a vision of an enlightened society—a vision
which had more in common with Montesquieu and even Burke than
with Voltaire or d'Holbach or Mably. It was a vision distinguished
by its fundamentally conservative character and by the fact that it
was educational and didactic in spirit rather than critical or
prophetic. Above all, it was built on Condillac's overriding preoccupation with method: how to think correctly about problems
of politics and society in order to act appropriately.

In his political writings Condillac relied heavily on the hypothetical empiricism so characteristic of his thought: a search for
the principles of society in its origins, which tends to become a
theoretical reconstruction of the origins of society on the basis of
principles already given, a half-conscious drift from inquiry into
what society has been to assertions about what society must have
been. Thus, concluding a description of the growth of religion and
government in the ancient Near East, Condillac observed:

> If my conjectures are not an exact picture of what happened
> in times so little known, they at least show you the effects
> that the general character of the human mind must have
> produced in the circumstances we have supposed men to be

in. You have seen the origin of laws, idolatry, and monarchies. You have seen the origin of royal power, which at that time included the legislative power, the priestly power, and the command of the army. Finally, you have seen the origin of everything that combines to form civil societies.[3]

The mixture of frank supposition, concealed supposition, and implied empiricism in this statement points up the genuine difficulties the eighteenth century encountered in trying to develop a valid methodology of the social sciences. Convinced that to understand anything we should look to its origins, Condillac was forced to deal with the fact that the origins of social institutions are largely lost in the obscurity of time. In the absence of sufficient empirical data, he tried to work out a fruitful method employing conjectures, but he insisted on plausible conjectures, not mere fantasies. In order to construct such plausible conjectures, he used the familiar technique of proceeding from the known to the unknown. The most certain knowledge Condillac possessed was that all men share a structure, a mode of experiencing, and a set of basic needs. These constitute man's "general character," a universal human nature which is "the first cause of events."[4] Therefore, by imagining human nature as subject to the conditions that we may reasonably suppose to have prevailed at the time societies were formed, we make the origins of social institutions accessible to investigation. Significantly, the measure of the usefulness of this reconstruction is its plausibility, not its historical accuracy. It does not matter whether things did in fact happen this way, so long as they *may* have done so: "By continuing to observe the general character of the human mind, and the circumstances in which men found themselves . . . we can make sufficiently plausible conjectures on the way in which the first civil societies were governed. If we are mistaken, we shall at least have the advantage of having studied government in its simplest form; and this study, preparing you to follow it in all the forms it

3. *Histoire ancienne*, in *Œuvres phil.*, 2, 22.
4. Ibid., p. 11.

can take, will give you a greater facility in making an exact idea of complex governments."[5]

"Government in its simplest form"—here is the key to Condillac's anthropological method. For to the eighteenth century the simplest form of anything was not so much a fact to be sought in time past—although it may also have been that—as an ideal construct of reason acting in the present. Whatever empirical data was available (e.g. the biblical record of ancient civilizations or travelers' reports of contemporary primitive societies) served to confirm or to illustrate a theory arrived at by other means. Condillac, along with some of his contemporaries, was engaged in the first tentative formulations of the technique of model-building—a technique which in time has become one of the major methods of the social sciences. The chief inspiration for this new technique, of course, was mathematical physics, which abstracts from the confusing and complex interplay of natural phenomena physical "reality" in its simplest form. Condillac's primitive society was one such abstract model. Another, in the *Traité des systèmes,* was his image of society as a machine—the classic form of eighteenth-century model-building. However, it was by no means the sterile and artificial mechanical model which critics of the Enlightenment are so fond of describing. There is in Condillac's machine-model an inevitable pattern of growth and decay which is certainly more organic than mechanical, even though he usually describes the process in mechanical terms; thus the simple machine of primitive societies becomes a complex machine as society advances, requiring a more elaborate set of springs to keep it functioning properly and to keep its parts in equilibrium. The social machine, in other words, is not static. It possesses a certain self-generating power. Machines are characterized by motion, after all, even though in the long run, in Condillac's historical perspective, the motion is circular or, at best, spiral. In short, the machine-model is no rigid application of an inappropriate metaphor but the creative borrow-

5. Ibid., p. 17.

ing of a set of relationships and images from an intensely productive discipline to throw new light on old problems. For its time, and given its limitations, this was an illuminating procedure.

Condillac's two models, primitive society and the machine, correspond to two distinct but overlapping problems of political philosophy. The first is the essentially ethical question of the end of social order, or, more precisely, the justification of political power. The second problem is the practical one of the best—that is, the most effective—means for achieving given social and political ends. The two questions meet when the determination of means emerges as more than a problem of pragmatic effectiveness for accomplishing certain purposes, to become in addition a problem of moral consistency with those purposes.

The first of these problems is simply the ancient one of might and right. How can the power of the state to compel a man against his will to behave in certain ways or to submit to certain deprivations be justified? This is a question of more than philosophical interest, because its answer, by setting the conditions of power, establishes its limits and its legitimate operations. Its practical consequence is to indicate whether an existing political situation is to be accepted, modified, passively resisted, or violently overthrown. The generally accepted answers to this question ceased to be convincing to a few thinkers in the seventeenth century and to most in the eighteenth. It was not so much that the traditional approaches to the problem had been disproven as that they had come to seem irrelevant. The argument from the divine will with its scriptural support: "the powers that be are ordained of God"; the argument from custom: "the mind of man runneth not to the contrary"; the argument based on an analogy of natural hierarchies: sun and moon, body and soul, head and members, and so on; the acceptance—optimistic or fatalistic, depending on one's temperament—of whatever is as right, or at least inevitable; the theoretical construction of an ideal society deduced from first principles—all these arguments, having contributed to the maintenance of a degree of stability in Europe for so long, could serve no longer. They were arguments appealing to authorities that no longer commanded universal respect, using a type of logic that appeared no longer valid, taking off from concepts and definitions that seemed to have not even the shadow, much less the substance, of reality. Appeals to Aristotle carried little weight after Descartes and Newton; appeals to Scripture or the Fathers rang hollow after Bayle. And as for tradition, was it not tradition which bestowed power and privilege on classes and institutions whose contribution to society no longer justified it (if, indeed, it ever had)? Was it not tradition which denied power and privilege to those very classes and institutions whose economic and cultural usefulness most demanded consideration? Under these circumstances, the mere age of a political order could not justify it. Nor, in an age in love with the methods of science, could the old deductive logic of classes and divisions compel assent. Who in the eighteenth century could be convinced by an argument that began with an abstract concept like justice or sovereignty, and from its definition deduced a political system? Such a system, even if geometrically perfect within its own terms, would have no bearing on the real world. To the men of the Enlightenment these arguments seemed to be the fantasies of a child or a madman, scarcely deserving serious refutation.

What was needed was a new beginning—one which truly began at the beginning by asking the crucial question: How did the power of the state come into existence in the first place? This was not a historical question. It did not intend an empirical investigation of man's remote past. The characteristic form of the answers to the question—a state of nature ended by a social contract—was not intended to represent historical fact (although it may, incidentally, have been a historical fact). The state of nature and the social contract were abstractions, arrived at analytically and intended to be instruments for further analysis. The state of nature, in all its variations, was determined by asking what there would be if there were no social or political order. The social contract, with its corresponding variations, was determined by asking what society and government add to this state of nature in order to end it, and

how and why. This line of reasoning was to open up a new understanding of the political order based on "facts," expressed in, or
perhaps symbolized by, the admittedly abstract state of nature and
social contract. The state of nature expressed the basic fact of
man's nature vis-à-vis his relationship to other men. The social
contract embodied the nature of the social order and man's obligation to that order. The difference between these abstractions and
the abstract concepts that figured in the older political philosophies
lies in the kind of definition they were given. Instead of being
defined in terms of other abstractions (e.g. Bodin's "citizenship is
subjection to a sovereign" and "sovereignty is supreme power over
citizens and subjects, unrestrained by law"), the social contract and
the state of nature were defined by describing an event or a state
of affairs and pointing to it: "Men lived in such and such a way—
that is the state of nature. Finding this way of life to be difficult,
they did such and such about it—that is the social contract." Thus
the terms were given a kind of empirical definition, a definition in
the form of a statement of fact, even though the state of affairs or
event described may admittedly have existed only in imagination.

Approached in this manner, the contract philosophy began in its
essentials with Hobbes in the middle of the seventeenth century,
gathered momentum after Locke through the eighteenth century,
and culminated in a series of revolutionary attempts to establish
might on a new right—the right of "the people" (variously defined) to consent to their government. That this is an outcome
which Hobbes would have regarded as perverse, illogical, and
destructive of the very end and essence of the contract, merely
points up the fact that not all contract philosophies were alike.
The chief variable factor was the state of nature, which every
man envisioned according to his special perception of man's nature
and the effect of society upon it.

By the time Condillac was thinking about the foundation of
society, it was a commonplace to begin with the state of nature
and a social contract, so he quite naturally adopted these notions
as the starting point for his analysis. But the imaginary character

of the state of nature was even more explicit in Condillac than in other writers. He did not try to describe it in concrete terms as if it had once been a way of life. All we can mean by the state of nature, he argued, is man abstracted from all social relations and considered solely in terms of the qualities intrinsic to his being.[6] Thus the state of nature, rather than figuring as a difficult and dangerous situation to be resolved by the formation of society, appears instead as a summation of those inner forces which impelled man to live in society from the first moment of his existence. Likewise, the social contract does not figure as an event, either real or imaginary, in Condillac's analysis. It is a legal fiction expressing and justifying the moral relationship among men, which society, by its very existence, implies.

Man in the state of nature is free but frail. He has certain natural needs which must be met if he is to survive, but each man's natural faculties are inadequate to the task if he must fend for himself. He has no superior but the God who created him; and his liberty is unlimited except by his weakness and by the fact that he does not have the right to get in the way of another man's equal right to self-preservation. Owing to man's individual weakness, the effect of such equal and unlimited liberty is equally injurious to all.[7] In short, men in a state of nature "are not as yet linked by any engagement; but all need to be helped, and all also have the power to give help."[8] To put it another way, man in a state of nature is man in need of society.

Society, then, springs from the cooperation that results from man's nature and circumstances, and this cooperation is symbolized by the idea of the social contract. The contract was never an explicit action; it was never deliberated on or its terms spelled out. It is, rather, a tacit agreement among the members of society by which they each limit their liberty in return for a measure of security. Each is pledged to do nothing injurious to another and to join with

6. Ibid., p. 122.
7. Ibid., pp. 15, 122.
8. Ibid., p. 123.

the others in the protection of each. Although Condillac occasionally writes about the contract as if it were an event,[9] this is merely figurative. He in fact regards the contract as implied in the behavior of men toward one another, impelled by feeling, not reflection, from the moment they are in contact with one another:

> They did not need to reason as I hypothesize, but the circumstances guiding them reasoned for them, so to speak. The obstacles they found in the way of their preservation when they were separated were enough to bring them together. Once brought together, they felt the need of acting in concert. Acting in concert, they all cooperated for the good of all, and from that moment, each of them limited his liberty, or rather, none had the time to realize that he had a right to unlimited liberty.[10]

The essence of society, then, is cooperation, and the essence of the state of nature is the need and the impulse to cooperate. For this reason, in Condillac's analysis, the social contract is not so much an act of renunciation, putting an end to the state of nature, as it is a direct expression and fulfillment of the state of nature. In other words, society and the state of nature are by no means in opposition to one another, although, as we shall see, society may in the course of its development go astray from the norms that the state of nature and the laws of nature justly establish.

Condillac unequivocally places the social order on the moral foundation of a natural law given and guaranteed by God. It is for the natural law to establish the form, rather than prescribe the content, of all morality. It is, simply, the will of God and cannot be defined more precisely. It becomes explicit, however, in two sets of natural laws (natural laws being distinguished from the natural law): those which establish rights and duties for man even in the

9. For example, "Society was formed when . . . each of them pledged to do nothing contrary to the welfare of all, and . . . all pledged to jointly protect each" (ibid., p. 16); and, "As soon as [the contract] was passed, each member was protected by the entire body of society, and society itself was protected by the united strength of all its members" (ibid., p. 123).

10. Ibid., p. 16.

state of nature, and those which are the basic conditions of all social organization. Man's very first obligation is, oddly, one which he cannot at first observe—the obligation to worship God. Knowledge of the one divine creator upon whom man depends for his existence does not come without reflection and sophistication. Since neither man in the abstract state of nature nor primitive man in the concrete historical past has .this knowledge, the first obligation remains ineffective until a later stage of social development. The other natural laws, however, are binding from the start. In the state of nature there are two such binding laws: all men are equal, since no one has any superior but his creator, and all men have an equal right to self-preservation, which no one has the right to interfere with. These laws are the foundation of all justice and may be reduced to the simple statement: each may only do to others what he would have them do to him.[11] These natural laws, then, establish the conditions of man's relationship to God and man's relationship to man prior to any agreement he might make or custom he might establish. Indeed, his agreements and his customs derive whatever validity they have from their correspondence to the first natural laws.

But if the natural law, the will of God, is manifest in the abstract rights and duties laid upon man even in the state of nature, it is even more manifest in man's need for society and in the basic conditions that permit a social order to exist. These conditions, stated in the imperative mood, become a second, a derivative, set of natural laws: the tacit conventions of primitive society. Such conventions are the same from one society to another, because they spring from man's nature, and because, without them, no society could continue in existence. Condillac finds five basic and universal rules binding upon men in society: (1) not to injure one another, (2) to be faithful to commitments, (3) to join against a common enemy, (4) to respect the security of person and property, and (5) to oppose whomever would disturb the established order. The observation of these rules is "the essence of civil society." Condillac explains how he came to

11. Ibid., pp. 122–24.

know this: "We shall discover [the usages] belonging to all times and all climates if we consider that men formed societies only because they felt the need of mutual help. Then we see that in general they *must have had* as rules . . ."—and the five rules follow.[12] It appears to be deduction pure and simple, beginning with the principle of society—the end for which it was formed. In fact, it is analysis and provides an example of the way in which analysis differs from a strictly empirical approach. Condillac does not, for he cannot, observe society in the process of formation, either directly or through evidence passed down from the event. He does not, for he would not, deduce the principles of society from an abstract First Principle given in the framework of a metaphysical system. Instead, he operates with a set of analytic abstractions—the elements out of which a viable, concrete society could be constructed.

The continued belief in a natural law, which was by no means peculiar to Condillac in the eighteenth century, ran up against epistemological difficulties. The natural law was essentially a rationalist conception. It has an a priori existence independent of human experience, and was traditionally made known to man by pure reasoning. Morality, society, and political order derive both their own existence and their validity from the preexisting natural law. Condillac provides one answer to the question of how such a belief can be reconciled with the eighteenth-century rejection of the rationalist metaphysics and epistemology in favor of empiricism.[13] He maintains the a priori ontological status of natural law as the eternal decree of God, but shifts the ground of man's discovery of it from reason (in the rationalist's sense) to experience.

It is essential to the character of natural law and natural laws that they be universally knowable. Most natural law theorists tended to make these laws—in keeping with their a priori character—accessible to man through something called his "natural reason," which appears to imply a degree of reflective thinking. Condillac, however,

12. Ibid., p. 96. Italics mine.

13. See Cassirer, *Philosophy of the Enlightenment*, pp. 243–48, for a discussion of this problem.

denies any role to reflection in the discovery of natural laws.[14] What makes them "natural" is precisely the fact that one need not reflect to follow them.[15] Circumstances, trial and error, the sanctions of pain and pleasure, all lead men into the tacit acceptance of the conventions on which society rests. But if man's reason no longer provides an open road to the discovery of natural law, man's nature does. There is a psychological congruity between man and natural law that makes its discovery certain and universal, except by those who do violence to their own natures:

> There is, then, a natural law; that is to say, a law having its foundation in the will of God, and which we discover by the sole use of our faculties. There are no men who are absolutely ignorant of this law, for we can only form a society, however imperfect it may be, when we obligate ourselves to one another. If there are those who want to ignore it, they are at war with all nature, and they are on bad terms with themselves; and this violent state proves the truth of the law they reject and the abuse they make of their reason.
>
> The means we have for discovering this law must not be confused with the principles that give it its authority. Our faculties are the means for knowing it; God is the sole principle from which it emanates. It was in him before he created man. It is what he consulted when he molded us, and it is what he wants us to be subject to.[16]

The faith of a rationalist-deist could not be more explicit. Yet, as an empiricist and sensationalist, Condillac must ground the psychological congruity between man and law in man's physical, not mental, makeup. He finds that, by and large, man tends to follow natural laws merely by obeying the promptings of his own nature—that is,

---

14. Except with respect to the prime obligation of worshiping God. Does this make it less prime than it appears?—an act of grace, as it were, on man's part, nice, courteous, but essentially superfluous?

15. *Histoire ancienne*, in *Œuvres phil.*, 2, 16.

16. *Traité des animaux*, in *Œuvres phil.*, 1, 370–71.

his needs and faculties. There is, in Condillac's scheme of things, a direct route from self-interest to that morality which is natural law. It is self-interest which makes us aware that we need help. Our need for help joined to our observation that others are in the same situation, and to our sense of identity with beings like ourselves, develops an attitude of reciprocity expressing itself in agreements on what behavior will be required, permitted, or forbidden. These agreements constitute the beginning of morality, which is, although not recognized as such at the time, the natural law.[17] Again, all this takes place without weighing the factors involved or spelling out the conditions. Men are guided into society and its conventions by sentiment.[18]

However, if it is unreflective sentiment, or instinct, which leads men to the discovery and observance of natural law—to its realization, so to speak, in their tacit conventions—it is also unreflective instinct which leads them astray. For society in its more advanced stages ought still to conform to the principles of natural law, but it does not. The ignorance and passions of men see to that: "The errors of men in this respect began with the first engagements, express or tacit, that they contracted. Guided by instinct they formed their laws the way they formed their worship; and if finally they have become enlightened in the art of governing themselves, it is only after having gone through many revolutions, and having recognized, in the calamities they brought upon themselves, the error of the prejudices they had taken for rules."[19] Where, it may be asked, does this leave the status of instinct? Is it a reliable or a false guide? Is reflection necessary, after all, before man can live virtuously or establish a just society? Perhaps the answer to the seeming contradiction can be found in Condillac's analysis of the development of our habit-systems in the *Traité des animaux*, and especially his analysis of the way disorders arise in our habit-systems. Man is made up of a complex set of idea-sequences which

17. Ibid.
18. *Histoire ancienne,* in *Œuvres phil.,* 2, 123.
19. Ibid., p. 122.

have developed at the instigation of the several passions. These sequences are the springs of action whereby the body obeys the commands of the soul, and, in general, man looks after his preservation. In theory, this process contributes to the development of a complete and well-functioning man, with all the faculties from sensation to reason operative:

> Nevertheless, disorder may occur in the habit-system of a man. It is not that our actions spring from several principles. They have only one principle, and can have only one. It is because our actions do not all work together equally for our preservation; it is because they are not all subordinated to the same end. And that happens when we put our pleasure in things that are contrary to our true happiness. Unity of goal joined to unity of principle is what gives to a system the most perfection possible.
>
> But because our habits multiply infinitely, the system becomes so complicated that it is difficult to have perfect accord among all the parts. The habits which, in certain respects, work together, injure each other in other respects. The bad do not do all the evil one could fear of them, the good do not do all the good one could hope. They fight against one another and this is the source of the conflicts we sometimes experience.[20]

Thus there is an ambivalence in man arising from his complexity. The very same forces which impel him unreflectingly toward the good become confused and contradictory and get in the way of the good. Societies are much the same. There is a parallel between the problems of the complex individual and those of the complex society. It is for this reason that while natural laws—tacit conventions—are adequate for primitive societies, they soon cease to be adequate as technological progress increases the needs of society and permits the appearance of conflicts for which there had

20. *Traité des animaux*, in Œuvres phil., I, 374.

previously been no occasion.[21] For it appears that even though the tacit conventions which form society are a direct expression of the natural law, there are certain inconveniences—Condillac goes so far as to call them "vicious"—inherent in the society organized on them alone. The viciousness lies precisely in the fact that they are tacit. No matter how reasonable, how essentially sound and just, these conventions are, their tacitness means that they are not clear enough, not precise enough, not familiar enough, to insure their consistent and continued observance. "Men adopted them without deliberation; they follow them by instinct. Men wander from them without meaning to, change them without having planned to, and they do not perceive the variations that develop."[22] Therefore these tacit conventions tend to become altogether arbitrary. Being susceptible of different interpretations and applications, it is not long before the most powerful members of the society begin to insist upon *their* interpretation and applications, which in fact are determined by their passions and caprices. Thus, if order and justice are to be preserved in society, natural laws must be made explicit, and their application must be developed and extended to cover situations arising in more complex forms of society than those in which the tacit conventions first appeared. Positive laws, then, are needed to implement and supplement natural laws.

The origin of the need for positive laws suggests the proper relationship between them and natural laws. Positive laws, if correctly made, are simply natural laws made explicit and related to a variety of concrete situations and relationships. But to make explicit laws, and above all to enforce them, requires a new entity in the social order: a sovereign.

Condillac's analysis of the concept of sovereignty tended to be empirical rather than normative. He is more concerned with how the sovereign does function than with how it ought to function. His definition of sovereignty, for example, is in simple de facto terms. Sovereignty exists in every society in which order is maintained. It

21. *Histoire ancienne*, in *Œuvres phil.*, 2, 17, 95–98.
22. Ibid., p. 98.

is that power which is respected by all. It makes laws and enforces them, and it makes war and peace. It may be divided, as in a republic, or it may be united, as in a monarchy. The sovereign is the physical and moral person to whom the sovereignty belongs. He represents the preponderance of private force.[23] Condillac made no attempt to relate the sovereign to the moral universe implied by the state of nature theory or to include him in the social contract. Rather, he assumes that as society grew too complex to subsist on tacit conventions, sovereignty—as a concrete function, not an abstract concept—appeared. If it did not, if no center of power respected by all developed, the particular society simply could not continue as a going concern, and no more would have been heard from it. The different types of sovereignty have reflected different circumstances, and no special merit, apart from circumstance, attaches to any one of them. What matters is that the sovereign be effective; that is, that he make and enforce positive law in such a way as to maintain order and ensure the security of goods and person which tacit conventions were no longer adequate to preserve.[24]

Although Condillac was not too concerned with the moral aspects of sovereignty, he did—almost inevitably—touch on the question of the limits of sovereignty. This, he pointed out, constituted a serious problem, for the burden is placed on the sovereign power to regulate itself. The aim of sovereignty is to ensure not only security and order but liberty, since genuine security cannot exist without liberty, nor liberty without security. A free government is one in which the sovereign power does not act arbitrarily and thereby endanger everyone's security, but is regulated by laws. Since, however, the sovereign is himself the source of all law, there are no laws but his own—subject to his own modification or repeal—to regulate him, which seems an imperfect and unreliable sort of control. One theoretical source of control is the classic French concept of *la loi fondamentale*. Condillac, who makes brief mention of the fundamental law, does not spell out its provisions or its source, but

23. Ibid., pp. 99–101.
24. Ibid., p. 116.

in general it may be regarded as a basic deposit of traditional law—the constitution, so to speak—which always has regulated, and therefore always should regulate, the fundamental political relationships of the state. Even if this law is held to be superior to the sovereign, however, there still is no force superior to the sovereign. The sovereign ought to choose to respect the limits of the fundamental law, but if he does not, there is no orderly recourse to correct it. History, says Condillac, is the story of the efforts of nations to break out of this dilemma.[25]

Since the sovereign power has, by definition—and, wherever order is maintained, in fact—a monopoly of power, it is apparent that there exists a danger of sovereignty becoming despotic. Condillac has as little use for abstract definitions of despotism as for those of any other of the traditional "types" of government. Despotism as it is traditionally defined is a vastly different thing from despotism as it works out in practice. It is customarily defined as a government in which the three powers—the legislative, the executive, and the power to make war and peace—are brought together in a single person who enjoys an absolute and arbitrary authority. He has sole proprietorship in the state; he may dispose of everything at will; he exercises over his subjects the power of a master over his slaves. In practice, such a system cannot exist, any more than total anarchy can exist. They are abstract ideal-types. Depotism is limited by the physical impossibility of exercising such absolute authority over everything and everyone at once. Condillac therefore modifies the definition of depotism to accord with reality: "what characterizes the despot is that he puts, as far as he can, his will in the place of laws, and that he does not acknowledge the fundamental laws which ought to serve as rules for him."[26] In reality, few people are directly affected by the despot's will at any one time, and those who manage to remain inconspicuous in society are left pretty much alone all the time. But all *feel* menaced, and justifiably so, for they have no protection against the despot's caprice should it turn against them.

25. Ibid., p. 101.
26. Ibid., p. 102.

Where there is no guaranteed liberty from the sovereign's will, or willfulness, there is also no security.

Here is the meeting ground of liberty and security, which Condillac like Burke, does not regard as polar opposites between which a just society must achieve a balance. For Condillac liberty and security are so interdependent as to be almost identical. In his view liberty means simply the absence of arbitrariness and violence, both public and private. A citizen does not possess liberty if he is not secure from arbitrary assaults on his person or property, whether they come by the authority of the sovereign or by the aggression of another private citizen. What is required to ensure the liberty of society, thus defined, is a sovereign power which is moderate and restrained, while being at the same time strong and effective:

> When the sovereign disposes of nothing arbitrarily, people enjoy what they have with security.
>
> Moreover, people do what they want, without being forced to do what they do not want. For, as long as the sovereign power is not arbitrary, it does not need to use violence to compel obedience . . . .
>
> It assures liberty, therefore, in the relationship the citizens have to itself; and, because it protects the weak, it also assures liberty in the relations the citizens have with one another. It is a power which makes the laws respected, which respects them itself, and under which no one can use violence with impunity.[27]

Condillac's equation of liberty with security sounds strangely out of touch with the most pressing problems of his age. One might think he was writing in the chaotic period of the Religious Wars or of the Fronde, longing for a Henry IV or a Richelieu, rather than under the oppressive calm of the reign of Louis XV. The notion of "liberty" in the Enlightenment conjures up visions of Montesquieu celebrating the legal guarantees of the British Constitution; of

27. Ibid., p. 101.

Diderot demanding recognition for the rights of passion in human life; of Rousseau calling for the liberation of the individual from the moral oppression of a corrupt and artificial society; of Voltaire crying out against the persecution of Calas and Sirven; and of all the philosophes fighting against the censors—or running away to live and fight another day. Condillac seems to be living in another world from theirs. It is true that one can easily argue that security from the arbitrary power of the sovereign implies a broad range of legal rights and civil liberties, but Condillac did not develop such an argument. Moreover, the only legitimate restraint on the sovereign that Condillac recognizes is the *loi fondamentale,* and that restraint leaves intact the whole legal and moral structure of the Ancien Régime: censorship, religious restrictions, the harsh and unjust administration of the criminal law, the legal disadvantages of the unprivileged classes, and the rest. Condillac's voice cannot be heard in the intellectuals' protest against the injustices of their society.

There is one exception to the silence and that exception does not speak loudly. Condillac did deplore the extremes of religious persecution. But in doing so, he held up no alternative ideal of freedom of conscience. His disapproval of intolerance was strictly limited to its more brutal forms: he was against violence, rather than for religious liberty. The "true religion," he argues, ought never to use violence, either as an offensive weapon against a dissident minority or as a defensive weapon against a hostile establishment. In the first case persuasion should serve; in the second, meekness and patience.[28] The methods of the Spanish Inquisition were genuinely odious to Condillac,[29] and King Ferdinand was to be condemned for having impoverished his country by his crusade against the Moors and the Jews.[30] But it must not be supposed that Condillac held the view that religious differences were entitled to respect as such. He agreed with the orthodox that heresy and idolatry were despicable,

---

28. *Histoire ancienne,* in *Œuvres de Condillac, 14* (23 vols. Paris, 1798), 290.

29. *Histoire moderne,* in *Œuvres de Condillac, 18,* 154–56.

30. Ibid., *15,* 296.

but "we are forbidden to hate the heretic, the Moslem and the idolator, and charity invites us to work for their conversion."[31] Condillac's unconcern for the principle of religious liberty is such that he sympathizes with the plight of the sovereign, who is responsible for religious policy. The Christian sovereign—responsible for the spiritual welfare of his people and for the protection of the true faith—must find a road between persecution and indifference. Toleration is no absolute virtue to Condillac, and only circumstances can determine the degree of toleration that a state may safely allow. The sovereign confronted by the necessity of setting the limits to toleration is likely to be confused by advisers urging him "either to indifference in the name of toleration, or to persecution in the name of zeal."[32]

Condillac has a few suggestions for the perplexed monarch. For example, the emperor Constantine might have moderated his policy of persecution, but he need not have permitted every religious practice. He could safely have suppressed any cult that was "contrary to good morals"; he should have silenced oracles where trickery was manifest, and prohibited "enchantments, magic, and all the grosser practices which were rather the abuse than the essence of the pagan religion."[33] For the rest, he should have relied on gentleness and persuasion to bring pagans to Christianity and Arians to the Trinity. Elsewhere, Condillac makes a distinction between policies toward internal religious innovators and polices toward whole nations of heretics and idolators. While the sovereign may attack innovators within his borders because they are a disruptive influence, he may not launch a crusade against a neighboring nation—or, presumably, given the references to Ferdinand, a well-established dissident community within the nation—on religious grounds.[34] A Luther or

31. Ibid., *18*, 72.
32. *Histoire ancienne*, in *Œuvres de Condillac*, 14, 303.
33. Ibid., p. 304.
34. *Histoire moderne*, in *Œuvres de Condillac*, 18, 72–73. "If you were sovereign somewhere, and an innovator undertook to spread a false doctrine among the people, you would be right to punish him, and even to put him to

a Mohammed (or a St. Paul?) should be silenced by his sovereign, but a Lutheran or a Mohammedan nation must be left alone.

In all this, much as he deplores violent means, Condillac is willing to assume that there is a true religion, that the religious unity of the nation should be maintained (although not by exterminating an already existing dissenting community), and that it is the sovereign's business to promote the true religion and to silence dissent. It is doubtful that anyone else bearing the title "philosophe" shared these sentiments. It may be objected that Condillac was himself limited by circumstances and could not have taken an open stand for religious liberty. All his references to the subject were in the *Histoires,* where he was instructing the future sovereign of Parma.[35] He may have felt that the most he could accomplish would be to instill in the young Prince a distaste for religious warfare and a willingness to deal with Protestant and Moslem nations on friendly terms (modest enough goals for the middle of the eighteenth century, when the international scene was governed by the realistic, nonideological principles of dynastic power politics). To promote genuine domestic toleration would have been, in this view, a hopeless goal, although secretly Condillac may have believed in it. Here one can only imagine what a Voltaire or a Diderot—both men eminently, although reluctantly, capable of caution if they felt it necessary—would have written in a similar situation. It may well be

---

death, if the nature of his crime merited it. Tolerance, in such a case, would be culpable. But because in Turkey the Koran is preached, would you undertake a war against the Turks until you had converted or exterminated them? Would you next march with equal zeal against the Persians, against the Indians, against the Chinese who are praised for their wisdom? Finally, still conqueror, would you overrun the earth, leaving only ruins behind you? You would then be the scourge of all the peoples who had not, like you, the fortune to be born in the true religion. Consequently you can live in peace with the Turks, without having to reproach yourself for a culpable tolerance."

35. The mere fact that he found no other occasion to mention it suggests a less than burning concern. Toleration was on the minds, and on the tongues, of all the other philosophes.

doubted that either would have spoken, seriously, of a "culpable toleration" or missed the opportunity to slip in some telling arguments, at least in a semidisguised form, for liberty of conscience. Condillac had the chance—and stood silent.

The inescapable fact seems to be that Condillac's political and social values were conservative values. His version of the enlightened society would have been neither an efficient, streamlined, benevolent depotism, nor a libertarian republic, but simply a wiser, more humane version of the Ancien Régime. He took for granted the constitutional organization of the Ancien Régime, not as a perfect system by any means, nor as existing by divine ordination, but simply as the system that exists in France. Actually, Condillac had no single ideal in mind for the organization of government or society. One must begin with what is there in fact, not with theories constructed in the mind. This pragmatic attitude toward existing institutions corresponds to his lack of interest in justifying sovereignty or placing it in some morally imperative place in the polity. For Condillac power is what it is and resides where it does. Sudden or radical changes in the life of a people will only shock them and promote resistance, thus breaking down the society completely, instead of effecting salutary reforms.

Certainly Condillac had no reservations about the legitimacy of social, economic, and political inequality in the Ancien Régime. He found inequality to be in no way incompatible with reason, justice, or the health of the state, in spite of the fact that society had originated in equality, that the social contract had presumed equality among its participants, and that the second natural law known and observed by men is that "all men are equal." Condillac regarded it as entirely acceptable that social conventions and positive law have modified this original law of equality. Indeed, he felt inequality to be the natural and inevitable result of a society grown more complex than the original, simple tribal order of the savage. The necessary division of functions in a more complex society, coupled with the unequal fruits of unequal labor and talents, must necessarily give rise to inequality of possessions, status, and power. So long as the one inherent and permanent equality of men—the equal right to self-preservation and the protection of society—is maintained, no injury is done to the natural law or to the rights of men.[36]

To be sure, social and economic inequality could give rise to certain evils tending to undermine the health of the society, and these evils must be guarded against. If wealth becomes a measure of esteem in the society, or, even worse, if it becomes the received opinion that one's talents and wealth are to be used for oneself alone instead of on behalf of the community, then civic virtue will be undermined and the society will decline. Further, if economic inequality becomes so extreme that those on the bottom are denied the very means of self-preservation, then a basic natural law is violated. On the other hand, within limits, social and economic inequality may be a positive benefit to the society. By stimulating healthy competition, by making it a source of self-esteem and public esteem to have more with which to serve the republic—more wealth, more talents, more industry, more prestige—the acceptance and encouragement of inequality can enable the state to draw on the best energies of its citizens, to command their expanded resources, and to prosper itself as its citizens strive to prosper for the sake of the state.[37]

Condillac's coolness toward social and economic equality is exceeded by his outright hostility to political equality. Indeed, he regards political equality as impossible to achieve and attempts to achieve it as destructive of good order. Democracy, for him, is by far the worst form of polity; after all, it was democracy that ruined Greece. Three elements underlie Condillac's unfavorable analysis of democracy: his notion of class as the political unit of society, his distrust of the multitude, and his belief in the necessity of a fundamental law which cannot be abrogated.

Condillac makes the rather startling statement that Solon, by giving the right of suffrage to all citizens, made an unequal division

36. *Traité des systèmes,* in *Œuvres phil.,* 1, 209; *Histoire ancienne,* in *Œuvres phil.,* 2, 123.

37. *Histoire ancienne,* in *Œuvres phil.,* 2, 118; *Histoire moderne,* in *Œuvres phil.,* 2, 155–56.

of the sovereignty[38]—unequal because the political unit of society is not the individual citizen but the class, and therefore Solon's disposition of the suffrage gave to the most numerous class, the fourth class of Athenian society, a preponderant, and unequal, share of the sovereign power. Condillac would have an equilibrium of power among the classes, so that the interest and welfare of each class is kept in harmony with the whole, with no single class overturning the balance in its own favor. This may be accomplished by the distribution of power among the classes or by the concentration of power in the hands of a single sovereign who is skilled in maintaining the equilibrium of the classes, and who is sufficiently above the contest not to be partial to any.[39]

Condillac's attitude toward "the people" was common to nearly all the philosophes (if one excepts Rousseau, and one must always except Rousseau). He regarded the multitude as capricious, driven by the passions and tastes of the moment, and incapable of holding a steady course regulated by reason, firm principle, or law.[40] He even refers to the people at one point as "a ferocious animal" requiring skilled but firm management by the magistrate.[41] If political power is parceled out equally to all citizens so that the mass of men control the state, the result must be a constant splitting into unstable factions—factions united by transitory issues and not by genuine common interest—and the continual change of the structure and policies of the government. In practice, even if the society has fundamental laws which are supposed to be inviolable, they will in fact be violated, so that there is no real regulation of the uses of power. There are no rules which the sovereign must respect and compel everyone else to respect. There is only caprice. Thus a democracy will necessarily tumble from revolution to revolution until it ends in either anarchy or slavery.[42]

38. *Histoire ancienne,* in *Œuvres phil.,* 2, 103.
39. *Traité des systèmes,* in *Œuvres phil.,* 1, 208.
40. *Histoire ancienne,* in *Œuvres phil.,* 2, 116–17, 128.
41. Ibid., p. 126.
42. Ibid., p. 103.

Condillac was more certain of the political orders he disliked than of those he liked, and in general he hestitated to lay down a single form for all times and places, believing that every people must develop its own best form of government according to its needs and circumstances—that is, according to the way geography and history modified the original universal human character. Nevertheless, if he had a preference, it was for a limited monarchy, and his chosen example of such a government was the rule of Pisistratus in Athens. By a limited monarchy he meant a government in which the power of the monarch was limited by fundamental laws that he was compelled to respect through the existence of other governmental bodies sharing power with him:[43]

> It is in such a monarchy that one is truly free. The license of the people has a check in the laws that the monarch makes them respect, and the license of the monarch has a check in the laws that the areopagus and the senate force him to respect. The citizens are safe from anarchy because it is not the people who govern. They are safe from despotism because the monarch does not govern with an absolute authority. Their liberty consists in being subject only to the laws, and as long as this government subsists, it can be said without fear of setting up a vicious circle, that the laws regulate the use of the sovereign power.[44]

More cautious than Voltaire or Montesquieu, Condillac did not point to defects in contemporary French political practice or cite contemporary political models, not even in his *Histoire moderne,* so one cannot be sure what he would have prescribed for France. But by transferring his exemplary moderate monarchy from ancient Athens to eighteenth-century Europe, it is not difficult to suppose that he had in mind something like the government of England, in which power is shared between the king and the parliament, or, closer to home, the government of France as it would have been if

43. Ibid., pp. 104–05.
44. Ibid., p. 104.

such fundamental institutions as the Parlements or the Estates-General participated effectively in the nation's sovereignty. At least we can be sure that he would not have prescribed the sharing of sovereignty with a significantly larger segment of the population, or a reconstruction of the French Constitution from the bottom up. When reform is necessary, he felt, conservative reform is the best policy.

The health of a society does not depend entirely on the soundness of its constitution or the efficacy of its fundamental laws. Of at least equal, perhaps greater, importance are the skill and wisdom of the magistrate. It is best, of course, if the ruler (variously termed king, minister, legislator, or magistrate by Condillac) has a good system to work with, made by himself or inherited from his predecessors. But all is lost if he is not adept at managing it. No political system will run smoothly or for long by itself.

The state as Condillac comments many times, is a machine, and the magistrate is its mechanic. Of course, the prosperity and stability of the state will depend upon how well the machine was put together in the first place. Do its parts harmonize and work together toward the optimum functioning of the whole? Do its gears mesh properly? Is friction among the parts kept to a minimum? But even the best machine needs supervision and occasional repair, and here the role of the ruler is decisive. How well does the magistrate-mechanic understand the system of the state-machine? If he made it in the first place, he probably understands it very well. But if he is not a Solon or a Lycurgus, if he is merely a successor to the original lawgiver, then he must work to understand it—to grasp its principle and see the arrangement of its parts and the force that keeps it moving. In less metaphorical terms, he must understand the division of the society into classes, what constitutes the interest of each class, and how to keep these interests in equilibrium so that no one class or order of society comes to dominate the policies of the state to the detriment of the rest. So long as he can keep the various interests of the state properly balanced, then will every citizen identify *his* interest with the general interest—a condition equally as necessary as the skill of the magistrate and the soundness of the system to the health of the state and the welfare of all.[45]

In time, every society will outgrow the system with which it began. The simple social and economic structure of primitive societies will inevitably be succeeded by the more complex structures caused by technological advances. These, in turn, will require more complex political systems to keep the parts in harmony. This means that at various times in the history of any society the magistrate-mechanic must be prepared not merely to manage the existing system well but to change it, perhaps even to replace it with an altogether new one. Almost certainly his innovations will be unpopular. For by and large, the mass of people tend to fear and resist change. They are governed more by opinion and prejudice than by reason, and they find it easier to cling to the ways of their fathers than to be flexible and imaginative enough to accept new ways, new ideas, new methods—always sources of insecurity. So the magistrate must have the courage to go ahead in the face of public resistance, the wisdom to understand just what changes ought to be made, and the tact to introduce innovations with minimal shock to the sensibilities of the people.[46]

How should the magistrate go about repairing or reconstructing a political system? What should be his guide, his models, his norms, and his method? He should not look to abstract theories or a set of absolute standards. Condillac holds no conviction that there is a universal political or social ideal to be found in the state of nature, the law of nature, social physics, or any other abstraction. The magistrate must understand *his* people, *his* society, and devise a system appropriate to *their* particular needs and circumstances. His approach, in short, must be pragmatic, concrete, empirical, and probably conservative and piecemeal; otherwise, if he attempts to impose theories or abstract norms upon his society, he courts disaster:

45. *Traité des systèmes,* in *Œuvres phil., 1,* 208–09.
46. Ibid., p. 209.

In order to make a system . . . he should not seek the most perfect government in his imagination. That would be only a fantasy. He must study the character of the people, investigate their usages and customs. . . . Then he will preserve what is found to be good, and replace what is found to be bad, but by means which conform most to the *mœurs* of the citizens. If the minister shocks them, it must be only on occasions when he has enough authority to prevent the troubles which naturally give rise to sudden revolutions. Often he will not try to destroy an abuse abruptly; he will seem to tolerate it, and he will attack it only by indirect methods. In a word, he will so well combine change with preservation, and with the power he enjoys, that change will come without being noticed, or at least with the approval of part of the citizens, and with nothing to fear from those who would be against it.[47]

Nevertheless, no matter how well-balanced the original constitution, how well-constructed the political system, how sound the changes introduced by the magistrate, or how skillful his management, every society sooner or later will decline. The stage of decadence can be delayed, just as the stage of enlightenment can be encouraged and then prolonged, but decadence cannot be staved off forever.[48] For Condillac subscribes to a cyclical view of history in which the stages of barbarism, enlightenment, and decadence succeed one another in the life of each society with the inexorability of the tides. The stage of barbarism is characterized by simplicity of social organization, limited technology, and the ignorance of the people. Progress occurs as they develop new techniques to make their material existence more secure, abundant, and comfortable, and as they develop a more complex social order, with positive laws to make natural laws more precise, with the division of economic functions and the distribution of political power. As the society

47. Ibid.
48. *Histoire ancienne*, in *Œuvres phil.*, 2, 96.

advances technologically and socially, new knowledge is acquired, so that understanding replaces ignorance and reason supersedes prejudice in the intellectual life of the society. However, the process of change neither stops at an optimum point nor continues to move upward. The progress of technology continues, but this ceases to be a blessing, because out of technological progress come new needs—needs which are not inherent in the nature of man or even in the nature of social man. Such "needs" are artificial, they involve luxuries, they bring greed, envy, and social discord in their train. As the simple civic harmony of earlier societies breaks down under the pressure of this new acquisitiveness and the wider range of economic divisions in the society, it becomes necesstry to devise ever more complex and restrictive forms of social and political organization to compel the semblance of harmony where the reality has vanished. Meanwhile the *mœurs* of the society have become totally corrupted by the pursuit of luxury—ever more refined, ever more delicate—on the part of the rich, while the poor sink into a level of poverty and destitution unknown to the era of primitive barbarism. The dominance of reason and understanding is supplanted by the reign of vice, of passions, and of caprice, until finally the society crumbles into anarchy or is taken over by a more vigorous society and reduced to servitude. This, in outline, is Condillac's view of social change and history. He offers no prescription for escape from the wheel, for he apparently regards it as built into the nature of things and utterly inescapable.[49]

The commonplace thesis that the French Enlightenment was a period of radical and abstract political theories based on a naïve faith in the goodness and perfectibility of man and in the inevitability of infinite progress cannot be supported by Condillac's views. Condillac has all the pessimistic realism of the political conservative. He has a keen sense of man's limits, of his imperfection, and of the inadequacy of theoretical constructions. He does not equate technological and moral progress. On the contrary, he feels that

49. Ibid., p. 17; see also p. 9.

after a certain point technological progress is a positive threat to moral progress.

In the end, for Condillac—and this is surely a conservative position—a society will only be as good as the citizens are virtuous and the magistrate is wise. No system can compensate for the moral failures of a society and its leaders, and no system can generate virtue in a corrupt society. On the other hand, where the citizens are virtuous and the magistrate is wise, almost any political system will work. But this is a condition both rare and fleeting. Condillac does not suppose that any society will ever be very good, so he offers no utopias in his historical reflections and social philosophizing. He offers instead a picture of chronic political instability, of human perversity and caprice, and of ignorance, prejudice, inertia, and an overriding tendency to corruption. Civil societies, he tells us, are slow to form and quick to be destroyed for the very good reason that men are perverse. They tend to hold blindly and obstinately to ancient customs at precisely those times when innovation is called for, and to reject traditional ways in order to chase after every novelty when stability and the maintenance of order are desirable.[50]

By the last years of his life, when he was revising his early works, Condillac had sharpened his pessimism about the possibility of social progress. Thus one reads in the *Traité des systèmes* a passage not in the 1749 edition but apparently written as a marginal note in the 1770s and added to the posthumous 1798 edition:

> Above all, it is necessary to see clearly. I mean, to see without prejudices, and that is just what is difficult, especially for sovereigns. For in a democracy, the sovereign has only caprices, in an aristocracy it is a tyrant, in a monarchy ordinarily it is weak and its weakness protects it neither from caprices nor from tyranny. If you run through the ages of history, you will be convinced of the maxim that "opinion governs the world." Now what is opinion if not prejudices? Therefore that is what guides sovereigns.

50. Ibid., p. 96.

Each government has its maxims, or rather each government has a way of proceeding which supposes maxims which it does not have, or does not know it has. It proceeds blindly, by habit, and without asking itself what it ought to do, it does what it has always done. Thus in general the nations are blind to their true interests, and hurl themselves against one another. Experience, which teaches all men, does not teach nations. Nothing can teach them. Still I do not claim that one ought not to try to enlighten them, for light will always produce some good effects—at least among nations that have preserved their *mœurs*.[51]

Condillac wrote this after the failure of the Turgot ministry, which no doubt made him even more pessimistic. Nevertheless, this dim view of the prospects of bettering man's lot through political enlightenment is by no means inconsistent with opinions expressed earlier. It may reflect a more deeply felt pessimism, a new discouragement, but certainly it does not signal a basic change of mind about the future of mankind. Still, he concludes with the brave words that one ought to try, even if only a little good will result. Enlightenment, after all, remained the Enlightenment's business, even when human perversity and apathy seemed to make it agonizingly fruitless.

51. *Traité des systèmes,* in *Œuvres phil., 1,* 209–10.

Epilogue: "Everything Being Connected . . ."

Condillac's philosophy—inconsistent, even chaotic, by turns radical and conventional, quasi-science and disguised fiction—was a philosophy caught and torn apart by the intellectual tensions of its age. There is a profound ambivalence in Condillac; indeed, there are at least two Condillacs—one for each horn of the Enlightenment's dilemma. There is the Condillac who seeks uncompromisingly to integrate man into the natural order as a creature of mechanical laws, and there is the Condillac who will sacrifice his intellectual integrity to preserve man's spirituality and uniqueness in a supernatural order. I would suggest, however, that there is a third Condillac—or, rather, that the first and real Condillac lurks behind and between these two expressions of his intellectual confusion, almost obscured by his uncomfortable empiricism and his tenuous conventionality: Condillac the rationalist.

Condillac is never more convincing, nor more intellectually attractive, than when he displays his genuine and deeply felt conviction that this *is* a rational universe. Deep in his heart he may well have had reservations about Catholicism that he did not let himself think much about. His religious assertions are always extraneous and often absurd. In his attempts at empiricism, on the other hand, he either lifted his material straight from Locke or forced his data (intuited, not experienced, data at that) into mathematical pigeonholes too symmetrical to accommodate an irregular concrete experience. But he understood and believed in causality, order, unity, and coherence. He loved the fact that the world is full of "systems"—man, animals, the planets, the principles of mechanics, the fine arts. These are all systems with parts related to one another in determinable ways, comprehensible, coherent, and elegant as an equation. Moreover, these systems are not atoms, coherent in themselves but unrelated to one another. They are themselves the parts of the whole universe, created and sustained by a rational and just God, whose confirmation of the cosmic order is reflected in the way the pieces fit together. Man is impelled by private instinct and by social need to sing and to dance, to chant and to draw, but when he reflects upon his activity, he discovers that nature has led him to create art, which may be classified into genres and which is governed by rules that he had known nothing of. Likewise, man learns entirely by the natural pursuit of pleasure to subject himself to moral laws, and then by reasoning about his experience and his situation, he learns that these very moral laws which he had arrived at by nature are really of supernatural origin. The supernatural cannot be reduced to nature for Condillac, nor in his sincerest utterances does it transcend or contradict the natural. Rather, the two are interlocked in a cosmic correspondence. The natural perfectly reflects the supernatural, and the supernatural expresses itself in the natural. Man himself, who is part of nature, but who is taught by nature to rise to a knowledge of God, is the clearest manifestation of the link between two worlds.

Condillac's notion of reason is as rationalistic as his universe. The perfect language of algebra, the perfect logic of analysis, the analogy that lies behind calculation, the grammatical structure of language —these are the very forms of reason, that reason which is taught to man by nature working through his sensations, his needs, and his passions, but which in its highest activity extends far beyond its origins. For all his reduction of reason to transformed sensation, and despite his professed conviction that passion is the mainspring of the human soul, Condillac's ultimate faith was in pure reason, mathematical reason, independent of sensation, untouched by the passions, free, autonomous, and in harmony with a harmonious universe.

Nevertheless, Condillac's faith in reason was not the sort that leads to a conviction of infinite progress or of human perfectibility, for it was tempered by a moral austerity, a realistic and sober consciousness of the gap between what man ought to be and what he is. Nature's guidance, to which he owes his reason, his morality, his society, and his culture, brings man just so far out of primitive barbarism when he inevitably and perversely renounces his guide and turns into strange paths, after strange gods. His culture becomes artificial and precious, his material existence luxurious and effeminate, his political activity self-seeking and capricious, until he sinks into the new barbarism of decadence, anarchy, and ultimate extinction. Yet reason, nature, and God's design demand that a man of enlightenment do his work in the world—cultivate his garden—in spite of the limits placed on his hopes for mankind, in spite of the apparent ineffectiveness of many of his best efforts, and in spite of the ingratitude of his contemporaries and perhaps even of posterity. In his sense of the public duty and private necessity of making all the difference one can in an unenlightened world, Condillac stood united with the other philosophes. His work in the world, his garden, was generally more restricted than theirs—less flamboyant, less public, and less daring. But limited though it was, he stuck to it to the end—soberly, conscientiously, doggedly pursuing his youthful vision of a new metaphysics, a new method, and a renewed philosophy.

Here, then, is Condillac: a Christian *manqué,* an empiricist by profession, a Cartesian in spite of himself, a traditionalist who has embraced a new way in philosophy, a philosophe who had no stomach for the philosophes' battles with authority, and above all, a lover of mathematics and of the logic of mathematics. The world, even as science from Galileo to Newton had declared, is mathematical. But for Condillac this has a special meaning. The world is not operationally mathematical; that is, it is not matter-in-motion to be measured and quantified. It is qualitatively mathematical, to be understood as a structure of logical identities, pure, harmonious, symmetrical—the perfect expression of a geometer's God.

Bibliographical Essay

Condillac's Works

There are two major editions of the works of Condillac: the classic edition of 1798 and the modern critical edition put out by Georges LeRoy in 1947–51. The first: *Œuvres de Condillac, revues, corrigées par l'auteur, imprimées sur ses manuscrits autographes et augmentées de La Langue des calculs, ouvrage posthume* (23 vols. Paris, 1798), was prepared by the Abbé de Mably from manuscripts left by Condillac at his death, containing his own revisions and corrections of the various works, as well as the unfinished *La Langue des calculs,* published for the first time in this edition.

LeRoy's edition: *Œuvres philosophiques de Condillac* (3 vols. Paris, 1947–51), was prepared for the fine series "Corpus général des philosophes français." It is based on the 1798 edition, but also contains all the textual variations that appeared in the earlier editions of the separate works. The text is complete except for the *Histoire ancienne* and *Histoire moderne,* of which LeRoy has presented only those portions which he felt had a bearing on Condillac's philosophy. Thus he has included Condillac's observations on historical method, on change and causation in history, and on the purpose of studying history, as well as his evaluations of past epochs and his account of the European intellectual revolution since 1500. LeRoy also published in this edition, for the first time, excerpts from the manuscript of Condillac's *Dictionnaire des synonymes,* including all articles that he felt would contribute, even slightly, to an understanding of Condillac's philosophy. This edition is completed by all that was known at the time of Condillac's correspondence: twenty-one letters, most of them disappointing as revelations of either his character or his philosophy. LeRoy's notes, identifying references, pinning down sources, and pointing out parallels in the writings of Condillac's contemporaries are painstaking and thorough. It is an excellent piece of work.

Shortly after this edition appeared, nine more letters turned up—all to the Swiss mathematician Gabriel Cramer—which LeRoy published in 1953: *Condillac, Lettres inédites à Gabriel Cramer,* ed. Georges LeRoy (Paris, 1953). These letters are of more interest than most of the previously published correspondence, because they are attempts to answer questions Cramer had evidently raised about points in Condillac's philosophy. There is, however, nothing really new or startling in them.

Between 1798 and 1947 there appeared two other complete editions of Condillac, in 1803 and 1821–22, and several editions of separate works. Although I shall not attempt to discuss the various minor editions, it is of interest to note that the chronological distribution of these editions corresponds to the fluctuations in Condillac's reputation. For the thirty-six years from 1798 to 1834, I have located fifteen separate printings of works of Condillac, the most frequently reprinted book being *La Logique.* In the forty-three years between 1834 and 1877, I have found only one printing: an edition of *Le Commerce et le gouvernement* (its only separate printing since its first appearance) in a series on economic thought. Then, in a resurgence of interest, there appeared five printings between 1874 and 1886, including three different editions of the *Traité des sensations* in two years. (Two of these, edited by François Picavet and Georges Lyon, are of special interest for their introductions, which I shall discuss below under "Secondary Works.") Between 1886 and 1947 there were two editions of separate works: Raymond Lenoir's careless 1924 edition of the *Essai sur l'origine des connaissances humaines* and an English translation of the *Traité des sensations.* Since the LeRoy edition of the *Œuvres* there has been nothing.

There have apparently been only three English translations of any of Condillac's works. The first appeared during Condillac's lifetime: *An Essay on the Origins of Human Knowledge,* trans. Thomas Nugent (London, 1756). The second was a version of *La Logique,*

which appeared at the height of its popularity as a text in French
schools, and was evidently intended for the same use in this country:
*The Logic of Condillac, Translated by Joseph Neef as an Illustration
of the Plan of Education Established at his School near Philadelphia*
(Philadephia, 1809). Finally, there is the twentieth-century translation of the *Traité des sensations,* an adequate but undistinguished
version, with a brief introduction linking Condillac to the idealist
tradition of Berkeley: *Condillac's Treatise on the Sensations,* trans.
Geraldine Carr (Los Angeles, 1930).

Conspicuously lacking is a good modern edition, in any language,
of any of Condillac's single works.

Secondary Works Dealing with Condillac

Because Condillac was a philosopher, he has been written about
primarily by other philosophers. As a result, most studies of him
are intended as evaluations of his thought. They discuss the merits
and weaknesses of his major doctrines; they analyze inconsistencies
in his methods in order to show that his ideas are not logically
tenable; they point out his role as a precursor of one or another
school of thought contemporary with the writer; and they consider
whether he deserves the charges previous critics had leveled against
him, or the tributes of his followers. The history of these works
about Condillac is itself part of the history of philosophy.

In the first quarter of the nineteenth century Condillac's work
was approached as a living philosophy to be adopted, modified, or
rejected. Pierre Laromiguière's *Paradoxes de Condillac* (Paris, 1805)
and his *Leçons de philosophie sur les principes de l'intelligence,
sur les causes et sur les origines des idées, 1* (4th ed. 2 vols. Paris,
1826), 72–96, 129–75, 219–63, which are lectures delivered at the
Sorbonne in 1811, represent the thought of an *Idéologue* and disciple of Condillac. Laromiguière's aim was to defend Condillac
against the charge of "materialism" and to defend his fundamental
contribution to our understanding of what we do when we think—
namely, the idea that sensation is the first faculty and that language

is the basis of method. At the same time, he wanted to correct Condillac's monistic analysis of the soul by endowing it with a self-generating activity of judgment.

Victor Cousin began as a student and disciple of Laromiguière, but later, under the influence of Maine de Biran and Royer-Collard, and after a trip to Germany to meet Hegel and Schelling, he reacted against *Idéologie* and formulated the philosophy of "Eclecticism," whose aim was to create a synthesis of sensualism, idealism, skepticism, and mysticism. In his *Philosophie sensualiste au dix-huitième siècle* (3rd ed. Paris, 1856), pp. 39–129, based on his Sorbonne lectures of 1819, and more briefly in his *Histoire générale de la philosophie depuis les temps les plus anciens jusqu'au XIXᵉ siècle* (11th ed. Paris, 1884; 1st ed. 1828), pp. 501–11, Cousin attacked Condillac for lacking the spirit of observation, for having no appreciation of facts, and for creating a purely verbal science out of an *esprit de système*. This marks the end of Condillac's thought as a living philosophy.

For a generation Condillac was in eclipse, unread and unregarded. He appears briefly in the pages of George Henry Lewes, *A Biographical History of Philosophy* (4 vols. London, 1845–46), and in Hippolyte Taine, *Les Philosophes classiques du XIXᵉ siècle en France* (Paris, 1855). Lewes, a Comtean empiricist, repeated the substance of Cousin's criticism, added that Condillac's clarity was largely owing to shallowness, but credited him with having been the first to see, albeit imperfectly, that our faculties are not innate. Taine, writing about Laromiguière and Royer-Collard, discussed Condillac only in passing as the object of their controversy.

In 1862 the spiritualist philosopher Jean Philibert Damiron inaugurated a new attitude toward Condillac: that he was an interesting, significant, and much-maligned philosopher who ought to be rehabilitated. In his "Mémoire sur Condillac: Son *Traité des systèmes*," *Séances et Travaux de l'Académie des Sciences Morales et Politiques,* 60 (1862), 5–28, and 61 (1862), 5–31, Damiron said that Condillac, too, was a *spiritualiste,* if not a refined one. Condillac had perhaps overemphasized the analysis of sensations, but he certainly was not a materialist, nor really even a *sensualiste*, at heart. While Damiron especially praised the solidity of Condillac's proofs for the existence of God and a spiritual soul, his tribute was not unqualified: he asserted that Condillac did not understand the philosophies he criticized in the *Traité des systèmes,* so that his criticisms were generally wide of the mark. Damiron's articles contain the first accumulation of the basic biographical data about Condillac, to which only a very little has been added since.

For the next twenty years the rehabilitation of Condillac continued, but not all who supported him agreed on their reasons for doing so. François Réthoré, *Condillac, ou L'Empirisme et le rationalisme* (Paris, 1864), was an entirely polemical work, defending Condillac as a sensationalist and empiricist, and denouncing Cousin and German rationalism. Damiron's argument that Condillac was fundamentally a spiritualist was taken up in M. Patru, "De L'Influence précédemment exercée par Condillac dans la philosophie et les lettres et de celle qu'il peut encore exercer aujourd'hui," *Mémoire lu à la réunion des Sociétés savantes à Paris* (Grenoble, 1866). Inspired by *dauphinois* partiotism, Lucien Pion, in "Condillac et sa philosophie," *Bulletin de l'Académie Delphinale,* 17 (1881–82), 13–30, summarized Condillac's life and major ideas, and deplored his temporary loss of favor after the rise of Royer-Collard and Cousin. In his "Réponse au discours de Réception de M. Pion," ibid., pp. 31–39, M. Auxias also celebrated Condillac as a fellow *dauphinois,* attacked the old materialist charges, and argued that Condillac's theory of the relation of thought to language points to a divine creation.

Somewhat later, but still preoccupied with Condillac's reputation, was Victor Delbos, "Condillac et les idéologues," in his *Philosophie française* (Paris, 1919), pp. 250–76, which was put together posthumously on the basis of his and his students' notes, from his Sorbonne lectures of 1910, 1914, and 1916. Delbos, very much concerned with labels, argued that Condillac was not a materialist, an empiricist, a rationalist, or a *sensualiste,* but a *sensationniste,* a spiritualist, a deist, an intellectualist, an idealist, and a logical formalist. The title of the chapter is misleading: there are only two pages on the *Idéologues*.

Not everyone was convinced by the new enthusiasm for Condillac. Louis Robert, *Les Théories logiques de Condillac* (Paris, 1869), argued that Condillac, although historically significant and a noble and distinguished mind, was dead past recall as a philosopher. And Antoine-Augustin Cournot repeated the standard criticisms in his *Considérations sur la marche des idées et des événements dans les temps modernes, 2*, ed. F. Mentré (2 vols. Paris, 1934; 1st ed. 1872), 38–44. Cournot, who was himself a mathematician, also criticized Condillac's notion that ordinary language could be given the character of numbers.

Although the program to rehabilitate Condillac as a living philosopher was not successful, there is no doubt that it did succeed in calling attention to him as a historical figure. As such, he became the object of still another approach—his thought as a stage in the history of philosophy to be understood, and perhaps praised or blamed, in the light of subsequent developments. Thus Taine, in *L'Ancien Régime* (1873), regarded Condillac as a chief representative of the eighteenth century's abortive effort to develop a good philosophic method, an effort which the nineteenth century, having abandoned the mathematicism and abstractness of the eighteenth, pursued with more success. In this country Lyell Adams, "Condillac and the Principle of Identity," *New Englander, 35* (1876), 440–66, set forth a sharp and sound criticism of Condillac's question-begging epistemology and "identical" reduction of reflection to sensation, but nevertheless credited him with having "cleared the continent of the Cartesian cosmologies, and . . . furnished the original draft of the final form of the Empirical Philosophy." François Picavet published an excellent edition of the first part of the *Traité des sensations* in 1885, distinguished by good notes and a nonpolemical attitude. In his introduction, a straightforward and accurate presentation of Condillac's major doctrines, Picavet argued that Condillac's continuing, if covert, influence on French philosophy had been underrated.

In 1892 appeared the first serious, large-scale attempt to analyze Condillac's writings: Léon Dewaule, *Condillac et la psychologie anglaise contemporaine* (Paris, 1892). This well-documented book is especially useful as a history of nineteenth-century opinions of Condillac. Its aim was to demonstrate Condillac's significance by proving that his work directly influenced the methodological and psychological formulations of such English associationists as Bain, Spencer, Mill, and Lewes. Dewaule fails for two reasons. First, proof of similarity is not proof of influence, except in a sense which Dewaule was not thinking of: the participation of all these thinkers in a common developing point of view, in which the earlier phases naturally influenced the later, but in a diffuse and unspecific way. In the second place, Dewaule failed because of the inherent limitations of his face-value approach. He compared single sentences and brief passages of the writers he was concerned with, not so far out of context as wholly to distort them, but without sufficient attention to the larger contexts, to meanings of words, to the purpose of the moment, etc. Thus he sometimes found identity of doctrine where there was little more than a common tradition which each employed in the service of his own interests. Still, this is a useful book for the intellectual historian in ways not intended by the author—in pointing up the continuing empiricist tradition and in giving leads to understanding the persistence and the transformation of ideas.

In the same tradition of evaluating Condillac's place in the evolution of modern thought are Alfred Kühtmann, *Zur Geschichte des Terminismus* (Leipzig, 1911), pp. 38–61, and a chapter in William Boyd, *From Locke to Montessori* (New York, 1914), pp. 30–35. Kühtmann's short essay placed Condillac in the nominalist tradition of William of Ockham; his primary concern was to show how scientific methodology had advanced since Condillac, but that Condillac was a significant step in its evolution. Boyd said, wrongly, that Condillac himself did not see the educational possibilities in his philosophy, but that through Rousseau he has nevertheless been an influence on the development of modern educational theory. Gabriel Compayré, *Histoire critique des doctrines de l'éducation en*

France depuis le seizième siècle (2 vols. Paris, 1911), contains a
routine description of Condillac's educational theories, with some of
the standard criticisms, and T. M. Moustoxidi, *Les Systèmes
esthétiques en France . . . 1700–1890* (Paris, 1918), summarizes
briefly Condillac's aesthetic ideas, somewhat overemphasizing their
potentiality for an aesthetics of expression. Both these books are
essentially catalogues of theories, historically arranged.

Raymond Lenoir, *Condillac* (Paris, 1924), contains the most
penetrating observations made up to that time on the effect of
Condillac's mathematicism on the substance of his thought. Lenoir
also has some good material on currents of ideas in the 1730s and
1740s in schools, salons, etc. The main part of this short work is a
book by book summary of Condillac's philosophy and an excellent
but very brief evaluation of it in the light of subsequent developments in psychology.

In Wladislaw Folkierski, *Entre Le Classicisme et le romantisme*
(Paris, 1925), there is a discussion of Condillac's aesthetic ideas as
they figured in a period of transition.

Zora Schaupp, *The Naturalism of Condillac* (Lincoln, Nebr.,
1926), aims to reevaluate his thought in order to point out "certain
healthy tendencies" which had been overlooked during the nineteenth-century reaction against materialism and sensationalism. She
finds these tendencies in his attack on superstitions through scientific method—e.g., his replacement of the mysterious faculty of the
"will" by the naturalistic "desire," or, in short, his elimination of the
"soul." She argues that Condillac should be vindicated as a psychologist because of his affinity to twentieth-century behaviorism. This is
a useful study, but limited in value for the intellectual historian
because the problems connected with the meaning of "nature" in the
eighteenth century are never discussed.

Gabriel Madinier, in his *Conscience et mouvement: Essai sur les
rapports de la conscience et de l'effort moteur dans la philosophie
française de Condillac à Bergson* (Paris, 1938), pp. 1–38, argues that
Condillac was a better psychologist than his explicit doctrines reveal.

According to Madinier, implicit in Condillac's philosophy are many of the favorite themes of modern psychology: the relationship of practical to theoretical knowledge, of spontaneity and instinct to reflection, and of nature to art. Madinier concludes that Condillac's system is weak but that his separate insights are often sound.

Paul Meyer, *Etienne Bonnot de Condillac: Ein Wegbereiter der ökonomischen Theorie und des liberalen Gedankens* (Zurich, 1944), is a monograph outlining Condillac's contribution to the development of economic liberalism.

Charles Coulston Gillispie, in his fine *The Edge of Objectivity* (Princeton, 1960), evaluates briefly Condillac's contribution to the evolution of scientific method, concluding that "Condillac's assimilation of science to language was the most fertile conjunction of empiricism with analytical rationalism in the Enlightenment."

The revival of interest in Condillac also stimulated an approach to him which was "historical" in a stricter sense of the word—that is, which judged his historical significance primarily by his relationship to his own century, rather than by his real or supposed affinity to ours. Georges Lyon's Introduction to his 1886 edition of the first part of the *Traité des sensations* was written in this spirit. Lyon took up the question of the sources for the statue-man, and, wishing to absolve Condillac of the charge of plagiarism, he gathered together all the evidence showing it to have been a commonplace of the eighteenth century. Auguste Lebeau, *Condillac économiste* (Paris, 1903), is a thorough discussion of Condillac's economic doctrines and their relationship to those of the physiocrats. Edouard Maynial, "Les Grammairiens philosophes du XVIIIe siècle; la grammaire de Condillac," *Revue Politique et Littéraire*, 40 (1903), 317–20, is too brief to make more than a single unelaborated point: Condillac made grammar conform to a universal philosophy of thought.

Gustave Baguenault de Puchesse, *Condillac, sa vie, sa philosophie, son influence* (Paris, 1910), is the first and only biography of Condillac. It pulls together the scanty and scattered data and augments it with family tradition about Condillac's life and habits. (Baguenault de Puchesse was a collateral descendant of Condillac.) It is for the most part without documentation. It contains a sketchy summary of Condillac's books and a brief discussion of his influence.

Gustave Lanson, "Les Idées littéraires de Condillac," *Revue de Synthèse Historique*, 21 (1910), 267–79, discusses *De L'Art d'écrire* as the link between the aesthetic absolutism of Boileau and the ideal of national self-expression of the *Idéologues*. Lanson summarizes Condillac's basic aesthetic attitude that taste is relative but that some tastes are more relative than others, and evaluates his literary theory as "the most coherent, the clearest, the most penetrating that French taste of the eighteenth century . . . could produce." This article is also to be found in the author's *Etudes d'histoire littéraire* (Paris, 1929).

Guy Harnois, *Les Théories du langage en France de 1660 à 1821* (Paris, 1929), contains a few pages on Condillac as the chief of the empiricist grammarians. Paul Kuehner, *Theories on the Origin and Formation of Language in the Eighteenth Century in France* (Philadelphia, 1944), points out the historical significance of speculation about the natural evolution of language. Kuehner compares Condillac to Rousseau and Diderot with respect to some specific theories.

Cay von Brockdorff, "Wahrheit und Wahrscheinlichkeit bei Hobbes und Condillac," *Veröffentlichungen der Hobbes-Gesellschaft, 8* (1937), 3–13, is an insignificant study, listing some similar ideas in Hobbes and Condillac, but demonstrating nothing except that they shared in a common tradition in philosophy.

Georges LeRoy's *La Psychologie de Condillac* (Paris, 1937) is not as good a job as his edition of Condillac's works. It is a fair monograph, with an adequate discussion of the background of Condillac's thought in the seventeenth-century philosophic tradition and in Newtonian science. LeRoy deals with the evolution of Condillac's thought from the *Essai sur l'origine des connaissances humaines* to the *Traité des sensations,* and with the influence of Condillac's tendency to think in logical structures upon his psychological doctrines. This is probably the best and most objective

twentieth-century study of Condillac. LeRoy has no axe to grind.
Ferdinand Pelikán, "La Méthode de Condillac et de Descartes,"
Travaux du IX Congrès International de Philosophie, Congrès Descartes, 3,* ed. R. Bayer (1937), 43–48, has a somewhat misleading
title. Pelikán points out that the search for *l'idée simple* is common
to both Descartes and Condillac, and then takes up Condillac's
analysis of the self and subsequent critics of it. His point is to show
that there is such a thing as a real self and that Condillac's analysis
is inadequate.

Mario dal Pra, *Condillac* (Milan, 1942), is a systematic analysis of
Condillac's whole thought, but it is really in the tradition of nineteenth-century rehabilitations. Dal Pra's aim is to demonstrate the
constant themes of spiritualism and idealism in Condillac's works
in order to show that he was not a wicked materialist. Special
pleading limits the value of this work as a contribution to an
understanding of Condillac.

Roger Lefèvre, *Condillac, ou La Joie de vivre* (Vienne, 1966), is
a brief, straightforward analysis of Condillac's major ideas. The
subtitle is puzzling.

Most of the general studies of the French Enlightenment give
Condillac one or two pages, whose content rarely varies. He is billed
as the foremost disciple of Locke in France and the creator of the
statue-man, which is usually briefly described. There are two exceptions to this pattern: Ernst Cassirer's masterful *Philosophy of
the Enlightenment,* trans. Fritz C. A. Koelln and James P. Pettegrove
(Princeton, 1951), to which all students of the period can return
again and again with profit, and Charles Frankel's *Faith of Reason*
(New York, 1948). Cassirer, it is true, presents no lengthy discussion of Condillac in any one place. Rather, he integrates his
discussion of Condillac into his topically arranged analysis, in which
he reveals a fine appreciation for what is important and what is
peripheral in Condillac's thought. Frankel's book contains an acute
discussion of the coexistence of a belief in empirical method with
a rationalist's sense of system in Condillac's mind.

Robert McRae, *The Problem of the Unity of the Sciences: Bacon to Kant* (Toronto, 1961), is a first-rate little study of a significant intellectual problem in its various formulations over two centuries. It is especially good on Condillac's concept of scientific method as an analytic logic, and the bearing this has on the unity of science.

Finally, Aram Vartanian's *Diderot and Descartes: A Study of Scientific Naturalism in the Enlightenment* (Princeton, 1953) contains some perceptive remarks about Condillac but no extended discussion of him.

Background Material

I shall make no attempt to present here a bibliography of the French Enlightenment or to list the many books and articles in which I have found pertinent information; the more important of them have been acknowledged in the notes, in any case. But there are some books that provide more than information—books that illuminate, that yield not mere facts but a deeper insight, that extend one's understanding of the material at hand. And these, which played such a role in the preparation of this work, I should like to acknowledge.

I have already discussed, in section II of this Bibliography, Cassirer's *Philosophy of the Enlightenment,* McRae's *Problem of the Unity of the Sciences,* and Gillispie's *Edge of Objectivity.* To them I would add: Edwin A. Burtt, *The Metaphysical Foundations of Modern Physical Science* (2d rev. ed. New York, 1932), for the relationship of the scientific revolution to problems of epistemology; Arthur C. Lovejoy, "The Parallel of Deism and Classicism," in his *Essays in the History of Ideas* (Baltimore, 1948), for insight into the way thought-patterns of an age reappear in different contexts; Louis Couturat, *La Logique de Leibniz* (Paris, 1901), for guidance in understanding some of the more abstruse aspects of analytic logic; F. H. Anderson, *The Philosophy of Francis Bacon* (Chicago, 1948), for his painstaking and scholarly analysis of the thought of one of Condillac's idols; and Aram Vartanian's "Introductory Monograph" to *La Mettrie's L'Homme Machine* (Princeton, 1960), for a fine historical analysis of an idea which was both characteristic and scandalous in the eighteenth century.

Finally I must acknowledge a special debt to Lester G. Crocker, *An Age of Crisis: Man and World in Eighteenth-Century French Thought* (Baltimore, 1959), one of those imperfect but indispensable books, whose value lies outside the point it wants to make. Crocker, as I have suggested above, in Chapter 5, distorts the thought of the Enlightenment by systematically treating its extreme expressions as if they were central, and its hacks and cranks as if they were minor philosophes. But in doing this, he has uncovered a wealth of forgotten material which, although certainly not part of the central thought of the age, is continuous with it, pointing up the tensions in that thought by focusing on some of the implications which its healthier representatives customarily repressed. Peter Gay is quite right to point out *(The Party of Humanity* [New York, 1964], p. 285) that the Marquis de Sade, one of Crocker's favorite points of reference, is a caricature of the philosophes. But it is surely not without significance that a caricature of the philosophes should turn out to be Sade.

Index

3